R. Kalley Miller

The Romance of Astronomy

Third Edition

R. Kalley Miller

The Romance of Astronomy
Third Edition

ISBN/EAN: 9783744679473

Printed in Europe, USA, Canada, Australia, Japan

Cover: Foto ©Thomas Meinert / pixelio.de

More available books at **www.hansebooks.com**

THE ROMANCE OF ASTRONOMY.

THE

ROMANCE OF ASTRONOMY

BY

R. KALLEY MILLER, M.A., F.R.A.S.

FELLOW OF ST. PETER'S COLLEGE, CAMBRIDGE
AND PROFESSOR OF MATHEMATICS IN THE ROYAL NAVAL COLLEGE, GREENWICH.

THIRD EDITION

London:
MACMILLAN AND CO.
1882.

CAMBRIDGE:
PRINTED BY W. METCALFE AND SON.

PREFACE TO THE FIRST EDITION.

The greater part of the following papers was originally written for delivery in the form of popular lectures. They were then published in a University Magazine, the *Light Blue*; and having met with considerable success in both these ways, they have now, at the suggestion of several friends, scientific and non-scientific, been partially rewritten and enlarged into their present form.

I have endeavoured, however, to keep their original object unaltered, and to write nothing which would not be at once interesting and intelligible to non-scientific readers. There is no lack of systematic, and yet easy works of Astronomy, such as those of Sir John Herschel, M. Arago, and W. Norman Lockyer; and I have, therefore, made it my object not so much to instruct as to entertain, and possibly in some cases to inspire a taste which might lead to the further prosecution of a most fascinating study. This must be my apology for passing over entirely many important parts of the subject, and simply selecting a few points here and there which seem to afford scope for striking or amusing amplification.

I have to thank two very distinguished Members of my own College, Sir William Thomson and Professor Tait, for kind suggestions and advice.

PETERHOUSE,
December, 1873.

The kind reception which the first edition of these papers met with from the public and the press encourages me to think that their object has been in some measure attained. I regret that the pressure of other work has so long delayed the appearance of the second edition. It contains a few alterations and additions.

August, 1875.

CONTENTS.

	Page
INTRODUCTION	1
THE PLANETS	5
ASTROLOGY	51
THE MOON	63
THE SUN	92
THE COMETS	110
LAPLACE'S NEBULAR HYPOTHESIS	132
THE STARS	151
OTHER UNIVERSES	190

The Romance of Astronomy.

THE Romance of Astronomy strikes one at first as sounding something very like a contradiction in terms. We might naturally be inclined to think that there is about as much of romance in astronomy as there is of poetic fire in Martin Tupper, or of charity in a Saturday Reviewer. Anyone listening to the conversation of two astronomers, and hearing them descanting enthusiastically about perigees, apogees, and syzygies, right ascensions and declinations, precession of the equinoxes, and the longitude of the moon's ascending node; or anyone opening at random the pages of a work on the science, and finding an incomprehensible mass of calculations, formulæ extending over twenty lines and using up all the letters of two or three alphabets, and diagrams like nothing in the earth beneath, or in the waters under the earth, and only bearing a very faint resemblance to things in heaven above; anyone, we repeat, on getting such an introduction to the subject, would be very much tempted to think that romance and astronomy were altogether incompatible. Science is said by rhetoricians to be the logical opposite of poetry, and whence then can come any element of romance into the sternest and loftiest of the sciences?

But if we consider not so much the study of the science itself, in its profound and recondite details, as the results to which it attains, the magnitude and importance of the subjects it treats of, and the beauty and grandeur of the phenomena it investigates, we shall have to acknowledge that somewhere or other in the ponderous tomes of astronomical science there must lie entombed rich stores of novel and unwonted interest. The science which fathoms the infinite and reckons up the eternal, which pierces the abysses of space, grasps the orb which we see now by the light that left it eighty thousand years ago, measures its distance, and traces its movements—the science which accomplishes such marvels as these, and the history of the great men who achieved these noblest triumphs of human intellect—must surely furnish many themes and contain many episodes of a character as wonderful and as truly romantic as we can find within the airy realms of fiction or of poetry. And besides the grandeur of the phenomena of astronomy and the romance which gathers round its history in all ages and casts a brilliant gleam here and there upon its sober annals, there often flashes even across the pages of the driest and most mathematical parts of the subject a glimpse of strange and unexpected interest; and a fact here and a figure there will start the mind in a train of fresh and novel speculation, and set the fancy to luxuriate in new and untrodden realms. Many of these points, moreover, to which we allude, though very interesting and wonderful in themselves, are yet of comparatively little importance from an astronomical point of view; their interest centres in themselves, and the results to which they lead must be regarded as rather curious than valuable; and hence they are but little to be met with in books, or if touched upon at all, are soon abandoned with the remark that it is time to quit such regions of endless and unavailing speculation. Now some of these speculations we purpose following out a little to their legitimate conclusions, trusting that from the above reason they may prove new to many of our readers. And in the other points which we take up—for we must not confine ourselves to so limited a portion of the romance of astronomy as this alone—we shall seek to select those which are likely to prove at once the most striking and the least familiar to non-scientific readers.

THE PLANETS.

WE turn naturally first to our sister planets. They are in all respects analogous to our own globe; they hold the same position in the great system of the universe that we do, and in them—if in any of the orbs of heaven at all—we might expect to find the face of nature presenting the same appearance, and the course of nature the same phenomena, that they do to us. But not such do we find to be the case. Some of them indeed will resemble us pretty closely in one thing and some in another, but in every one the points of contrast will be much more numerous and striking than those of similarity.

In looking over a table of the elements of the planets, one of the points which most attract our attention is the very great differences in size which they present; and as this circumstance is the cause of some of their most striking physical peculiarities, we may commence with it our examination of them. It affords, too, a remarkable illustration of the statement we have made, that a fact of apparently little importance in itself often leads indirectly to very unexpected and startling consequences. The magnitude of a planet is a point we should never expect to find in any way necessarily connected with the nature of the beings who inhabit it and the general character of life at its surface, and yet we shall find it intimately related to these matters, and that to the production of very singular consequences indeed. Take for instance the case of one of the minor planets—Ceres, or Pallas, or Vesta. Astronomers tell us that the diameter of the earth is 7912 miles, and that of Ceres 160 miles; and the words may very easily pass in at the one ear and out at the other, without leaving any impression behind; or if we pause for a moment to think over them, it will likely only occur to us what a compact little world Ceres must be, how easy it must be to get from one place to another in it, and how delightful to be able to sail round the world, pay a visit to one's friends at the Antipodes, and get settled at home again,—all within the short space of a week. But if we look at the subject a little more closely, we shall find that it involves far more extraordinary consequences than these. We know that by the law of gravitation, the force with which one body attracts another varies directly as its mass, and inversely as the square of its distance; and also that a sphere attracts any external object as if its own mass were all collected at its centre. Now the diameter of the earth being fifty times as great as that of Ceres, it is altogether 125,000 times as large; but this disproportion being partially counteracted by the greater distance of its surface from the centre, it follows that on the whole the force of gravity here is fifty times greater than at Ceres—or, in other word, any object here is fifty times as heavy as it would be there. Now let us look for a moment at what is implied in this. The first and most obvious consequence is, that a man will be able to lift fifty times as great a weight there as here. A ton would be an easy load, boys would play at ring-taw with huge round boulders instead of marbles, and a rattle intended for a stout baby might be made as heavy as a moderate sized cannon-ball. If the tower of Siloam had fallen there instead of here, the men, instead of being crushed by its weight, would have lifted themselves and it up with the greatest of ease, and felt nothing the worse for the accident. But there are more singular consequences yet. We know that if a body be once set in motion, it would continue moving to all eternity, if not brought to rest by some external force. Thus when a man leaps up into the air, he would continue ascending for ever, were it not for the attraction of the earth, which very speedily brings him down again. But at Ceres, this force is so small that it will be much longer before it takes effect, and a man might consequently leap to an enormous height before the attraction would check his ascent. Jumping over a house-top would be a very trifling exploit, while a good leaper would think nothing of clearing, with a short run, the new tower of St. John's Chapel, or the great Pyramid itself. Staircases might be abolished, for even a stout old lady could easily jump in at a three-story window. The range of projectiles would be increased in proportion. Ensign Humphry, with a good telescope, would put a ball into the bull's-eye from a distance of twenty miles.* An economical war-minister could no longer build on the security afforded by "the streak of silver sea," for Great Britain might be swept with artillery, from the Land's End to John O'Groat's House, by batteries erected far inland on the continent.

Nor have we exhausted the wonders of Ceres yet. When Swift made Gulliver describe his adventures among the Brobdingnagians, he probably had no idea that they were even farther removed from reality than the other creations of his fancy—that they were not

---

* Provided that he could see round a corner, as on so small a globe as Ceres an object at that distance would be far below the horizon.

only myths but absolute impossibilities. A giant here would be crushed by his own weight. A very easy calculation will shew this. Suppose a man twelve feet high, and stout in proportion. He will be twice as long, twice as broad, and twice as thick as an ordinary mortal, and thus eight times as heavy. Now if we take a cross section of his leg, the cut surface will be twice as broad and twice as wide as usual, and thus four times as large altogether. We shall thus have eight times the ordinary weight to be supported by only four times the ordinary surface; and hence the stress on the bone will be twice as intense as usual. In the same way, in a man three times the ordinary height, the stress would be three times as great, and so on. Such a stress might perhaps be borne, but when we got the length of a giant sixty feet high, the stress would be ten times as great, and that the bone certainly could not bear. It would either be crushed outright if the giant attempted to stand erect, or else his legs would totter, his knees would bend, and his mighty body come thundering down to the ground. Once down, it would be utterly impossible for him to get up. A sitting posture he might perhaps compass; but if he were a very big giant indeed, that too would be out of the question—and he could do nothing but lie along on the ground. But transport him to our queer little friend Ceres, and he is all right at once. In a moment he becomes fifty times lighter than he was, he leaps to his feet with ease and rears his huge head sixty feet into the air, his legs recover their strength, his aching bones grow well, and he may proceed, if he please, to astonish the acrobatic natives of the planet by gymnastic exploits far surpassing even their own.

Indeed, all the wonderful feats we have seen that an ordinary man would be capable of at the surface of Ceres must be multipled fifty-fold when we take into account the superior possible size of the inhabitants of that planet. Muscular exertion there goes fifty times as far as it does here; and as these gigantic beings will be able to put forth at least fifty times as much of it, the exploits they will be capable of achieving must be no less than 2500 times as great as anything that could be done here. Upon this enlarged field of speculation we can scarcely venture to enter. The wildest flights of fancy, and the most exaggerated visions of fairyland, will be more than realized. Like Milton's angels, they could tear up the hills by their bases and hurl them at their foes. Stronger than the vanquished Titans of old, fetters of iron would be to them as threads of gossamer; and mountains piled on the top of mountains would not suffice to crush or imprison them with their load. Like the genii of the Arabian Nights, they could spring at a bound from the earth to the clouds, or clear half-a-dozen miles at a single leap. The seven-league boots would be no longer a fable. Puck said he would put a girdle round the earth in forty minutes; but one of these giants of Ceres would stride round his planet in less than half the time.

Of course all the other denizens of the asteroid will have their size and strength increased in the same proportion. The race-horse will rear its crest two hundred feet into the air, and gallop five thousand miles an hour. The giraffe on the plain will lift his stately head, and browse on the trees that crown the mountain-top. The ponderous elephant will cover three acres of ground, and surpass in strength the most powerful steam-engine. The lion's roar will be more dreadful than the thunder-peal, and his resistless spring more terrible than the lightning's flash. Snakes two hundred feet in circumference and a thousand in length will roll their huge coils through the forest; while the sea will boil and foam with the gambols of its mighty inmates, and the gigantic carcase of Leviathan extend for a mile along the deep.

If we reverse the circumstances and go to a world larger than our own instead of smaller, the case will of course be exactly opposite. If we ourselves were transported to the sun, we should feel as much like fish out of water as the colossal inhabitants of Ceres would do here; and in fact it will be readily seen that if the sun were inhabited by beings constituted like ourselves, its population could consist only of dwarfs two or three inches in height. Very singular it surely is that the larger the world the smaller its denizens must be, that the inhabitants of the earth should be men, those of the sun dwarfs, and those of the tiny asteroid giants.

We must remind our readers—what they might well be excused for forgetting—that we are not romancing about what might be the case in some absurd and impossible circumstances and if the laws of nature were to undergo some extraordinary and unheard-of change, but that we are speaking in all truth and soberness, and that what we have stated is absolute and demonstrable fact.* If any man were transported at this moment to the

---

* See Herschel's Astronomy, end of Chap. VIII., where some of the above ideas are hinted at. Our mathematical readers will see that there is not the slightest exaggeration in the extent to which we have carried them.

planet Ceres, he would be able to do everything we have mentioned; and the actual inhabitants of that planet, if constituted like ourselves, must be able to do the same. Whether, if they exist at all, they are beings like ourselves or not, of course we cannot tell; their frames may be feebler and their powers more limited than our own, and life at the Asteroids may be after all not so very different from life on the earth itself.

And now to consider a few other points connected with the planets—those namely which arise from their various positions relatively to the sun, and from the character and velocity of their movements. The general celestial phenomena, and the periodical changes connected with them, must of course be the same at all the planets. They have the same alternation of day and night, of summer and winter that we have. For them, as for us, the sun has been set to rule the day, and moon and stars to rule the night. But though their times and seasons, their days and years, are exactly analogous to our own, yet the differences in their positions and movements will produce corresponding differences of a very marked kind in the lengths of those periods and in the vicissitudes of climate occasioned by them. The most important of these differences are caused of course by the very various distances from the sun at which the planets are situated. Mercury is three times nearer to it than we are, and Neptune thirty times farther away. It follows from this that at Mercury the sun will appear nine times as large as it does to us—the intensity of its light and heat being of course increased in the same proportion; while at Neptune all its influences will be nine hundred times feebler than they are here. Hence at the former planet the average heat must be greater than that of boiling water; and if at its creation it contained any seas or rivers like our own, they must have been long ago dissipated in vapour by the sun's overpowering beams. At Neptune, on the other hand, that luminary will appear no larger than one of the planets does to us. How cold and drear an abode it must therefore be!—its brightest noon-day more dusky than our winter twilight, and its hottest midsummer far colder than our frozen poles.

Another consequence of the varying distances of the planets is a great diversity in the length of their years, some of them being as short as three of our months, while one extends over no less than a hundred and sixty years. How long and dreary the circle of the seasons must be there!—forty years of spring, forty of summer, forty of autumn, and forty of winter.

The contrast between the seasons will be in some of the planets greater, and in some much less than our own; at Jupiter especially there will be no perceptible change of seasons at all, and day and night will everywhere last for twelve hours each, just as at our equator. Every region will be temperate; the climate a universal and perpetual spring. At Venus we have just the reverse. No region is temperate; the torrid and frigid zones extend so far as to blot out the temperate zone altogether, leaving in its place a belt which is at once between the tropics and within the polar circle. This unhappy region must combine all possible disadvantages of climate. At one period of the year it has perpetual night; at another perpetual day,—and not the mild perpetual day of our arctic regions, but a real hot day, with the sun high above the horizon. Twice in the year he will be vertically overhead, pouring down his scorching rays with a force beyond what we ever experience, on account of our greater distance from him. Truly that "girdle of Venus" must be an unpleasant dwelling-place!

The orbit of Mercury presents a very marked eccentricity;—in other words the planet is much nearer the sun at one period of its revolution than at another; so much so that that luminary will appear twice as large, twice as bright, and twice as hot, when Mercury is in perihelion as when in aphelion; a circumstance which cannot fail to be productive of very serious effects to its inhabitants. Even at our own earth, whose orbit is so much more nearly circular, the same cause produces a quite perceptible effect. The earth is nearest the sun in December, and the consequence of this is that in our northern hemisphere the winter is rendered milder than it would otherwise be, while south of the equator the heat is considerably aggravated. In June the opposite will be the case, and the whole result is evidently to make the northern hemisphere more temperate than the southern. Accordingly, we find that the intense heat of the sun is much more complained of in the Australian and South African deserts than in those to the north of the equator. The eccentricity of the earth's orbit is at present diminishing at a small uniform rate,* and the effect of this, in a sufficiently long course of time, would be to decrease these annual variations of temperature. In some of the other planets, however, it is on the increase, and when this fact was first discovered it excited great interest among astronomers. The increment, though extremely

---

* Due to the perturbing influence of the other planets.

small, appeared to be perfectly regular, and if continued long enough it must infallibly cause such frightful vicissitudes of cold and heat as to destroy any life which might exist at their surfaces. Lagrange, however, succeeded in establishing a beautiful and simple relation between the eccentricities of the planetary orbits, which showed that none of them could ever exceed certain definite limits, and that although they might increase for almost countless ages, a maximum would in time be reached, and a compensating period of diminution would ensue.

Lastly, the rotations of some of the planets on their own axes are performed in much shorter periods than that of the earth. The effect will be to shorten the length of the day, to make the planet bulge out at the equator, and to diminish gravity by reason of centrifugal force. We all know that if a stone be tied to a string and whirled round, it will acquire a tendency to fly off, which will be greater the faster it is whirled. In the same way some of the planets spin round so rapidly as to communicate to any body on their surfaces a very powerful tendency to fly off, which is, however, counterbalanced by the effect of gravity. But if Jupiter's rotation were only four times faster than it is, the centrifugal force would be so great that all the inhabitants would be sent flying off through the air—or rather along with it, for it would go too. When the impulse with which they started was lost, they would of course fall back to the ground, but only to be shot off again at once; and in this state of perpetual oscillation, bouncing up and down like an india-rubber ball, they would spend all their lives, unless they took some means of anchoring themselves to the surface of their planet.

The class of phenomena which we have been last considering depend all of them upon the positions and movements of the planets, and are hence common, with various modifications, to the whole of them. But besides these there are connected with all of them special points of individual interest, arising from circumstances peculiar to themselves alone, and over these we must cast a rapid glance before we proceed in our excursion to visit a new set of worlds.

Of the first of the planets, Mercury, we know but little. From the closeness of his proximity to the sun he can never be seen with the naked eye, except occasionally for a few moments close to the horizon, immediately after sunset or before sunrise; and even these hurried glimpses cannot be got except at considerable intervals and under very favourable circumstances.* Hence, though his existence seems to have been known from a very early period, he was comparatively seldom seen before the invention of the telescope. Copernicus lamented upon his death-bed that he had never been able to catch a glimpse of Mercury at all, the mists from the marshes of the Vistula too obstinately fringed the morning and evening horizon round the Observatory of Thorn. A distinguished French

---

* It is calculated that Mercury, Venus, and the Earth will, from a similar reason, never be visible at all from the surface of Uranus.

astronomer of the same period only saw him twice. The telescope when turned upon him shews us little but a small round disc, which exhibits phases, like the moon, according to its relative positions with regard to the sun and to the earth. Recent observations have revealed enormously lofty mountains upon his surface, eight times as high in proportion to their planet as the Himalayas are to our own globe. The proximity of Mercury to the sun, the eccentricity of his orbit, and the fact that he is unattended by any satellites, rendered the determination of his mass and other elements a matter of much difficulty, and great discrepancies exist between the earlier estimates of them. Fortunately his small size, and the consequent insignificance of the perturbations he produces in the other planets, diminished the importance of having an accurate knowledge of him. Any similar uncertainty about one of the larger planets would have interposed most serious obstacles to the progress of science, and would, for example, have rendered the discovery of Neptune impossible.

It is at present uncertain whether there are any planets within the orbit of Mercury. If there are, their light must be so overpowered by that of the sun as to render them visible only when he is under eclipse, or when they are passing across his disc, in which case they would appear as small black spots. Astronomers have occasionally fancied that they detected planets under the latter circumstances, but they have never felt certain that what they saw were not merely some of the ordinary spots on the sun. A French astronomer, M. Lescarbault, felt pretty confident on one occasion that he had found a real planet, to which he gave the name of Vulcan; but twenty years have passed away, and the discovery has never been confirmed. It was hoped that at the recent total eclipse Vulcan might have been seen near the edge of the moon's disc when the sun's light was cut off; but if he really exists, he lost the glorious chance then offered him of proving the fact, by perversely hiding behind the sun, or between it and the moon.

With Venus we are all familiar. It is the most brilliant of all the planetary or stellar orbs; and the "Star of the Evening, Beautiful Star," has been sung by poets of every age and clime, from Homer to the Christy Minstrels. Like Mercury, and for the same reason, Venus is seldom seen except about sunrise or sunset; but as her elongation from the sun, though limited, is much greater than that of Mercury, she is very frequently visible. Sometimes even, though at rare intervals, she is sufficiently near us to be seen when the sun is above the horizon; and the sight of the little planet, shining softly out in fearless companionship with the dazzling orb of day, is described as singularly striking and beautiful. Varro relates a tradition that Venus shone thus at noonday, a most auspicious portent, upon Æneas' voyage from Troy to Italy. And on the occasion of one of the first Napoleon's triumphal entries into Paris after a successful campaign, Venus joined in the pageant of the procession; exciting the intensest enthusiasm among the populace, who regarded her daylight appearance as a miracle, and flattering even the stern heart of the conqueror with the thought that Heaven itself had sent its fairest orb to grace the brilliance of his triumph. It was long before it was discovered that the morning and the evening star were one and the same planet, and hence we meet with it in the classics under a double name,—Lucifer, Son of the Morning, and Hesperus, Star of the Eve.* A similar confusion prevailed with regard to Mercury, which as a morning star was styled Apollo, the Lord of Day, and as an evening star Mercury, the Patron of Robbers.

The phases of Venus are readily shewn by the telescope, and were detected by Galileo soon after the invention of that instrument. Delighted at his discovery, but unwilling to

---

* Ἦμος δ' Εωσφόρος εἶσι, φόως ἐρέων ἐπὶ γαῖαν,
 Ὅν τε μέτα κροκόπεπλος ὑπεὶρ ἅλα κίδναται Ἠώς.
                                   Homer Il. 23. 226.
 Ἔσπερος ὃς κάλλιστος ἐν οὐρανῷ ἵσταται ἀστήρ.
                                   Homer Il. 322. 18.

publish it until verified by fuller observations, he shrouded it in the following line:

Hæc immatura a me jam frustra leguntur,*
which, anagrammatically transposed with a little license, gives

Cynthiae figuras emulatur mater amorum.†

This ingenious way of embalming a discovery until ripe for publication was a favourite one with the mediæval astronomers, as it enabled them to claim priority, if any one else, by making the same discovery, should take the wind out of their sails.‡ The result of Galileo's first observation upon Saturn was communicated to the scientific world in the form

aaaaabeeegiiiillmmmmmnnoprrstttuvv,
letters which he afterwards arranged thus:—

Ultimam planetam trigeminam observavi.‖

---

* These things, yet unripe and not understood, are read by me.

† The mother of loves emulates the phases of the moon.

‡ Simon Mayer, a Bavarian astronomer, contested with Galileo the priority of the discovery of Jupiter's satellites, but his claim appears to have been not only unfounded but absolutely dishonest.

‖ I have perceived the most distant planet to be threefold.

Huyghens' discovery of the real nature of the ring was first made known thus:—

aaaaaaa ccccc d eeeee g h iiiiiii llll mm nnnnnnnnn oooo pp q rr s ttttt uuuuu,

which, when he had fully satisfied himself of its truth, he interpreted into

Annulo cingitur tenui plano nusquam cohœrente ad eclipticam inclinato.*

As every one knows, the interest of the scientific world is at present very much concentrated on the approaching transit of Venus, or passage of the planet across the sun's disc. The importance of this phenomenon arises from the following cause. The relative dimensions of the solar, and even of the stellar system, are known with great accuracy; but in order to determine them absolutely, it is necessary to know with precision some one distance in terms of which the others may be calculated. The distance required for this is that between the earth and the sun, and the

---

* It is surrounded with a thin plane ring, nowhere adhering to it, and inclined to the ecliptic.

only accurate way of determining this is on the occasion of a transit of Venus. The rarity of this phenomenon renders each recurrence of it of special importance. It only takes place twice in rather more than a hundred years, the last occasion having been in 1769. Doubts are entertained as to the accuracy of the sun's distance as then determined, and it is hoped that more certain results may now be obtained. The nature of the observations and calculations required is not simple enough to be explained here, but any one with a moderate knowledge of the science may obtain a clear idea of them by referring to Mr. Proctor's works.

The dazzling and uniform brilliancy of the disc of Venus, which renders it very difficult to get a good telescopic view of it, is supposed to be caused by the reflection of the sun's rays off a dense cloudy stratum; and in fact it seems probable that we never see its surface at all, but only its illuminated atmosphere. In Mars, on the other hand, which is the next planet, we can trace with perfect distinctness the outlines of continents and seas. The bright ruddy light which distinguishes this planet from all the others proceeds from its solid parts, and is caused, doubtless, by a prevailing reddish tinge in the soil, something the colour of our red sandstone, only much brighter. The seas are distinguished by their blueish tinge, while at the north and south poles are large and irregular patches of a brilliant white. These have been conjectured with great probability to be vast tracts of ice and snow; and this idea is confirmed by the fact that they are of variable size, being largest during their winter, and diminishing very perceptibly on the approach of summer. These conclusions have recently been confirmed by spectroscopic observations. The spectroscope indicates the presence of aqueous vapour in the atmosphere of Mars, and therefore of water on his surface; and it also shews that the reddish hue does not proceed from the atmosphere, and must be inherent in the soil.

Leaving this planet of the "Red, White, and Blue," and passing over the asteroids, to which we shall return presently, we come to Jupiter, the largest and most important of all the planets. This great orb is no less than thirteen hundred times as large as our earth, and everything connected with him is on the grandest scale. His years last for ten thousand days, his motion on his axis is so rapid that the heavenly bodies must be seen changing their places every minute, and his nocturnal sky is illuminated by a band of four large and beautiful satellites.* His surface is divided into bright and dark belts parallel to the equator. The former are supposed to represent dense masses of clouds, reflecting the sun's rays more perfectly than the solid body of the planet. Their paral-

---

* These satellites have played a very important part in the history of science. Their discovery was hailed as a valuable confirmation of the Copernican theory of the solar system, of which they present a miniature picture. They have proved of great service to the navigator; the time of their eclipses can be calculated with great accuracy, and, when compared with local time, gives a simple method of determining that important and difficult geographical element, the longitude. And some discrepancies between their calculated and observed positions first suggested the great discovery of the finite velocity of light.

lelism to the equator, and their comparatively uniform breadths, are probably to be accounted for by steady atmospheric currents, of a character similar to our trade and return trade winds, but much more violent, in consequence of Jupiter's more rapid rotation on his axis.* In fact, all the observations upon his atmosphere tend to shew that the wind blows at his surface with overwhelming fury, sometimes surpassing a thousand-fold our most terrific hurricanes.

The moons of Jupiter were among the earliest revelations of the telescope. They were discovered by Galileo, who at first supposed them to be stars, and was much puzzled for a few nights by the irregular manner in which Jupiter appeared to move

---

* Some writers think that the sun's heat at the distance of Jupiter cannot be sufficiently great to produce such powerful effects in the same way that it produces our trade winds. They, therefore, attribute them to some cause inherent in Jupiter himself, and conclude that he is still in that unsettled and unsolidified state in which our earth formerly was. This hypothesis is rendered more probable by the fact of Jupiter's very small mean density.

about among them. He had great difficulty in getting the scientific world to acknowledge their existence. Some of the contemporary philosophers thought that they were optical illusions due to an imperfection of the instrument. Many absolutely refused to look through such an unnatural and diabolical engine as the telescope, and of course there was no other way of proving to them that the moons were really there.* One of these sceptics, Libri of Pisa, died during the heat of the controversy; and we find Galileo, in a letter to a friend, charitably hoping that

---

* It is not quite certain that Jupiter's satellites have not occasionally been seen with the naked eye by persons of very powerful sight. In an early Japanese plate Jupiter is represented with two small stars beside him, which very possibly are meant for two of his moons. At a time when this subject happened to be exciting a little discussion in the scientific world, a German lady declared that she could see one of the satellites. Unfortunately for her probity, it was soon found that she always saw it on the wrong side of the planet—to the right when it should have been to to the left, and *vice versâ*. The explanation was easy. She had got hold of some diagrams representing the apparent relative positions of Jupiter and his satellites from day to day, but they were constructed for using with the common astronomical telescope, which is an inverting one.

the way to heaven lay past the planet Jupiter, and that Libri might be convinced at last. Another unbeliever, a rather eminent astronomer of the name of Sizzi, delivered an elaborate harangue against Galileo, which is still extant, and in which he argues as follows:—"There are seven windows given to animals in the domicile of the head, through which the air is admitted to the tabernacle of the body, to enlighten, to warm, and to nourish it; which windows are the principal parts of the microcosm, or little world—two nostrils, two eyes, two ears, and one mouth. So in the heavens, as in a microcosm, or great world, there are two favourable stars, Jupiter and Venus; two unpropitious, Mars and Saturn; two luminaries, the Sun and Moon; and Mercury alone, undecided and indifferent. From these, and from many other phenomena of nature, which it were tedious to enumerate, we gather that the number of planets is necessarily seven. Moreover, the satellites are invisible to the naked eye, and therefore can exercise no influence over the earth, and would, of course, be useless; and therefore do not exist. Besides, as well as the ancient Jews, other nations as modern Europeans have adopted the division of the week into seven days, and have named them from the seven planets. Now if we increase the number of planets, this whole system falls to the ground."

Absurd as this tirade is, we wonder at it the less when we find the illustrious Huyghens talking in a similar strain after his discovery of the first satellite of Saturn. He says:—"The solar system is now complete. It consists of six planets and six moons, and from this equality, and from the fact that they together constitute the perfect number twelve, we infer that no more satellites will be discovered." The philosophers both of the ancient and middle ages had great belief in perfect numbers, but their superstitions have, in the nineteenth century, been thrown completely into the shade by the wild ravings of Comte, the high priest of Positivism, about primes. Like Sizzi, he had a great partiality to the number seven, because it was a prime, and because it was "composed of two progressions followed by a synthesis, or of one progression between two couples." For these reasons he wished it to be made the basis of our scale of notation. The latter reason we frankly confess our inability to comprehend; the former is intelligible, but singularly inconsequential. Most people would think a prime the worst number possible to found a scale on. His favourite number of all, however, is thirteen, and that for the following reasons: It is a prime; it is the seventh prime; seven is a prime; it is the fifth prime; and five is a prime. Here, unfortunately, he has to stop; five is the fourth prime, and four, on Comte's principles, is a very poor number indeed. It is a perfect square, and nothing on earth can twist that into a prime. Comte sincerely regrets this little flaw; if only twice two did not make four, thirteen would be an absolutely perfect number. Still it is so near it that it cannot be so very unlucky as it is popularly considered; and we trust none of our readers will ever again think it necessary to count the number of guests at a dinner-table.

Undeterred by the cogent arguments of Sizzi, Galileo, so far from giving up his moons or abandoning his infernal machine, turned his telescope, after investigating the orbits of Jupiter's satellites, to other bodies of the system, and soon detected those most extraordinary appendages of the next planet, the rings of Saturn. The highest magnifying powers shew these rings merely as thin luminous threads crossing the disc of the planet and projecting slightly beyond it at either side, but to the inhabitants of Saturn itself their appearance must be inconceivably grand. To the dwellers on one side of the planet the rings must present the magnificent spectacle of two vast luminous arches spanning the sky from horizon to horizon and rotating with enormous velocity; and to the people on the other side the appearance will be the same, only that the arches will be dark instead of bright; while the regions which lie beneath their shadow will be reduced for long periods at a time to a state of dusky twilight.

It was long supposed that the rings were solid, and indeed no telescopic observations could suggest to us anything to the contrary, their appearance being that of perfect continuity. Laplace was the first to discover a mechanical difficulty in the existence of a solid ring revolving round a planet. He perceived that such a ring would be in a state of what is technically called unstable equilibrium, and would naturally tend to split up into fragments. Still there the rings were, to all appearance, solid and continuous, and he and his successors were led to frame a variety of hypotheses—possible, though anything but probable—to get over this mechanical paradox. But Professor Clerk Maxwell, in quite recent years, has demonstrated the insufficiency of these theories, and proved that the rings must consist of separate fragments or meteoric stones, so numerous and so closely packed together as to be, at our distance from them, indistinguishable from a solid mass.

The feeble telescope with which Galileo discovered the rings only revealed to him two protuberances beyond the disc of the planet at the opposite ends of a diameter. They appeared to him to be detached bodies, and he was much surprised to find that they did not change their positions relatively to the planet, and therefore neither revolved round it nor rotated with it in its daily course. But extraordinary as this phenomenon appeared, it became still more so when these two objects gradually diminished in size, and finally disappeared altogether. Galileo was utterly baffled. "Is the legend of mythology," he asked in amazement, "no longer a fable, and has Saturn really devoured his children?" The explanation of course was that the planet advancing in its course, and changing its position relatively to the earth, had brought its equator into the same plane with us, so that the rings only presented their narrow rim to us, instead of their broad flat surface. But it was not till long afterwards that Huyghens, with improved telescopes, detected their real nature. Maupertius started a quaint theory for their origin. He supposed that they might be the mangled remains of an unfortunate comet, which had incautiously come too near Saturn, and got his tail wound round the planet and twisted off. Another theory we shall meet with further on.

Till within a comparatively recent period these five planets—Mercury, Venus, Mars, Jupiter, and Saturn—were believed to be the only ones besides our own earth in the system, but in the year 1781 Uranus was added to the number by Sir William Herschel. He did not suspect at first that it was anything but a comet, but, as every observatory in Europe immediately set to work to calculate its orbit, it was soon recognised as a planet. Herschel wished to call it Georgium Sidus, after his kindly and munificent patron, George the Third. Several of his brother astronomers urged that it should be named after the illustrious discoverer himself, but the advocates of uniformity insisted upon the classical nomenclature being adhered to.

The rival claims of all the old gods and goddesses were discussed. The name of Neptune found considerable favour in this country, Englishmen being then justly proud of the exploits of their fleet, but the foreign astronomers would not agree to this. Many other names were suggested, and backed up by fanciful and epigrammatical reasons. Uranus was finally adopted, on the suggestion of Bode that the most distant of the planets might appropriately be called after the most ancient of the gods.

It was soon found that the planet had been observed no less than nineteen times before in different parts of the heavens, but from its great distance, and consequently insignificant apparent magnitude, it had always been taken for a star.* This remarkable discovery excited the greatest interest among

---

*Lemonnier, in especial, seems to have narrowly escaped detecting its real nature, as he had observed it several times. But his observations were not registered and compared with sufficient care to lead to any results; indeed one of the most important of them was afterwards found by Bouvard scribbled upon a confectioner's paper bag.

astronomers, and the hope began to be entertained that other distant planets also might have been mistaken for stars, and that the number of the planets might be thus still further added to. The only other discovery, however, which has yet been made of the character anticipated is that of Neptune, whose existence was first suspected by Bouvard in 1821, from the perturbations in the motions of Uranus caused by his disturbing influence. The problem of determining from these scanty data the distance, the orbit, and the mass of the disturbing planet, was evidently a possible one; but the analytical difficulties which it presented to the mathematician were so enormous, that for more than twenty years no one attempted to grapple with them. Our own University had the great honour of first undertaking the task, and of prosecuting it to a successful conclusion. Mr. Adams commenced his ever-memorable researches immediately after taking his degree in 1843, and on the last day of September, 1845, his calculations of the place in which the supposed planet should be sought for were tendered at Greenwich Observatory. Before commencing the search, which was likely to prove a laborious one, the Astronomer Royal requested Mr. Adams to make some further calculations, with a view of confirming his results;* but while he was engaged on these, M. Le Verrier (who had been, unknown to both of them, employed in similar researches) published the results of his calculations on the first of June, 1846. As they agreed exactly with Mr. Adams', Professor Airy's hesitations were removed, and he wrote to Mr. Challis, recommending a careful search with the great Northumberland refractor in the Cambridge Observatory. This advice was immediately followed, and an accurate map of the part of the heavens in question was commenced, with the hope that, on a second survey, some star in it would be found to

---

* Mr. Adams had based his calculations on the perturbations of Uranus in longitude, and Professor Airy suggested that he should examine whether those in radius vector would lead to the same result.

have changed its place, and thereby shewn itself to be the planet sought for. But before this labour was completed, Dr. Galle, a Prussian astronomer, who had the advantage of having a good map already in his possession, found a new star not laid down in his chart; and a little investigation established this at once as the long sought for orb. Professor Challis found that it was one of the bodies he had already mapped down, and that a few nights more must have infallibly led to its discovery by him also. Considerable jealousy was felt at the time between England and France with regard to the priority of claim between Adams and Le Verrier, the French Astronomer being much disappointed to find that our countryman had vanquished the difficulty first, although his discovery was not made public at the time. But after all, the question of priority is a small one; each of the astronomers completed the task by his own unaided genius, and the names of Adams and Le Verrier will be handed down to posterity with equal honour as the solvers of the hardest mathematical problem which has yet engaged the attention of scientific men.*

No planet more distant than Neptune has yet been discovered; but more than a hundred and fifty tiny orbs have been added to the system, whose existence had been previously unsuspected—not from their distance, but from their minuteness. We allude, of course, to

---

* The problem was the solution of a series of simultaneous partial differential equations with nine unknown quantities, namely, the mass, mean distance, eccentricity, epoch, and perihelion longitude of the unknown planet, and the corrections to the latter four elements of Uranus. The smallness of the perturbations in latitude shewed that the inclinations and nodes might be neglected, or, otherwise, the number of unknown quantities would have been thirteen. Many of our readers will understand the impossibility of solving such a problem by any ordinary mathematical methods, and even the usual devices of the Planetary Theory, evolved by the genius of Laplace and Lagrange, failed in application in consequence of the inverse character of the problem. In fact, the old armoury of Science was unavailable, and Adams and Le Verrier, in fighting their great battle with Nature, had to invent a fresh weapon for every stage of the conflict. For an interesting sketch of their labours we may refer our mathematical readers to Grant's "History of Astronomy," while the question of priority will be found discussed in Airy's "Historical statement of circumstances connected with the discovery of the planet beyond Uranus."

the asteroids. The history of their discovery is very interesting, and affords a remarkable contrast to that of Neptune, being the result of a bold and fortunate guess, while the other was the fruit of years of patient toil. Soon after the elements of the planets came to be accurately known, a remarkable empirical law was observed to connect their several distances from the sun. These were found to form a series, the difference between each of whose terms were twice as great as the preceding difference; in other words, the distance of any planet from the next without it was twice as great as its distance from the next within it. The only exception to this rule was in the case of Mars and Jupiter, whose distance from each other was much too great; in fact, it seemed as if there was a planet wanting between them to complete the perfect series. This fact, which was first noticed by the Baron de Zach, was considered so remarkable, that a company of astronomers banded themselves together to institute a search for the missing orb, and shared out among themselves the part of the heavens in which it was expected to be found. The leading men of the day considered the idea as altogether chimerical, arguing with perfect truth that there was no reason to believe that the law in question was anything more than an accidental coincidence,* and that it was thus utter madness to attempt reasoning upon it at all. The madmen, however, pursued their quest; and after a long and interesting search, the first of the asteroids was discovered; and shortly afterwards, to the astonishment of everybody, a second, revolving in an orbit nearly coincident with that of the first. This remarkable departure from the established analogy of the whole solar system attracted universal attention; and when a third and a fourth asteroid had been discovered about the same place, Dr. Olbertz propounded the idea that the large planet which ought to have been found in this position had been, by some internal convulsion

---

* It has since been found to be broken in the case of the planet Neptune.

or by the shock of a comet, split into fragments—each of which was now pursuing its separate course as an independent orb about the great common centre of the system. This theory was at first almost universally received, being strikingly borne out by a remarkable fact with regard to the orbits of the then-discovered asteroids. If such a catastrophe occurred, the fragments would be hurled off in different directions and with different velocities, and would thus take up different orbits; but as the orbit of each would be ever the same, it follows that they would all at some period of their course pass again through the position from which they originally diverged. And this was found to be the case. There was a particular part of the heavens through which the four asteroids at one time or another passed, and which was therefore set down as having been the scene of the great original disruption. It was conjectured by some that the aërolites, or shooting stars, were small fragments from the same mass, which had been projected so far inwards towards the sun as to come within the range of the earth's attraction, and be deflected down to its surface. This latter hypothesis received a good deal of support, being at least as probable as that of Laplace, which refers the origin of these meteors to volcanoes in the moon, and holds that they are hurled forth from those luna craters with force sufficient to reach the earth. But the explosion theory is now itself exploded. Many of the more recently discovered asteroids do not pass near the place of the supposed disruption; and, therefore, as we have seen, can never have been at that spot at all. It is true that the perturbations caused by the other planets would by this time have partially affected their orbits; but the discrepancy seems too great to be accounted for in this way, and the theory has now been generally abandoned. The only other attempt to account for the phenomenon of the asteroids is based upon the great Nebular Hypothesis of Laplace, which we shall explain hereafter.

These minor planets being all included within a belt of very moderate extent, it follows that numbers of them will at some times be comparatively near together, and the appearance of the heavens at one of these will be peculiarly striking. Many bright planets will be scattered over every part of the firmament—some appearing as thin silver crescents like the new moon, some as half-moons, and others with fully illuminated discs; some so distant as to be indistinguishable from stars, and others surpassing the moon itself in magnitude and splendour; their orbits crossing and overlapping in every direction, and the planets thus circling in and out among each other as if in the mazes of some majestic dance—some winging their flight far away to the most distant parts of their orbits beyond the sun, and others perhaps approaching so near as to fill half the firmament with their glorious blaze, and travelling along for days and weeks together, so near that their gigantic inhabitants might almost clear at a bold leap the airy gulf that separates their worlds from each other.

ASTROLOGY.

WE can scarcely turn away from the subject of the romance of planetary astronomy without alluding to the mysterious influence which those bodies of our system were for many ages supposed to exert on the affairs of men. The science of astrology—for a science, and a most elaborate science it was—comprehended, of course, the other heavenly bodies as well as the planets. But although the sun and moon are far more important luminaries than the planets, and although the stars incomparably exceed them in number, yet the simple regularity of their movements rendered them far less interesting to the astrologer than the "wanderers" of the nightly sky. To the ancients, unfurnished with the master-key of Copernicus, the motions of the planets, with their fitful loops and backward sweeps, appeared altogether arbitrary and irregular, and these orbs were therefore naturally selected as those most fitted to represent the varying terms of Fortune's wheel, and to preside over the changing lots of men, of nations, and of the human race.

The origin of astrology, or the foretelling of events from the configuration of the heavenly bodies, is lost in the mist of a remote antiquity; but it was undoubtedly practised by the old Egyptian magi, before the time of Moses. The father of the written science was the illustrious Ptolemy, whose astronomical researches seem to have been prosecuted mainly for astrological purposes, and whose elaborate work, the Tetrabiblos, is the text-book of all succeeding votaries of the science. According to him, the planet in the ascendant at the time of birth was the chief ruler of the character and fortunes of the "native," as the entrant on this world's stage was technically called. Mercury presided over the mental faculties, and literary and scientific occupations. He caused a desire of change—though in this respect his influence was less than that of the moon —and a love of travelling. Venus was a benefic planet, styled the Lesser Fortune. She tended to produce a mild and benevolent disposition, with an inclination to pleasure and amusement; and her favouring influence brought good fortune to the native in his or her relations with the other sex. Mars, on the other hand, was the Lesser Infortune. His influence was not altogether evil, but he was decidedly risky, and needed to be well aspected by other planets to lead to any good. The man born under him was high spirited, quarrelsome, and defiant of danger. The woman was probably a virago, or at the least what Ptolemy, if he had lived in a less favoured age, would have been familiar with as "strong-minded." Mars, of course, ruled over war-like pursuits, and also over such trades as were concerned with iron and steel.

Jupiter was regarded as far the most propitious of all the heavenly orbs, and styled the Greater Fortune. He ruled all high and dignified offices, especially the Church. The favoured mortal born under him might be expected to prove high-minded and honourable; charitable and devout; liberal, wise, just, and virtuous. Happy the kingdom ruled by a sovereign on whose birth he shone! English astrologers of the present day tell with pride that our gracious Queen was born when Jupiter rode high in the heavens, right upon the meridian. So, they say, was the Duke of Wellington; but as both the date and the place of his birth were uncertain, the astrologers must be as clever as Daniel— they can not only interpret the dream, but supply it when forgotten. The Greater Fortune smiled also, though less brightly, on the birth of the Prince of Wales.

Next him we have the grim and ill-omened Saturn, the Greater Infortune; "and justly," says Lilly, "does he merit the title, being the cause, under Providence, of much misery." Those born under him are gloomy and reserved in character; faithful, indeed, in friendships, but bitter and unforgiving towards an enemy. Failure, disease, disgrace, and danger beset the steps of the child of Saturn with frequent and terrible pit-falls. The only pieces of good luck that appear to be attributable to him are the gloomy ones of legacies; while his special favourites are sextons, undertakers, and mutes. Of Uranus, of course, Ptolemy tells us nothing, but modern astrologers think him on the whole malefic. He causes eccentricity and abruptness of manners; and whether he brings good or evil, it is always of some peculiar and unexpected kind. We cannot find how Neptune is regarded by the astrologers: probably they have not yet made up their minds about him. But we may hope for his credit that Adams and Le Verrier, to whom he owes so much, are watched over by him with special favour.

Although the ascendant planet is the chief element to be considered in Genethlialogy, as Ptolemy styles the science of nativities, its influence may be modified by its combination with other planets, or its position in the zodiac. Thus, while Mars in general begets military men, they must, if he be in the watery sign of Cancer or of Pisces, find vent for their fighting tastes in the navy. And so on, from the soldier and sailor, through the "tinker, tailor, ploughboy, and apothecary," down to the "thief," who is born under the moon, "afflicted by Mars." The tailor is the only one of the list we cannot trace. Probably, from his fractional character, he belongs to one of the asteroids.

The signs of the zodiac were supposed to have a good deal to do with personal appearance. Thus Pisces produced a short figure, pale and fleshy face, round shoulders, and a heavy gait; Taurus a well set person, with broad face and thick neck; and so on. If parts of two signs occupied the ascendant together, a portion of the body would belong to one sign and the rest to another. Wild as the whole system of astrology is, it seems especially strange that the great philosophers of antiquity should have thought that human fortunes could be swayed, not merely by the constellations themselves, but by the arbitrary and fanciful names which men chose to assign to them.

Definite portions of human life were allotted to the different luminaries:—infancy to the Moon; childhood to Mercury; youth to Venus; the vigour of manhood to Mars; maturer age to Jupiter; and second childhood to the ominous Saturn. And lastly, the visible firmament was divided into twelve equal portions, meeting in the zenith. The first was the house of health; the second that of wealth; the third that of brothers and sisters, and also of short journeys—the latter being probably put in to fill up the space if the former should be wanting; the fourth that of parents; the fifth that of children and of amusements; the sixth that of sickness; the seventh that of love and marriage; the eighth that of death; the ninth that of scientific pursuits and distant journeys; the tenth that of trade or calling; the eleventh that of friends; the twelfth that of enemies. The connection of these houses with the rest of the system is, of course, obvious. Thus Saturn in the fifth house foretells misfortune with one's children; Mercury in the sixth house, mental disease; and Mars in the eighth house, a violent death.

Probably few persons have their horoscopes erected now-a-days, but we have before us that of the Prince of Wales, calculated at the time of his birth by Zadkiel, according to Ptolemy's rules. The Prince was born at forty-eight minutes past ten, on the morning of the 9th of November, 1841, at Buckingham Palace, lat. 51° 32′ N., long. 6′ W. The sign in the ascendant was Sagittarius, which, in Ptolemy's words, produces "a tall upright body, oval face, ruddy complexion (with a tendency to duskiness), chestnut hair, much beard, good eye, courteous, fair-conditioned, noble deportment, just, a lover of horses, accomplished, and deserving of respect." The Sun, being well aspected, prognosticated honours; and as he was in Cancer, in sextile with Mars, the Prince was to be partial to maritime affairs, and win naval glory. The house of wealth was occupied by Jupiter, aspected by Saturn; and this, as we have already seen, betokened " great wealth through inheritance "—a prognostication which, in spite of republican shoemakers and baronets, is not unlikely to come true. The house of marriage was unsettled by the conflicting influences of Venus, Mars, and Saturn, but fortunately the first was to predominate, and the Prince, " after some trouble in his matrimonial speculations," was to marry a princess of high birth, and one not undeserving of his kindest and most affectionate attention. His marriage was to be expected in 1862. There are few other predictions of particular events; the one put forth with most confidence is that of an injury from a horse in May, 1870, when Saturn is exactly stationary in the ascending degree. Zadkiel says, however, that this evil might be guarded against by prudence, which we presume was done, as the accident did not come off. There was also danger of a blow on the left side of the head, near the ear; but it does not appear whether this was to be administered by the horse, or to be a separate accident. The house of sickness shewed a predisposition to fever and to epileptic attacks. The position of Saturn in Capricorn betokened some loss or disaster to the native in one or other of the places specially ruled over by Capricorn, which we find from a table to be Brussels, India, Greece, Mexico, part of Persia, the Orkney Islands, and Oxford. We hope that the place indicated was the last of these, as if so the disaster is probably well over by this time, and was nothing more serious than some slight scrape with the authorities of Christ Church.

But while we have few particulars about the Prince's history, we are overwhelmed with information about his character. Each planet contributes an enormous list of characteristics, depending on its position and aspects at the moment of birth. When put together alphabetically, they give the somewhat complex character, which we subjoin. The infant Prince was to turn out "acute, affectionate, amiable, amorous, austere, avaricious, beneficent, benevolent, brave, brilliant, calculated for government, candid, careful of his person, careless, compassionate, courteous (twice over), delighting in eloquence, discreet, envious, fond of glory, fond of learning, fond of music, fond of poetry, fond of sport, fond of the arts and sciences, frank, full of expedients, generous (three times), gracious, honourable, hostile to crime, imperious ingenious, inoffensive, joyous, just (twice), laborious, liberal, lofty, magnanimous, modest, noble, not easy to be understood, parsimonious, pious (twice), profound in opinion, prone to regret his acts, prudent, rash, religious, reverent, self-confident, sincere, singular in mode of thinking, strong, temperate, unreserved, unsteady, valuable in friendship, variable, versatile, violent, volatile, wily, and worthy." It will be seen that the good qualities largely predominate; the bad ones are due to Saturn, who, of course, must have his envious cut, but who is happily pretty well kept down by the cumulative influence of the propitious planets.

Zadkiel finishes thus:—"The square of Saturn to the Moon will add to the gloomy side of the picture, and give a tinge of melancholy at times to the native's character, and also a disposition to look at the dark side of things and lead him to despondency; nor will he be at all of a sanguine character, but cool and calculating, though occasionally rash. Yet, all things considered, though firm, and sometimes positive in opinion, this royal native, if he live to mount the throne, will sway the sceptre of these realms in moderation and justice, and be a pious and benevolent man, and a merciful sovereign."

God grant that it may be so, and that the life recently spared in answer to a nation's prayers may, while crowned with every good and perfect gift itself, be blessed to the promotion of that nation's truest welfare.

THE MOON.

PASSING now from the planets to the other bodies of the solar system, we turn in the first place to our next door neighbour—the Moon. While the interest with which we view the planets arises from their close analogy and consequently great probable similarity to ourselves, that attaching to the moon is caused mainly by its remarkable proximity to us, and the clear view which we accordingly have of its surface and configuration. It is, in fact, the only one among all the heavenly bodies of whose state and constitution we can ever hope to learn much by actual observation. With regard to the rest, we must for the most part reason from analogy alone, and hence we can seldom arrive at any results of which absolute certainty can be predicated. With the moon on the other hand, we have ocular demonstration; and though we do not know very much about it—not half so much as we should like—still what we *do* know we can be perfectly certain of, and that is a very great matter indeed.

Before we touch at all upon the vexed and difficult questions of the existence or non-existence of a lunar atmosphere, lunar seas, and lunar inhabitants, we may glance in the first place over those points of interest which depend simply upon the position and movements of the moon—points therefore in the determining of which there can be no difficulty, and about the results of which there can be no difference of opinion. The first ideas which the ancients conceived of the nature and constitution of the moon were very wide indeed of the truth. The old Chaldean astronomers supposed that it was a globe, one half of which was made of fire, and which, by revolving upon its axis, presented its different sides to us in succession. This idea accounted sufficiently well for the phases exhibited by it; it was, however, anything but a probable one in itself; and when Thales observed the fact that the bright portion of the moon is always that which is turned at once to the sun and to ourselves, the old hypothesis was at once exploded, and the true explanation—that our satellite shines with reflected solar light—came to be universally received. Next to the phases of the moon, the most noticeable point about the appearance which it presents to us is the fact that the configuration of its surface is always the same. From our earliest childhood that configuration, with its quaint resemblance to a human face, has been familiar to all of us; the large eyes and arched eyebrows of the "man in the moon," his irregular nose, and his long melancholy mouth, are among our first recollections of the nightly sky. Nor is the idea only a tradition of the nursery. It is of the most venerable antiquity (though the ancients assigned to the moon's face a softer sex than we do); for we find in Plutarch the following quotation from a very early

Greek poet, Agesianax, whose works are lost:—

πᾶσα μὲν ἥδε πέριξ πυρὶ λάμπεται, ἐν δ' ἄρα μέσσῃ
γλαυκότερον κυάνοιο φαείνεται ἠΰτε κούρος
ὄμμα καὶ ὑγρὰ μέτωπα τὸ δ' ἐρυθρὸν ἄντα ἔοικεν,—

lines which Amyot translates thus:—

> De feu luisant elle est environnée,
>   Tout à l'entour ; la face enluminée
> D'une pucelle apparoit au milieu,
>   De qui l'œil semble être plus vert que bleu,—
> La joue un peu de rouge colorée.*

The earliest attempt at explaining the fact that the moon's surface presents a constant appearance to us, notwithstanding its revolution round us, is found in Clearchus, a follower of Aristotle, who says that "the moon must be the most beautiful and perfect mirror, in regard to smooth polish and lustre, in the world; for that in it we see to appear reflected the images and figures of our great continents and oceans." A little consideration

---

* Over the orb shines a resplendent light,
    In midst of which a damsel's face is seen;
  Whose cheeks suffused display her blushes bright—
    Her eye cerulean, or a pale sea-green.

sufficed to shew that this hypothesis, besides its inherent improbability, was insufficient to account for the phenomenon in question; and astronomers were shut up to the conclusion that the moon rotates on its own axis in a period exactly equal to that of its revolution about the earth. This perfect agreement of two periods so independent of each other (in the case of the earth, for example, the angular motion about the axis is 365 times as rapid as that in the orbit) was long regarded as the most marvellous coincidence in the economy of nature; but a recent ingenious mechanical explanation, too difficult to be given here, has cleared away a good deal of its à *priori* improbability.*

The idea of Clearchus about the moon being a mirror was revived in a singular

---

It has been shewn that if the two periods were originally at all nearly equal, the attraction of the earth on the protuberant parts of the moon would tend to bring them in time to exact equality. See Arago's *Astronomy*, vol. II. p. 283. Routh's *Rigid Dynamics*, p. 449. The same peculiarity has since been found to hold in the case of the satellites of Jupiter and one of those of Saturn.

manner in the middle ages. Some pseudo-philosophers maintained the possibility of communicating between distant parts of the earth by reflection at the surface of its satellite. "Do we not," they said, "see objects sometimes reflected by mirrors, even in positions in which, by reason of the interposition of screens, we cannot see them direct? Accordingly, writing on paper, either in characters of the ordinary size, or magnified by optical arrangements, might be reflected up to the moon, and from thence be transmitted to some point of the earth. They might then be magnified by some means so as to become visible."

The necromancer Agrippa had the effrontery to maintain that he had actually communicated in this manner with the distant east. Nothing goes down so readily with the ignorant as a good round lie, coated with a flimsy varnish of science; and, accordingly, these marvellous asseverations were received with very general credence, and the scientific men of the day found considerable difficulty in combating them. The energy with which they controverted these fabrications made them perhaps the less ready to detect the grain of truth which lay concealed under the mass of fiction. The faint ashy light which irradiates the dark part of the lunar disc, and which produces the appearance familiarly known as "the old moon in the young moon's arms," was long a matter of discussion and debate among astronomers. Some supposed that the moon's surface was slightly self-luminous, others that its mass was partially transparent, and that the sun's rays penetrated to a small extent through it. But both these theories were disproved by the fact that in a total eclipse the ashy light was altogether wanting. It was reserved for an amateur—the painter Leonardo da Vinci —to suggest the real explanation; namely, that the illumination was produced by the sun's rays being reflected from the earth's surface to the moon's and back again to the earth. The astronomers gladly availed themselves of the suggestion, and being once put upon the right track, they had little difficulty in shewing that it presented a most perfect accordance with facts. It need not surprise us that the sun's light, even after two reflections, should remain bright enough to be discerned by the eye. When we consider the brilliant illumination which our own surface receives on a clear night from the full moon, it is evident that it must be quite possible for the lunar inhabitants to see their own light reflected back to them from us. And as the earth is so much larger than the moon, the effect will clearly be increased in proportion when we take the case of our light returned to us from them.

The general aspect of the heavens from the surface of the moon will not be very different from what it appears to us, except that on account of the lack of a lunar atmosphere, or at least its extreme rarity, the celestial phenomena will be greatly increased in brilliancy, none of their effects being wasted by atmospheric absorption. The sun will be, of course, the great luminary in the firmament of the moon as it is in ours; and the great source of lunar—as of terrestrial—light and heat. The nightly revolutions of the stars also will be the same, and the place the moon itself occupies in our nocturnal firmament will be supplied to it by the earth, which will present the appearance of a splendid moon, thirteen times larger than the sun. Its revolution on its axis will present its different faces to the moon in rapid succession, and when our sky is free from clouds, the configuration of land and water on our surface will probably be clearly visible to the lunar inhabitants. They must know more of our circumpolar regions than we do, and could doubtless tell us whether there is open sea around the north pole; though, unless their telescopes are much more powerful than ours, they could not settle the question of the legendary Scotchman.

This great orb will appear immovably fixed in one particular part of the heavens, while the stars pass slowly beside and behind it. It will display the same phases, and cause and suffer the same eclipses, that our moon does. It is scarcely proper perhaps to speak of our suffering any eclipse from the moon at all; for the shadow of that body is so small that it will never cover any large part of our surface, and will in fact appear only as a small black circle passing slowly across our disc. But solar eclipses on the other hand will be at the moon far more frequent and striking phenomena than they are here. From the large size of the body behind which the sun appears to pass, a total eclipse will sometimes last as long as four or five hours, during which time the whole surface of the moon will be plunged in midnight darkness.

In consequence of the slow rotation of the moon upon its axis, its day and night must each be a fortnight long; and as its year is just the same length as ours, each of its seasons must consist of only three days and three nights. But the distinction of the seasons will be much less there than on the earth, and will besides be almost entirely lost in the far greater difference between night and day. If the atmosphere at the other side of the moon be as attenuated as it is at that which is turned towards us, this fact, combined with the great length of time for which the sun continues above or below the horizon, will render the lunar days more scorching than the sirocco, and its nights colder than the frigid zone; and thus each of its long days will be in reality a summer, and every night a winter—the morning twilight spring, and the evening twilight autumn. The hemisphere turned towards the sun, or the part of the moon which appears bright to us, must have any moisture which it may contain dried up by its scorching beams; while on the other, or dark side, the ground must be frozen hard to the depth of several feet, the mountains covered with glaciers, and the seas blocked up with icebergs. At the very margin between the two hemispheres there will be a narrow temperate zone, which will of course move round the moon, as the latter turns round its axis and presents its different faces successively to the sun; and the only way in which we can see that life could be supported with comfort at the moon (supposing the atmospherical difficulty surmounted) would be by moving constantly round it, so as to keep always in this temperate zone. A queer Noah's Ark-like sight it would be to see the whole inhabitants of the moon, side by side, in a huge procession extending from pole to pole, and hurrying quickly round it at the rate of ten miles an hour—some riding, some driving, and some travelling in slow railway trains; beasts, wild and tame, galloping by their side, and all the birds of heaven flying along over their heads!

But this brings us to the great question whether the moon can really have any inhabitants or not. Of all the problems which the science of astronomy is called upon to answer, none perhaps is possessed of deeper or more general interest than that of the plurality or non-plurality of worlds. We have all often wondered, as we have gazed on the star-spangled sky, whether those distant orbs are teeming hives of busy life like our own, or whether all the inhabitants of the universe have been indeed collected upon this one tiny and insignificant ball. And as the moon is the only one of the heavenly bodies with regard to which there has ever been a chance of arriving at any positive and definite evidence upon this subject, it follows that upon it have been concentrated almost all the researches and arguments of astronomers on the point. We can fancy the eagerness with which Galileo first turned his tiny telescope to its mottled face, and his disappointment when he found himself unrewarded by any revelations of life at its surface. And as the instrument has received each fresh accession of magnifying power from his day to our own, every succeeding observer has felt the same anxiety and experienced the same disappointment. Kepler thought that he saw, in the regular circular valleys with which the moon's surface is so closely dotted, artificial excavations, under the sides of which the inhabitants sheltered themselves during their long and scorching days; but when he found on measurement how large the dimensions of some of these craters were, he was compelled to abandon the idea. Even within the last half-century, an eminent German observer, in using a new and powerful telescope, fancied that he had discovered a series of colossal fortifications in one part of the moon's surface, closely resembling the gigantic wall which the Chinese have erected against the outside barbarians. But these lunar ramparts could not stand against the tide of optical improvements, and the next big telescope shewed them to be only basaltic formations, though of such singular regularity that their first observer might well be excused for attributing to them an artificial origin.

The fact is, that no satisfactory traces of inhabitants or of their works have ever been detected upon our satellite. The smallest space that can be distinctly seen with the best telescope at the surface of the moon is a circle of about a mile in diameter, and therefore no ordinary creation of human hands could be seen with sufficient clearness to place its character beyond doubt.

An old philosopher suggested, half in earnest and half in jest, a method of settling the point, which certainly possessed at least the merit of ingenuity. He argued that any race of rational beings must have discovered the leading principles of geometry, and would doubtless be aware that the square on the hypothenuse of a right-angled triangle is equal to the sum of the squares on its sides. He therefore suggested that a huge figure of the forty-seventh proposition of Euclid should be built on some great plain on the earth's surface. If the moon were inhabited by rational beings, they would be sure to recognize it as an old friend, and would doubtless divine that their terrestrial brethren were wishing to open communication with them. They would accordingly reply by the construction of some other important mathematical diagram—possibly, if their geometry is in advance of ours, they might send us down a method of squaring the circle. Thus we should at once have settled the existence of lunar inhabitants, and started a method of communicating with them. Probably our next move would have been to construct the figure of a man, to shew our new friends what we were like, and to hint that we should be glad to know something of them.

An improvement upon this suggestion was that enormous bonfires should be simultaneously kindled at points on the earth's surface forming the angles of a regular polygon. The symmetry of this phenomenon would strike the people in the moon with the idea of design, and suggest to them the existence of terrestrial inhabitants; and they would doubtless make known to us in return their own existence by some similar device. But neither of these experiments was tried, and neither of them is likely to be tried now; for in more recent periods some delicate investigations have thrown serious objections in the way of the inhabitant theory, by proving almost beyond a doubt the lack of water, and of all but an extremely attenuated atmosphere, on, at any rate, that side of the moon which is turned towards us. These conclusions were resisted as long as possible by Sir David Brewster, and other enthusiastic patrons of the "Selenites," or "men in the moon;" but latterly the weight of proof was becoming fairly too strong for them, and they were being obliged to take refuge in the somewhat unsatisfactory argument that after all the Selenites might be so constituted that they could get on without either water or air.

Some twenty years ago, however, the sun of the Selenites shone out from the clouds which were gathering round it with a gleam of such sudden and unexpected brilliancy as to fill Sir David Brewster and his friends with extreme exultation, and to carry confusion into the ranks of those who had begun to triumph over them. And though, alas, this light was destined to be soon and speedily eclipsed, yet as the incident to which we refer forms one of the most striking and interesting episodes in the history of science, it would be a mistake to pass it over unnoticed.

It was discovered on a certain occasion that the moon had absolutely got no less than three seconds behind her proper calculated time!

What connection a fact like this has with the question of the moon's being inhabited or not it is not at first easy to see, but we shall find that it is really connected with it in the closest manner, and that in fact it very nearly cleared out of the way all the objections which have ever been started against the moon's capability of supporting animal life at its surface. Of course it was not to be thought of for a moment that so great a discrepancy between fact and theory as that mentioned above should be allowed to remain unexplained. An express train on a journey of an hour's length would be granted at least a couple of minutes' grace, but not even three seconds could be allowed the moon after its long circuit of nearly a million miles. Many astronomers, both of this country and of the continent, were soon engaged on the question; and as they failed to explain the observed irregularity by the disturbing influence of any other body, they concluded ere long that it must arise from something anomalous in the figure or constitution of the moon itself. After an elaborate analysis, Professor Hansen, of Gotha, found that it could be accounted for by supposing that the side of the moon nearest us was lighter than the other, and hence that its centre of gravity—or the point to which any object on its surface would be attracted—was not at its centre of figure, but considerably nearer the side of it which is always turned away from us. He calculated the distance between these centres to be nearly thirty-five miles, evidently a most important eccentricity, when we remember that the radius of the moon is little over a thousand miles. It would probably have been produced by some great internal convulsion after the moon assumed its solid state; but the forces required to produce this disruption are less than might at first sight appear necessary, owing to the fact that the force of gravitation, and the weight of matter, are six times less at the moon than with us.

Assuming this peculiarity of the moon as proved, the rest of the argument is easy. It is clear that any fluid substance at the surface of the moon, in its attempt to get as near as possible to the centre of gravity, must have flowed round to the other side, and taken up a position of equilibrium there—just as a drop of water let fall upon a smooth globe of any kind would trickle round it and hang suspended from the lowest point. In fact, we can readily see that the circumstances at the part of the moon nearest to the earth must be the same as at the summit of a mountain on our own globe more than two hundred miles high; and we know that at such an elevation as that, the atmosphere would be so rare as to be utterly indistinguishable. At the edges of the moon's visible disc, the conditions would be the same as at a considerable altitude on the sides of such a mountain. And as we find from actual observation that there really is a certain attenuated atmosphere at those parts of the moon's surface, we are led to the unquestionable conclusion that on its other side, which would correspond to the level surface of the earth, the atmosphere must attain a very considerable density, such as we have every reason to suppose would render it perfectly well fitted for the support of animal life.

The water difficulty is got over in a similar manner. It is true that when the seas flowed away from the side of the moon next us, large bodies of water would be left behind in lakes and in the depths of the ocean. But the withdrawal of the atmosphere would lead to their immediate evaporation, and as soon as they were converted into vapour, they too would be free to gravitate round to the other side. Indeed the visible disc of the moon presents every appearance of having been, in former ages, to a great extent under water. Its enormous level plains surrounded by lofty mountains, its huge basins or craters opening everywhere among the rocks, and the vast ravines dividing its mountain chains, are altogether unlike our terrestrial scenery; but they are exactly similar to what we should see if all our oceans, lakes, and rivers were dried up, and their beds laid bare. In fact, we can scarcely doubt that there were formerly great bodies of water on this side of the moon; and if there were, it is equally certain that they must now be upon the other side.

We see, then, argued Hansen, that we might have predicted à *priori* the absence of air and water from this side of the moon; we see also that there must be air, that there probably is water, and that there is no reason why there should not be inhabitants upon the other side. These are the conclusions to which his theory certainly leads, and they were of course warmly welcomed by those who wished to believe in the habitability of the moon. Perhaps the interesting and attractive nature of the results, founded on them, caused Hansen's calculations to be received with less criticism than might otherwise have been the case. Be that as it may, they certainly met with very general acceptance, and will be found referred to in all the astronomical works of the period.

But—alas for the Selenites!—our greatest mathematical astronomer, Professor Adams, in the course of some refined investigations into the smaller inequalities of the Lunar Theory, fell foul of Hansen's views, and shewed that the celebrated three seconds' discrepancy could be accounted for by more natural causes. The stern facts of astronomy came into ruthless collision with one of its most pleasing romances, and the weaker had to go to the wall. Adams proved that the moon's eccentricity was both unnecessary and untenable, and dealt a death-blow to the antipodean Selenites by cutting off their water supply and putting them under an air-pump.

But although the moon has been shewn to be uninhabitable by beings like ourselves, it would be monstrous presumption in us to conclude that it must therefore be destitute of life of every kind. It would be quite as easy for the Creator to form beings capable of thriving in a vacuum, as in the particular combination of oxygen and nitrogen which is necessary for our existence. The fact that our own soil swarms with creeping things, and our own seas teem with myriad beings, that never see the light or breathe the breath of heaven, and lead a life which we should deem impossible if we did not actually see it, should teach us not to place limits to the possibilities of animated existence. It is true that not even the planets nearest and most like to us would be suitable abodes for ourselves, and that the sun, moon, and comets must be utterly uninhabitable by any beings such as our experience can give us any conception of. But this does not in the least diminish the probability of their having denizens "after their kind." The fact is that the plurality of worlds is not a question for the man of science. It belongs to the province of the inductive philosopher and the natural theologian, and must be handed over to them, to be judged of by analogy, and by a consideration of what we otherwise know of the general economy of Providence. This part of the argument falls without our sphere—it belongs to the Religion of astronomy, and not to its Romance. The arguments, however, in favour of the plurality of worlds are patent to everyone, and each of us may arrive for himself at what conclusion he pleases upon it. For our part, we cannot bring ourselves to think that our globe is the only inhabited one in the universe. Besides the *primâ facie* improbabilty that a small and insignificant planet, forming not a million million millionth part of the universe, should be in reality the most important body in creation, we think it is utterly impossible, on any common-sense grounds whatever, to believe that the larger and more distant orbs that spangle our firmament should have been created for our sakes at all. If their object were to afford us light, this purpose might have been far more effectually served by giving us another moon not a thousandth part as large as any of them; if it were to beautify our celestial scenery, this end, too, would have been equally attained by fixing some small luminous bodies within the limits even of our own atmosphere, instead of by placing these gigantic spheres at such incalculable distances from us. Nor is it probable that the Divine Architect should have created them for His own contemplation and that of the angelic hosts alone. It is contrary to the whole analogy of nature, and repugnant to all the ideas of the Divine wisdom and goodness which we have been accustomed to entertain, to think that these mighty orbs should have been framed for no other end than this. In all the economy of Nature we find nothing like waste of material or aimless expenditure of creative power; and while we see every blade of grass around us furnished with inhabitants and every drop of water teeming with a world of its own, it seems impossible to believe that those glorious stars should be in reality nothing more than so many waste and gloomy deserts.

Before we pass on to the next part of our subject, let us glance for a moment at a singular train of speculation suggested by Hansen's idea of the eccentric gravitation at the moon. Again, assuming for a moment the correctness of the idea (and it is not at all impossible that such a peculiarity may exist in some of the other heavenly bodies), we have seen that any object at the surface of the moon would be attracted not towards the centre but to a point at a considerable distance from it. This eccentricity, though enough to bring all the lunar atmosphere and water round to the heavier side, would yet probably be insufficient to cause any serious practical inconvenience to the dwellers upon its surface; but if it were carried to a somewhat greater extent, the results would be very singular. The reason why the natural position of any object at the surface of the earth is an upright and not a slanting one, is that the centre of gravity being exactly beneath our feet, the direction of its attracting influence is of course perpendicular to the surface. But if the centre of gravity were removed somewhat to one side, its attraction would now be oblique, and all formerly upright objects, such as men, buildings, and trees, would be compelled to take up a slanting position in order to the preservation of their equilibrium, while any round and easily movable body would immediately bound off in the direction of the new centre. Practically speaking, this state of affairs would be much the same as if the level surface were suddenly, and without any change on itself, transformed into a steep hill-side; for on such a surface, though at right angles to the sea-level, we yet occupy a sloping position relatively to the face of the hill. But the eye would doubless inform us that we were upon a level surface; and, in fact, in order to arrive at an idea of the matter, we must combine the appearance of a level plain with all the properties of a steep incline. At the part of the surface nearest the centre of gravity, this "slantindicular" state of things, as the Americans would call it, would be especially singular. Though the surface all round would be evidently level, yet to whatever side we started off the feeling would be the same as if we began to ascend a steep hill; and while at the central spot a man would stand upright, when he walked away in any direction his head would seem to go faster than his feet, till he took up his natural inclined position. In fact, to use a slang expression in a strictly literal sense, it would be a regular case of "sloping off."

THE SUN.

THE next of the heavenly bodies which claims our attention is the great centre of the system itself. When seen with the naked eye, the uniform and dazzling brilliancy of the sun's disc prevents us from getting any idea of the configuration of his surface, as we can do in the case of the moon; and even when viewed through a telescope, the overpowering brightness of the greater part of it renders it impossible to distinguish anything of the surface from which that intense illumination proceeds: just as when the eye catches the glare from a fragment of glass lying in the sunshine, it sees only the light proceeding from it, while of the object itself it sees nothing. But fortunately for astronomers, the brightness of the sun's disc is not altogether uniform, and by a contemplation of those remarkable phenomena known as the solar spots, they have been able to arrive at an idea, and no doubt an approximately correct one, of the nature and constitution of this extraordinary luminary. The spots on the sun, though varying much in size and shape, yet in their general appearance partake very much of the same character. They consist of a black central spot or nucleus, surrounded by a well-defined fringe less dark in colour, which is known as the penumbra. Sometimes the nucleus is absent, more rarely the penumbra; but the great majority of solar spots show both. Round their edges there are generally seen small patches of light of intense brilliancy, surpassing even the ordinary radiance of the sun's disc: these are called faculæ. The spots are by no means permanent, but undergo changes, and often very rapid ones, in magnitude and position; while after a comparatively limited period they close up and disappear altogether, to be succeeded by new ones, and those again by others, in varying and never-ending succession.

The discovery of the spots on the sun was as stoutly resisted by the metaphysicians as those of Jupiter's satellites and the earth's orbitual revolution. They could not in this case, like the superiors of the Inquisition, twist Scripture into contradiction with facts; but they took their ground on what with them was a still higher authority—the dictum of Aristotle. The illustrious Stagyrite had proclaimed the heavens incorruptible and immutable; it was beneath the dignity of the great orb of day to be affected by any physical changes such as our paltry planet is subject to. The Jesuit Scheiner, one of the earliest observers of the solar spots, was prevented by his provincial superior from publishing his results. "I have," says he, "read Aristotle's writings from end to end many times, and I can assure you that I have nowhere found in them anything similar to what you mention. Go, my son, and tranquillize yourself; be assured that what you take for spots in the sun are the faults of your glasses or your eyes." But other glasses and other eyes gave the same results, and only the most bigoted of Peripateticians could deny that their master's infallibility had received its death-blow.

The next discovery was a most important one. It was found that any individual spot, if it did not break up, moved across the sun's disc in a period of about fifteen days; that it then disappeared, and after an equal interval presented itself again on the opposite edge. This evidently pointed to one or two conclusions. Either the spots were solid bodies revolving round the sun, or else that luminary had himself a motion about an axis and carried his spots round with him. Scheiner and some other astronomers leant to the former hypothesis, but the latter was soon received as the correct one, and numerous theories were started as to what the nature of the spots really was. Galileo supposed them to be clouds. La Hire imagined that they were huge cinders from the burning body of the sun, rising to the surface of the fiery ocean which surrounded it, floating for a time upon it, and then being again engulfed within it, to rise a second time in another place. Derham and Wollaston referred them to volcanic agency, supposing that they were great clouds of smoke and scoriæ ejected from craters in a state of eruption, and that the faculæ consisted of flames and streams of molten lava. The least improbable hypothesis was that of Lalande, who believed them to be high mountains rising above the general solid surface of the sun, and sometimes covered, sometimes laid bare, as the tides and waves of the solar sea surged backwards and forwards around them.

But about a hundred years ago, Dr. Wilson, of Glasgow, established, from simple optical considerations, the fact that the spots are depressions below the general luminous surface, and not eminences above it. It also came to be recognised that the rapidity of their fluctuations, and the gigantic scale on which they take place, are incompatible with anything but a gaseous state of existence. Accordingly, the old idea of a luminous liquid ocean was discarded; and the following theory, propounded by Sir William Herschel, is now, in its main points, almost universally received. He supposes that the sun has two separate atmospherical strata, or rather gaseous envelopes of cloud-like consistency, both several thousand miles in thickness; the outer one—the photosphere, or source of the solar light and heat—being of some extraordinarily phosphorescent character, while the inner one is non-luminous in itself, but possessed of a highly reflective surface. Upon this theory the spots are caused by atmospherical agitations on a most enormous scale. A huge chasm, sometimes not less than fifty thousand miles in diameter, opens in the outer stratum, while a corresponding rift of lesser size in the inner one reveals the dark body of the sun itself behind. This accordingly constitutes the black nucleus of the spot, while the penumbra is caused by the light from the luminous atmosphere being reflected back to the eye from the surface of the inner one. If, as not infrequently

H

happens, the rift in the photosphere does not extend through the inner envelope, the spot will be all penumbra without a nucleus. And when we have the rarer occurrence of the inner opening exceeding the outer in size, the whole spot will be uniformly black. The phenomenon of the faculæ, which Dr. Wilson shewed to be great prominences or waves on the photosphere, is due to the piling up of the luminous matter thrown out from these gigantic chasms.

Not to enter further into details, which would be familiar to scientific readers and irksome to others, we may just say that this theory accounts in the most satisfactory manner not only for all the changing phenomena of the spots, but for other remarkable peculiarities which have been detected upon the sun's disc. Sir John Herschel has completed his illustrious father's theory by suggesting the probable physical cause of these convulsions in the solar atmosphere. He supposes them to be analogous to those terrible whirlwinds or rotatory storms which form so appalling a feature in the meteorology of our own tropical regions. Into this theory also it is impossible to enter in detail; but the whirlpool-like appearance of the spots, the situation of them all within a small distance from the sun's equator, their apparent rotation about an axis of their own, and the direction in which they move along the solar disc, all bear out Sir John Herschel's explanation in the fullest and most satisfactory manner. A *primâ facie* objection to his theory is that the terrestrial whirlwinds are caused by the great differences of temperature between the equatorial and other regions of the earth's surface, and that as the sun is the source of his own heat, there is no reason why such differences should exist in his case. But Herschel meets this objection by an ingenious answer. The sun has an ordinary non-luminous atmosphere of great extent, exterior to the photosphere; and his rotation on his axis will cause this atmosphere to bulge out considerably round the equator. And this greater depth of atmosphere, by retarding radiation from the equatorial regions, will give rise to the differences of temperature which the theory assumes.

Our knowledge of the physical constitution of the sun has been greatly increased within the last few years by the wonderful revelations of that most powerful engine of physical research—the spectroscope. A careful analysis of the solar spectrum formed by a prism, and a comparison of it with the spectra of terrestrial elements in a state of incandescence, reveal to us the presence in the solar atmosphere of many familiar substances, such as hydrogen, and the vapours of iron, sodium, and other metals. Line for line the solar spectrum agrees with the known peculiarities of elements which form constituents of our own globe, and we have the interesting fact established that the gorgeous parent of our system is, so to speak, bone of our bone and flesh of our flesh. The same powerful analysis, when extended to the stars, discloses similar results; and we are led to the inference that our own tiny globe, though such an insignificant fraction of the universe, contains, represented within its narrow bounds, all the materials of which that gorgeous system is built up. Unfortunately the spectroscope can tell us nothing of our satellites, though it is so much the nearest and most distinctly visible of all the orbs of heaven. Moon-light is simply reflected sun-light; and hence its spectrum is, as we should expect, but a faint reproduction of the more brilliant solar one.

The spectroscope has lately been applied successfully to those singularly beautiful phenomena which accompany a total solar eclipse, and which are generally known as the rose-coloured protuberances. As soon as the sun's light is wholly cut off by the moon, cloud-like prominences, of a bright roseate hue, are seen projecting from its surface beyond the moon's edge; and occasionally traces of a layer of the same material are seen at their bases, which lead us to suppose that the whole sun is encompassed by a ring of this matter. Whether it is a distinct solar envelope, or only a part of the photosphere, is at present uncertain; but pending the settling of the doubt, it has received the specific name of the chromosphere. The spectroscope shews it to consist of incandescent gas, of which hydrogen is the chief constituent; and the rose-coloured protuberances are huge masses of this flaming substance, which have been hurled up into the solar atmosphere to a height, sometimes, of fifty or a hundred thousand miles above their ordinary bed.

Another interesting phenomenon which appears at the time of a total eclipse is the solar corona—a great halo of light surrounding the darkened sun and stretching far out into space. This halo was at first supposed, naturally enough, to be the solar atmosphere, lighted up by the sun's rays streaming through it and imparting to it a portion of his own effulgence. But here again the spectroscope comes to our aid. It tells us the degree of pressure to which the incandescent hydrogen composing the rose-coloured protuberances is subjected, and shews the impossibility of their being burdened by such an enormous atmosphere as the whole corona would represent. The progress of modern science has left little doubt as to its real nature. We have learnt that the whole solar system is traversed by numberless tiny planetoids, some moving singly, others in small clusters, and others in enormous groups, containing countless myriads of these little units. These aërolites pursue their proper paths about the sun as truly as the largest bodies of the system, save when they get entangled in the atmosphere of our own or any of the other planets. When this is the case, the sudden checking of their enormous velocities by the resistance of the air reduces them instantly to a state of incandescence, and we see them flashing across our firmament as shooting stars, the next moment to be dissipated into vapour. The periodical meteoric showers of August and November are caused by our orbit carrying us, at those periods of the year, right through great clusters of these aërolites. It has been estimated that not less than a hundred thousand million of them are annually caught by our atmosphere; and when we consider the comparative smallness of the ring which we traverse, we can see that the absolute number of the meteorolites belonging to our system must be something incomparably exceeding the highest flight of human circulation. In the immediate neighbourhood of the sun, where his attraction exercises the most direct and potent influence, they will be found in special abundance; and it is to the fact of their existence that we must look for an explanation of the corona, and perhaps of yet greater and more interesting mysteries of our system. The corona is simply the sun-light reflected from their surfaces, as it is from the discs of the moon and planets. For a vast distance round the sun the whole firmament is powdered with them as thick as hailstones, and the reflection from them produces a continuous luminous glow, lost indeed in the overpowering brightness of ordinary sun-light, but shining out with exquisite lustre when his direct beams are cut off from us.*

These meteorolites have played a most prominent part in the scientific speculations for the last twenty or thirty years. The meteoric theory of the sun's heat was first propounded by Dr. Mayer, a German physician of great scientific attainments, and was warmly espoused and worked out by Sir William Thomson. There can be no doubt that the sun is constantly receiving great accessions of heat from the meteoric fragments which compose his corona. Countless myriads of them rain into his atmosphere every instant, with a force sufficient to convert their solid mass into a puff of vapour; and it was for some time thought that the heat derived from these terrific impacts might keep the solar envelope ever ablaze with undiminished in-

---

* It appears probable that it is also, under favourable circumstances, seen after sunset in the form of the zodiacal light.

tensity. No grander or more striking theory has ever been propounded in the history of astronomy. That the mighty centre of our system should recruit his marvellous expenditure of energy from the tiniest of his satellites; that these fragments, each so insignificant in itself, should collectively supply light and heat and life to the great Sun himself, and through him to all his attendant orbs; that it should be through their agency that the Creator of the universe has ordained that all His creatures should live and move and have their being,—is one of the most striking conceptions that can possibly be imagined. But more recent observations have led Sir William Thomson to a modification of his theory. He has calculated that if the meteoric shower were sufficiently heavy to make up for the sun's whole expenditure of heat, the matter of the corona must be so dense as seriously to perturb the orbits of certain comets which pass very close to his surface—a result which is found not to be the case. But the meteoric theory is only thrown back a step. If the sun's mass were originally formed, as is not at all improbable, by the agglomeration of these particles, Sir William Thomson has calculated that the heat generated by their thus falling together would be sufficient to account for a supply of twenty million years of solar heat at the present rate of emission. And thus though the meteors are not sufficient to maintain the energy of our system unimpaired, they may yet have been the original store-house from which all that energy was derived.

The fact, now placed beyond doubt, that the sun's heat is gradually wasting away, naturally leads us to cast a glance into the future. Far, very far, distant the time must be; long before it comes, in all probability, the firmament will have been rolled together as a scroll, and the old heavens and the old earth will have passed away. But if the economy of our system be spared long enough, the day must come when the sun with age has become wan; when the matter of the corona has been all drawn in and used up without avail; when the lavish luxuriance with which he has showered abroad his light and heat has finally exhausted all his stores. He has still power, aided by the resisting medium,* to drag his satellites one by one down upon his surface; and the shock of each successive impact will, for a brief period, give him a fresh tenure of life. When the earth crashes into the sun† it will supply him with a store of heat for nearly a century, while Jupiter's larger mass will extend the period by thirty thousand years. But when the last of the planets is swallowed up, the sun's energies will rapidly die out, and a deep and deathly gloom gather around nature's grave. Looking into the ages of a future eternity, we can see nothing but

---

* See the Chapter on Laplace's Nebular Hypothesis.

† In the chapter above referred to we have depicted the earth as falling into the sun, still an intensely heated body. But it is scarcely possible to say whether such a catastrophe, should it ever occur, would not find the sun already a comparatively cold mass.

a cold and burnt-out mass remaining of that glorious orb, which went forth in the morning of time, joyful as a bridegroom from his chamber, and rejoicing as a strong man to run a race.*

---

* The scope of these pages does not admit of our entering at greater length into the interesting and important subject of recent solar research. Upon this point our readers must of course refer to larger and more systematic works, or to the original papers scattered over various scientific periodicals. A clear and interesting discussion of solar heat will be found at the close of Professor Tyndall's work on Heat; while the invaluable spectroscopic revelations of Kirchoff, Lockyer, Huggins, and others, which have added so vastly to our knowledge, not only of the sun but of other astronomical bodies, will be found well described in Roscoe's Spectrum Analysis and Proctor's work on the Sun.

THE COMETS.

IN a sort of "debateable territory" between our own solar system and the infinite stellar universe around, we come upon those erratic and anomalous bodies—the Comets; some of which have accidentally become permanent attendants upon our sun; others have only paid it a single casual visit in the course of their wanderings through space, and are not likely again to come within the range of its attracting influence; while countless millions are doubtless scattered throughout the realms of the Infinite, whose existence will never be revealed to human ken at all. The extraordinary appearance and anomalous character of these meteors, the apparent irregularity of their movements, the suddenness with which they blaze into the firmament, the gigantic trains of light which they throw out as they near the sun, the frightful velocity with which they whirl round that body, and the sudden diminution of their glory as they recede from it, till they seem to be extinguished in the primæval darkness from which they emerged, —all these circumstances, combined with the mystery in which their real nature is shrouded, have caused these knights-errant of astronomy to be regarded at all times with the deepest interest, generally not unmixed with superstitious dread. In fact, for ages they were hailed by the universal consent of all classes of the community in the light of portents. One was believed to have portended the birth of Mithridates, another the assassination of Julius Cæsar, a third the great plague of 1310. One of the most remarkable on record made its appearance at the time of the Saracenic invasion of Christendom. As the hosts of the Crescent swept on their irresistible course, the comet waxed brighter and brighter, till at last, as the Caliph Mahmoud laid siege to Constantinople, it filled half the sky with its splendour, and hung night after night over the doomed city in the guise of a blazing scimitar. The Pope scarcely knew at first whether to pray to, or curse it, but adopting the latter course as more congenial to a true Catholic spirit, he fulminated the thunders of the Church against it, and in the same Bull excommunicated both Moslems and comet.

Though the superstitious terrors which used to greet the appearance of a comet have now for the most part passed away, yet the mystery which involved them, and which in a great measure gave rise to those terrors, has by no means been altogether dispelled; for our ideas of the constituent matter of their several parts is still involved in the utmost uncertainty. The general history of the changes of form undergone by a comet is as follows: When first discovered, and when at a considerable distance from ourselves and from the sun, it appears simply as a round patch of filmy light, with a brighter spot in the centre. This round mass gradually lengthens into an oval form, the bright spot, or nucleus, moving from the centre towards the end nearest the sun. On approaching the sun the nucleus is visibly disturbed by his powerful but mysterious influence; it appears to throw off masses of its own matter, sometimes in the form of nearly spherical envelopes, sometimes as jets or fan-shaped protuberances. On a nearer approach this agitation becomes more intense; fresh matter bursts forth, proceeding at first for a short distance towards the sun, but almost immediately swept back from him by some irresistible influence, and streaming far away into space behind. When the comet wheels round the sun, this tail, which is usually curved like a scimitar, whirls round along with it, keeping always away from the sun; and as the mysterious visitant recedes from the centre of our system, the tail, which now lies nearly in front of it, gradually shrivels up, and the comet resumes its original indistinct globular appearance before finally passing away from our ken.

Such is the general history of cometary transformations, but in several cases there have been abnormal peculiarities. Some comets have been nearly or wholly tailless: that of 1744 had no less than six tails streaming out behind it, that of 1823 had two (one turned towards the sun and the other away from it), while others have thrown out their tails in oblique or lateral directions. In fact, the term 'tail' is not particularly appropriate, for, unlike the sheep of the nursery rhyme, comets do not always "carry their tails behind them," but wave them about in all directions. The old term 'coma' or 'hair' would be preferable, but that is now commonly restricted to denote the thicker hair of the comet close round its head, as distinguished from its more loosely flowing locks. In former times the hairy appendage, when worn in front, was called a beard; but the distinction has now ceased to be drawn, and front-hair and back-hair alike go by the name of tail.

If, as was universally assumed until within

the last few years, the tail of a comet be composed of continuous matter, it must unquestionably consist of some extremely rare gaseous substance, incalculably lighter than our own atmosphere. This is inferred from their inappreciably small weight. Though a comet is often many million times larger than the sun, its mass is yet so insignificant that the most delicate tests fail to detect it at all. The most striking illustration of this was given by Lexell's comet. It plunged right between Jupiter and his moons; but, while its own orbit was completely distorted by the planet's influence, it failed to produce the slightest effect upon the satellites, shewing that, even compared with those tiny masses, its weight was inappreciable. We have also optical proofs of the extreme tenuity of the cometary material. We see stars shining with undiminshed brilliancy through the thickest parts of their tails. The lightest cloud-wreath would conceal them altogether, and yet the filmy texture of the comet, though millions of miles in depth, cannot dim their lustre. And a still more delicate proof is afforded by the fact that the comets are absolutely wanting in refractive power. The rays of light from a star, in passing through our shallow atmosphere, are very perceptibly bent aside from their path; but they pierce their way through the vast depths of a comet's tail without suffering the slightest deflection.

The motions of a comet's nucleus are perfectly accounted for by the law of gravitation, and present no difficulty whatever. On the gaseous hypothesis, the enormous development in size of a comet when near the sun is sufficiently explained by attributing it to expansion by heat. The great rarity of its mass would render it extremely sensitive to variations of temperature, and account readily enough for its rapid expansion when near the sun, and contraction when receding from it. So far the cometary peculiarities are explainable by the action of two simple and familiar solar influences—the attractive effect of his mass and the expansive effect of his heat. But the great mystery is the peculiar form and position of the tail, and the sun's apparent repulsive influence during its formation. Though many attempts have been made, no satisfactory theory of this has ever been built up on the simple grounds of heat and attraction, and it seems clear that we must look to some other, and yet unknown, solar influence for the solution of the remaining difficulties. Professor Tyndall seeks for this influence in chemical action. He recently found that the actinic rays of the sun—those, namely, towards the violet end of the spectrum, which produce the effects in photography—are capable, on passing through certain rare and invisible vapours, of converting them into visible clouds, and he thinks that when the sunlight passes through the head of a comet, the heat and light rays of the middle and red end of the spectrum may be cut off, while the actinic rays pass through, and, freed from the counteracting influence of the others, convert the invisible atmosphere behind the comet into the glorious cloudy effulgence which we see.

But all former theories have received a severe, and probably fatal, blow from some very startling recent discoveries, which tend greatly to revolutionize all our ideas about the constitution of the comets. It was observed that notable showers of shooting stars, indicating the earth's passage through great clusters of meteoric stones, had repeatedly taken place on the 13th of November. From all these showers occurring when the earth was at the same place, the natural inference was that they were all due to the same group of meteors, and that the path of that group round the sun intersected our orbit at the spot to which we always return on each 13th of November. Professor Adams calculated their path, and assigned them a period of revolution of thirty-three years. The meteoric showers take place only in three years, and those consecutive ones, out of the thirty-three. During the remaining thirty the meteors are circling round the more distant parts of their path, but for these three they are near enough the sun to be within our reach. And the vast length of the stream in which they fly, estimated at not less than fifteen hundred million miles, is such that it takes three years for all to pass a single spot, so that at three successive circuits the earth still finds them there, and plunges through them, upon the 13th of November.

Adams' results having been published, an Italian astronomer, Schiaparelli, happened to observe that the orbit assigned by them to the November meteors agreed exactly with that of a small comet, known as Tempel's comet. Wondering whether there was anything more than chance in this apparently meaningless coincidence, he turned to the annual August showers of shooting stars, and found that they indicated the existence of a meteoric system with a period of a hundred and forty-five years. In this case, however, on account of the showers being seen every year, it is evident that instead of an isolated flight of meteors moving round a comparatively long orbit, we have a continuous and unbroken stream, forming a gigantic revolving elliptical ring round the sun. This vast ring is no less than twenty thousand million miles in circumference, and four million miles deep where the earth's path strikes through it.

Eagerly comparing this elliptic ring with a list of cometary paths, Schiaparelli found again the same extraordinary coincidence; the orbit of the August meteors was identical with that of the comet of 1862. It was scarcely possible that these two coincidences should be the result of chance, and, as they have been since confirmed by others, everyone now admits that many comets have connected with them, in some way or other, flights of meteoric stones.

What that connection is is at present one of the chief questions in astronomical polemics. Many people still cling to the old gaseous theories, regarding the meteors as minor and unimportant accompaniments of the comets, and refusing to assign them any essential part in the wonderful transformations which those bodies present to the eye. Others, discarding at once all old ideas, have struck out a bold and entirely novel theory. Weary of the endless speculations, hypotheses, and assumptions with which scientific men were formerly obliged to content themselves upon the subject, and seizing gladly hold of the one *fact* we have now learnt about the constitution of comets, they resolved to confine themselves to it, and, without making further assumptions, to endeavour to build up a cometary theory upon it alone. They accordingly start by supposing a comet to consist of nothing more nor less than a vast assemblage of aërolites, distinct solid masses—stones, rocks, and lumps, of metal—flying together through space, and rendered visible, in favourable positions, by the sunlight reflected from them.

It is at once evident that two of the most important cometary peculiarities are satisfactorily explained by this hypothesis. The smallness of their aggregate mass, and the fact of their not eclipsing any heavenly bodies which pass behind them, are as well accounted for by this supposed discontinuity of their material as by assuming them to be gaseous. So are the facts which we have learnt from recent spectroscopic and polariscopic observations. These show us that the tail of a comet shines largely by reflected sunlight, while both in it, and to a much greater extent in the head, some of the light proceeds from incandescent gas, and from luminous or red-hot solid matter. The explanation of this necessitates no addition to the meteorolite theory. Throughout a comet, and especially in the nucleus, where its component fragments are most closely crowded together, there must be very frequent and violent collisions between them; and the heat generated by these impacts will convert them into a state of incandescence, or into vapour, just as we know to be the case when they strike our own atmosphere.

The sudden changes in shape, size, and position of the tail, present less difficulty upon this hypothesis than on any other. No tail will be seen except when the comet is in such a position as to turn a sort of flat edge towards us, so that we can look at once through a great depth of its mass. For the reflection from each elementary fragment will be so slight, that it will be only when an enormous number are ranged along the same line of vision that their aggregate light will be sufficient to affect the eye. To borrow a felicitous illustration from Professor Tait, the principal advocate in this country of the new theory, we may see the same thing represented in miniature by the flight of a flock of sea-birds. Great numbers of them often fly about, approximately in one plane; and if they are at such a distance as not to be discernible singly, they will be equally invisible when their plane has its face turned towards us. But when a sudden sweep brings them into the plane of our vision, so that we get a number of them in one line, they start into sight at once, as a black streak against the face of the sky.

The greatest difficulty under all other material theories is to suggest any physical influences sufficiently powerful to account for the inconceivable velocity with which the matter of a comet's tail is whirled round at the perihelion passage from a position behind it to one in front of it. Under the meteorolite theory this difficulty vanishes. The meteors composing the tail after perihelion are entirely different from those which constituted it before, and a comparatively slight relative displacement among the particles of a comet is sufficient to produce a great change in the position of their layer of greatest depth. The meteorolite theory is, of course, not yet full-grown, and there are many difficult points of detail which it will have to grapple with. Its advocates have not yet published much on the subject, and some promised papers by Professor Tait will be looked for with much interest.

The paths pursued by the comets are very various indeed. Many of them, like the planets, move in ellipses round the sun, some traversing their orbits in three or four years, while others roam so far away that many centuries elapse before they again revisit our neighbourhood. A great number, however, only circle once round the sun, and never return to it again. The orbits into which, in accordance with the law of gravitation, they are bent, are so inconceivably long, that before they can reach the farther parts of them they come within the attracting influence of other stars, and are drawn off to pursue new orbits around new centres; and in this way a comet may wander through the universe for countless ages, seeking rest and finding none, till at last some star seizes it with a firmer grasp than the rest, compels it into a smaller orbit, and thus secures it as a perpetual attendant upon itself.

The most singular history on record is that of Lexell's comet, which made its appearance in 1770. On it elements being calculated, it was found that its orbit was exceedingly small, and its period no more than five and a half years, and consequently astronomers were much surprised that it had never been observed before. But on tracing back its path, it was found that it had just passed close to the planet Jupiter, and the inference was arrived at that in winging its long flight round some distant sun it had found its way into our system, and, impinging almost directly on the powerful Jupiter, had its wings clipped, its roving tendencies restrained, and its long period of millions of years reduced to a quiet revolution of between five and six. But it was soon set at liberty again by the same power which had first restrained it. Jupiter's period is eleven years—just double that of the comet—and accordingly after the latter had twice circled round the sun in its diminished orbit, the two bodies must have again encountered at the very scene of their former collision. What then took place we know not; Jupiter must have again asserted his potent influence, powerful enough at such close quarters to overcome that of the sun, twisted the comet's orbit as it pleased him, and again dismissed it on its long wanderings through space.*

---

* It is not improbable that all the comets of short period, whose orbits lie entirely within the limits of the solar system,

The question used often to be asked—whether there was any likelihood of one of these nomadic bodies coming into collision with our own earth, and if this event *did* take place, what its effect would be upon us? The answer which we can now give to this question is a startling one. The earth *does* come into collision with a comet regularly twice every year, and the result is simply a shower of shooting stars more or less numerous and brilliant, according to the density of the portion of the tail which we encounter. But we must by no means conclude that every such collision would be attended by equally harmless consequences. Fortunately the comets which we encounter are composed of small and widely-scattered fragments, but many will probably consist of far larger masses more densely crowded together. Numbers of meteoric stones are too large to be converted into vapour

---

have been drawn into them by the action of some of the larger planets as above described, and that in course of time they may again be dismissed from our neighbourhood as Lexell's has been.

during their passage through our atmosphere, and reach the ground in a solid but red-hot state. Several of these are on record which weighed more than a hundred pounds, and one, which fell in Spain in 1810, measured thirty inches in length and weighed three-quarters of a ton. An encounter with a comet composed of such masses as this would be a frightful ordeal for the earth to pass through. Its whole surface would be bombarded for some minutes or hours with great lumps of red-hot rock, which would burn and destroy everything upon which they fell. The only chance of the human race surviving such a catastrophe would lie in the fact that astronomers would probably forsee its advent, and warn everyone to take refuge in cellars or under bomb-proof casements, from which they would emerge, after the storm was over, to find all around them a mass of blazing ruins.

Nor is even this the worst from which a collision with one of these dangerous bodies might take. An account with the head of a comet would be a far more destructive event than a passage through its tail. And such an event, though extremely improbable, is yet a perfectly possible occurrence. Arago estimated the chances against any particular cometary nucleus striking the earth to be about three hundred millions to one; but still these chances, great as they are, must be by no means confounded with certainty; and indeed we find that on more than one occasion such a collision has very nearly happened. The nucleus of the comet of 1832, for instance, would have struck the earth if it had only been a month sooner. The consequences of such a catastrophe are almost too horrible to be contemplated. If, as is possibly the case in most comets, the nucleus consists of incandescent gas, we should find ourselves plunged in an instant into a mass of blazing vapour, which would scorch every trace of life off the earth's surface, and, not impossibly, dissipate its solid mass in smoke. If, on the other hand, as several astronomers of note have believed, certain cometary nuclei are composed of one solid mass, the results of a collision would be little less disastrous. Laplace describes them thus:—"It is easy to represent the effects of the shock produced by the earth's encountering a comet. The axis and the motion of rotation changed; the waters abandoning their former position to precipitate themselves towards the new equator; a great part of men and animals whelmed in a universal deluge, or destroyed by the violent shock imparted to the terrestrial globe; entire species annihilated; all the monuments of human industry overthrown—such are the disasters which a shock of a comet would necessarily produce." And even if, returning to the old hypothesis, we suppose ourselves coming into contact with a purely gaseous comet, though no mechanical shock of the above nature would be experienced, the chemical consequences might yet be equally fatal. Whatever the cometary material may be, it is not likely that it will be the same as that which composes our own atmospheric air; and, as our lungs are not adapted for the inhalation of any other kind of gas, the probable effect of the intermingling of our atmosphere with the substance of a comet would be at once to render the former utterly unfitted for the support of animal life.

LAPLACE'S NEBULAR HYPOTHESIS.

WE have now completed our survey of the great system of which we ourselves form a part. Sun, planets, satellites, and comets—all the elements of the solar system—have successively passed before us; and the only heavenly orbs we have left to consider are the more distant stellar ones, which are so far removed from our own immediate ken. But before we proceed to visit those distant realms, we must glance for a moment at Laplace's great theory of the origin of our system, one of the grandest and most magnificent speculations which it has ever entered into the heart of man to conceive. It is true that Newton's discovery of the law of gravitation furnished us with a key to much that was dark and inexplicable before; it reduced the motions of the planets to harmonious symmetry, and replaced the elaborate eccentrics, cycles, and epicycles of the ancients by simpler and more familiar curves. That law, as all our readers are aware, explains why the planets move in ellipses, and accounts for their different periods and ever-varying velocities; but there are questions which it does *not* answer—such as why all those elliptical orbits are so nearly circular, and why the planets and satellites all revolve round their primaries and rotate on their axes in the same direction—namely from east to west; all those orbits being moreover very nearly in the equatorial planes of the primaries.* On these points Newton's law throws no light; the solar system would be equally possible, and, with certain limitations, equally stable, and equally fitted for the support of life if this remarkable uniformity did not exist. To what then are we to attribute it? Is it likely to have been a direct and arbitrary exercise

---

* These laws are indeed broken by the satellites of Uranus, but it is impossible to doubt that this single exception arises from accidental circumstances, and that the otherwise unbroken uniformity must be explained by some common cause.

of the Creative will, or a less direct result of that power, working by natural means from some prior form of existence? Were the sun and planets called suddenly into being in their present forms and with their present motions, or were they developed by slow and gradual steps from some simpler original creation? Science tells us that both hypotheses would accord sufficiently well with known present facts; reverential thought pronounces neither of them inconsistent with the loftiest views of the Divine power and wisdom. But the latter is certainly the more interesting and attractive to us, and, we may perhaps add, apparently the more consonant with what we see of the Almighty's working in the lesser world around us. We see the perfect man developed from a helpless babe; we see the loftiest tree developed from a tiny bud; and there is nothing incongruous in supposing that our glorious system itself may have sprung from some vast but equally simple germ. This is a subject which must be handled with humility and diffidence; for we are leaving the regions of mathematics and entering upon those of uncertain speculation; we are treading on sacred ground in seeking to enter into the counsels of the Great Architect of the Universe. We are endeavouring to go deeper than the laws of Nature will take us; we are seeking for a key to the mysteries of our system in the probable circumstances of its creation. For this it is that the bold and lofty speculation of Laplace seeks to do; it reaches back into the unfathomable ages of a past eternity, and takes its stand beside the Almighty Author of all things at the first exercise of His creative fiat, when the foundations of the earth and the heavens were laid, when the morning-stars sang together, and all the sons of God shouted for joy.

The Nebular Hypothesis is briefly and poetically summed up as follows by the Poet Laureate in "The Princess:"—

> "This world was once a fluid haze of light,
> Till towards the centre set the starry tides,
> And eddied into suns, that wheeling cast
> The planets."

Laplace supposes that the first great act of creation—possibly the only one which strictly merits the name, the only one in which things that are seen were made not of things that do appear—was the calling into existence everywhere throughout the infinite regions of space a huge, chaotic, and nebulous mass of matter, such as was supposed to form the substance of the cometary bodies.* This is the only hypothetical step in the whole argument, all the rest following from it, as we shall see, by a course of the most rigid deduction. And against his hypothesis we think no reasonable objection can be urged. It accords with the language of Scripture—"The earth was without form and void, and darkness was upon the face of the deep." It harmonizes with the other sciences; the

---

* We give in the text Laplace's own theory unaltered. Those who accept the mordern hypothesis of the nature of comets would have to replace his "fluid haze of light" by a vast cloud of meteoric stones. But this supposition would not invalidate the theory; it would accord equally well with the rest of Laplace's speculation; and every step in the after development would be the same in either case.

geologist, in particular, having often to suppose the existence at a former period of a state of things springing from some such origin as this. Nor is it only to the man of science that the idea commends itself; it is a favourite theme with the poets. We find it in the pages of Hesiod, of Ovid, and of Dante. Milton gives it expression thus:—

> "A hoary deep, a dark
> Illimitable ocean, without bound,
> Without dimension, where length, breadth, and height,
> And time, and place, are lost; where eldest Night
> And Chaos, ancestors of Nature, hold
> Eternal anarchy, amidst the noise
> Of endless wars, and by confusion stand.
>   A wild abyss,
> The womb of Nature, and perhaps her grave;
> Of neither sea, nor shore, nor air, nor fire,
> But all these in their pregnant causes mixed
> Confus'dly........Chaos umpire sits,
> And by decision more embroils the fray
> By which he reigns: next him, high arbiter,
> Chance governs all."

But the Spirit of God moves upon the face of the waters, and the first elements of order begin to emerge from primeval chaos.

As all the particles of this nebulous mass

would exert a mutual attracting influence upon each other, it follows, in accordance with the law of gravitation, that they would begin to settle down and condense gradually around certain centres, the matter at which, from the intestinal workings of the whole, had become denser than the general mass around. And each of the nuclei thus formed contains the embryo of a separate sun; in each void chaotic mass the eye of the philosopher can already detect the germ not only of the great central orb, but of all its gorgeous band of attendants—planets and asteroids, satellites and rings. Let us follow the history of one of these nebulæ—say the parent of our own system—and trace the steps of its gradual elimination from chaos and conversion into the glorious cosmos which we now behold it.

The particles of this mass will all, of course, gravitate towards the centre, and a spherical form will thus be assumed by the whole body; but as the particles will approach the centre from opposite sides and with different velocities, a motion of rotation round an axis will necessarily be generated—slow at first, but rapidly increasing in velocity. As the ball condenses more and more, and shrinks into smaller bulk, it will, by a familiar mechanical law, spin round faster and faster; till at length the centrifugal force at the equatorial parts will overbalance the attraction of gravity, and a ring of surface-matter will detach itself from the general mass, and remain poised in mid-air behind as the ball within shrinks further and further away from it. The same process will be repeated over and over again, until at last the central mass becomes sufficiently solidified to resist any further separation of its parts. Now if we look at the case of any of these rings, we shall find that the form it eventually assumes will be different in different cases. If its material, as it is detached from the central mass, should happen to be of extremely uniform consistency throughout and to be poised with extreme accuracy about its centre, it might possibly cool down and solidify in the ring-shape;* but the chances against this are so great that we should expect it to be a very rare phenomenon indeed. If the density of the ring were at all irregular, it would inevitably split up into fragments, as the cohesion of its parts would be very slight. The largest of these fragments would, by its superior attraction, assume the others into its mass, and the whole would solidify into one globe of considerable size, except in the rare case of all the fragments happening to be about the same magnitude, when they would continue separate, and revolving round their primary in very nearly

---

* This part of Laplace's theory must be somewhat modified to render it consonant with the discoveries of modern science. It has been shewn that a ring, such as Saturn's, could not possibly exist in a solid state, but that it must be composed of separate fragments, or meteorolites, such as constitute the matter of the solar corona, and probably of the comets. But the theory readily adapts itself to the explanation of such a phenomenon. The ring would be detached from its primary in a viscous state: and as it would be impossible for it to solidify as a whole, it would break up into small fragments, which would solidify separately and move in nearly coincident orbits, thus preserving the general form of a ring, although not one composed of continuous matter.

coincident orbits. Of course the planets, as they were thrown off from the sun, would proceed, in turn, to develope satellites of their own in the same manner and with the same possible varieties.

Now all of these results we find actually occurring in nature. The perfect rings we have in the case of Saturn; the groups of small planets near together are represented by the asteroids; while in every other case we meet with the arrangement which we have seen would be the most likely to occur— a large satellite revolving round its primary, and situated at a considerable distance from any of the others. All the peculiarities of planetary motion, too, are accounted for by this theory. The planes in which the planets move are nearly coincident with the plane of the sun's equator, because the matter of which they are composed is thrown off from the tropical parts of that body. Their orbits are nearly circular, because such would be the motion of their particles while yet in the ring condition. And the direction in which they revolve is the same as that in which the sun turns on its axis, because they would acquire an impulse in that direction before they parted company with it.*

The nature and origin of the comets are also easily explained on this hypothesis. When the original nebulous material of the universe began to gravitate towards its several centres, large masses of it seem to have been in many cases left behind, too evenly balanced between the different attracting influences to yield to any one of them. But as their position would be one of unstable equilibrium, in the course of time the attraction of some one or other of the centres would come to predominate, and the filmy and uncondensed mass would gradually yield to its sway, and descend towards the controlling orb. Another very mysterious

---

* The theory also accounts for the fact of the planets rotating about their axes in the same direction as that of their orbitual revolution. When a fragment was detached from the ring, its outer particles would have a greater velocity in the general direction of motion than its inner ones, and there would be on the whole a moment of momentum in that direction about the centre of gravity.

point which the nebular hypothesis accounts for is the existence of a resisting medium around the sun, and extending to a considerable distance from it. The existence of such a medium is now undoubted. Encke's comet, which possesses the smallest orbit of any connected with our system, is sensibly drawing nearer and nearer to the sun at every revolution; and this fact cannot be accounted for in any other way than by supposing this medium to exist. On Laplace's hypothesis its origin is readily explained; it must evidently be part of the original solar nebula, which, from its extreme rarity, has never undergone condensation at all.* The terrible part which this resisting medium may be destined to play in the great drama of the universe is indicated but too plainly by the effect it has already begun to produce on the comet which comes most immediately under its influence. Slackening by sure though

---

* On the more recent theory, it will probably be simply the matter composing the solar corona.

imperceptible degrees the speed of every planet and comet in the system, and thus stealing away their power to resist the sun's attracting force, it will, by its insensible influence, bring them all in time within that orb's resistless grasp, till one by one they drop through his firey atmosphere and sink to rest upon his surface. Thus, to quote the words of Professor Nichol, one of the warmest advocates of the nebular hypothesis—"The first indefinite germs of the great organization of the universe, provision for its long existence, and finally its shroud, are all involved in that master conception from which Laplace endeavours to survey the mechanisms amid which we are. Not in confusion, however, shall this majestic system finally pass away—not with the jar and confused voice of ruin, but even in its own quiet and majestical order, like the flower which, having adorned a speck of earth, lets drop its leaves when its work is done and falls back obediently on its mother's bosom."

The terms in which the final destruction of our earth is spoken of in Scripture, and the comparatively short existence which seems to be in Providence destined for it, render it pretty certain that this globe at least will not meet with its doom in the above-mentioned manner. But as such an event is not only a perfectly possible one in the economy of nature, but an absolute certainty supposing that the resisting medium were allowed time enough to do its work,* it may not be out of place to pause for a moment and consider what is involved in such a catastrophe. Let us think, for example, what the case would be with our own earth, if no speedier destruction were to come upon it from some yet unanticipated and possibly miraculous cause. Many centuries no doubt —it may be many milleniums—would elapse before the most delicate observations could reveal the working of the mysterious agent. But at length some astronomer detects a

---

* The fact of the gradual dissipation of the energy of our system, established by Sir William Thomson, points also to the final destruction of the earth, and would tend to hasten the catastrophe we describe.

L

minute change in the elements of the earth's orbit which cannot be accounted for by any of the ordinary perturbations, and he is compelled to the belief that the resisting medium is beginning perceptibly to influence the planet. This discovery, when publicly announced, could not fail seriously to impress the most thoughtless of hearers. The first step has been taken by the earth on its way to a doom as fearful as the imagination can paint and as inevitable as the unchanging laws of nature can make it. Still generation after generation passes away; the end is—visibly—no nearer, and but for the figures of the astronomers the whole thing might be denounced as an idle fable. But not the less surely does the unseen destroyer fulfil his mission; and in time the effects of his work become palpable to every eye. The sun's disc is perceptibly enlarged, the intensity of his light and heat are increased, the length of the year is diminished. At first the change of climate is a pleasant and grateful one, except between the tropics, and even there it is not so marked as to be very severely felt. But slowly and surely the influence becomes more potent, and when we look again some ages later, the face of the intertropical regions is scarcely recognizable. The rich vale of the Nile, the fertile plains of the Ganges, the cotton plantations of the south, have disappeared; the sandy deserts of Africa and Asia have extended their bounds and stretch without an oasis far on either side of the equator. The inhabitants retreat, some to the north and some to the south, but the fiery belt between steadily pursues them, and mile after mile, league after league, falls under its devastating sway. Some ages more pass away, and when we look again the vineyards of Spain, the olive-groves of Italy, the fig-gardens of Turkey, are gone; their cities still stand with all their splendid palaces, their gorgeous temples, but they are like Tadmor in the wilderness—cities without inhabitants. Look again, and Mont Blanc has lost his diadem of snow and rears his head, a bare cone of granite, above the dry and rocky table-land which was once the Mer de Glace. Look again, and our own land has, in its turn, become a burning desert. And now the whole inhabitants of the globe are collected in two narrow circles around either pole. The ice and the snow have disappeared, and the frozen plains of Greenland and Labrador teem with tropical vegetation. But the narrowed limits of the habitable earth can no longer support this vast increase of population, and famine begins to mow down its victims by millions. Now, indeed, the end of all life on the earth draws on apace. The resisting medium, from the increased proximity to the sun, grows rapidly much denser, and its effect is proportionately increased. The heat and drought become more and more insupportable. Rain and dew fall no longer. All springs of water fail, and the rivers dwindle down to streamlets, and trickle slowly over their stony beds. And now scarcity of water is added to scarcity of food. Those who escape from the famine perish by the drought, and those who escape from the drought are reserved for a fate more awful yet. For a time, indeed, the few remaining inhabitants of the earth are partially screened from the overwhelming power of the sun by a dense canopy of clouds. From the excessive evaporation, thick columns of mist are constantly rising from the surface of every lake and every sea, and forming into dense banks of cloud, which hang like a funeral pall over the dying earth. But soon the sun scorches up these vapour-banks and dissipates them into space as fast as they can be formed by evaporation. Then the fiery orb shines out in unutterable splendour without the lightest cloud-wreath to interpose between himself and his victims. Then, truly, the heavens become as iron and the earth as brass. Then the last denizens of the world are stricken down and consumed, the last traces of organic life are blotted from its surface. How different the "last man" here from Campbell's picture of

"The last of human mould,
Who shall creation's death behold
As Adam saw its prime!"

Then the last drops of ocean are dried up, and nothing but a bare and blighted mass of rock is left of that earth which once, even in its Maker's eyes, was altogether good. Still the doomed planet rushes on to its awful fate. Swiftly and more swiftly it circles round the sun, like the bark which once drawn within the influence of the whirlpool is sucked irresistibly into its fearful vortex. At last it seems to get paralysed by the iron grasp that is tightening upon it —it staggers, pauses for a moment in its headlong career, and thus checked in its onward progress the sun draws it straight down to itself. A hurried rush through the tossing sea of fire, a swift plunge through the cloudy stratum behind, and the earth sinks to its eternal resting-place on the face of its parent globe.

THE STARS.

WE must turn now to realms lying beyond our own solar system. Beginning with ourselves and our sister planets, we have considered in succession the lesser light which rules the night, the greater light which rules the day, the comets which wing their wild flights around it, and the mysterious ether which encompasses it, and which in time will bring all the rest—planets, satellites, and comets—within its remorseless grasp. And now it remains to wind up by taking a glance at the great stellar universe around us, compared with which our own system, mighty as it is, counts but as a drop in the ocean. And here, as formerly, our subject naturally divides itself into two parts. We have to consider, first, those facts relating to the stars which depend upon their general physical character and their individual peculiarities; and, secondly, those which depend on their collocation in space and their movements through the realms of the infinite. As for the first, the great distance at which the stars are from us prevents us from knowing almost anything whatever about their condition, except what we can infer from analogy. They hold the same place in creation that our own sun does. They are not satellites of any other body, but primary orbs, independent sources of light and heat, and probably the centres of systems not less varied and gorgeous than our own. Hence we may argue with a high degree of probability that those facts which have been ascertained concerning the general nature of the sun, hold equally true of the stars. And as for their individual peculiarities, we are for the most part equally in the dark about them also, and that for the same reason. All the stars appear to us as mere luminous specks without any perceptible magnitude. And although "one star differeth from another star in glory," though even the naked eye can detect many degrees of brilliancy among them, yet it is often impossible to say whether this is due to a real difference in size and lustre, or only to the fact of the brilliant star being much nearer to us than the faint one. But there are two classes of stars which form marked exceptions to the general rule, and stand out prominently from the rest. These are binary stars, and periodical or temporary stars.

The existence of the binary stars was discovered by Sir William Herschel towards the close of last century. It had long been noticed by astronomers as a remarkable coincident that in several instances a pair of bright stars were found in very close proximity to each other, much closer than we should have expected supposing the stars to have been scattered up and down at random over the whole face of the heavens. Still it was never thought that this was anything more than a coincidence; it was supposed that these stars had no connection with each other, but were altogether separate bodies, which merely happened to be situated in one straight line with ourselves. But Herschel having, for some scientific purposes which it would take too long to explain, determined to make a series of minute and careful observations upon these double stars, soon found to his surprise that they were rapidly shifting their positions relatively to each other; and, in short, he was ere long led to the conclusion that the two stars were in reality situated close together, and revolving in orbits round one another. Many pairs of stars of this kind were observed and registered, while in some cases the combinations were found to consist of three stars, and even four, instead of two.

But one of the most remarkable features about these multiple stars is that they are very frequently of two different colours. In the case of the double stars the two colours are usually complementary; colours, that is, which when mixed together, in proper proportions, produce white. Thus one will be green and the other red, or one orange and the other blue, or one violet and the other yellow. Similarly in the triple stars we may have a blue, a red, and a yellow, or a green, an orange, and a violet. In a quadruple star we may have blue, green, orange, and red; and so on, in endless combinations. If there be any planets in attendance upon these multiple suns, as in all probability there will be, the celestial phenomena at those planets will be of the most extraordinary character indeed, and everything that depends on these phenomena—their times and their seasons, their days and their years—will be involved in the most intricate complications. If, indeed, any of them happened to be situated in very close proximity to one of the primaries, things with it would not be so confused. It would always revolve round the same sun, though in a very irregular and perturbed orbit; and hence its days and its years would follow each other pretty much in the natural and regular order. But its seasons will vary much both in length and temperature, and its nights, though much darker than its days, will yet differ from them far less than is the case with us. For when the primary orb sinks beneath the horizon, the secondary ones will shine out in full splendour, much smaller and more distant than the primary, but yet far exceeding in brilliancy the borrowed light of the brightest of full moons. But most of the planets, not nestled close enough beside any one of their suns, will come pretty equally under the influence of all. Take for instance the case of a planet in a quadruple system at a time when it happens to be about equally distant from all its four suns. A green and a red sun are above the horizon, and when we look directly at either, its colour is clear, brilliant, and well-defined. But their rays meet and mingle and unite into a dazzling snowy white, which imparts to the whole landscape the pure radiant look which seems to fill the firmament on a sunny day when the ground is covered with snow. A light cloud-wreath steals over the green sun, and a faint rosy blush overspreads the face of the sky. The cloud thickens and the rosy hue deepens into a mellow crimson. Then the green sun sets and a blue one rises, changing the red light of the sky into a rich purple, veined here and there with pale amethyst, as a few rays from the green sun struggle through the clouds just as it sinks beneath the horizon. The purple changes into a deep gold as the blue sun is succeeded by an orange one, and the gold pales down as the red sun sinks to his rest in turn. The orange is left alone, and when it, too, sets, night comes on apace. And now the moons rise and shed their radiance on the scene. But how differently do they show from the pale uniform light that beams from our own plain satellite! Every colour of the rainbow glows from their faces; in belts, in spots, in lunes, their chequered discs reflect every shade of hue that the artist's palette can produce. The parts illumined by one sun alone reflect, more faintly than the rest, the colours of their respective orbs; those which come within the light of two or three of them will shine more brightly and with gayer combinations of colours; while in the parts on which all the four suns shine at once we find again the snowy white, so bright as to sparkle almost with the light of day. But where there are four great lights to rule the day, night will be of unfrequent occurrence and of short duration; and soon the four suns, their nocturnal course ended, begin at once to draw nigh to their rising. Pale, slender threads of red, green, blue, and orange steal out from the darkness in four quarters of the horizon; and these widen and lengthen till they mingle together at their extremities in softly shading hues of white, indigo, and gold. Brighter and broader they grow, and the gorgeous variegated belt spreads rapidly from horizon to zenith, till at last the suns have fairly risen, and their many-coloured rays combine again into the dazzling white of the perfect day.

Nor are the annual phenomena of these planets—those, namely, which are connected with their seasons and their years—less extraordinary than their diurnal phenomena, which relate to their days and nights. Take the case of a planet in circumstances such as we have supposed above, situated at about equal distances from its several suns. It has just returned from performing a revolution about one of them, and while away on the farther side of that body it was pretty far removed from the influence of the others; and hence it has enjoyed a tolerably quiet and orderly year. Its days and its seasons have followed each other in due succession, though in their length and their temperature there were many and varied irregularities. But now, completing its circuit, it comes again into the region of confusion and anarchy. New suns wax and brighten till they rival the old one in splendour. Distinction of day and night there is none. Universal summer prevails over the planet —in some places mild, in others extreme— these patches of different climates being seemingly scattered up and down arbitrarily over the face of the globe. But gradually one of the suns—not the same one as before

—begins to exercise a markedly more potent influence than the rest; and they slowly dwindle in the distance, while the victorious orb grows larger and brighter as it draws its captive down towards it. And now the planet starts to perform again a new revolution in a comparatively undisturbed orbit. Day and night, summer and winter, seedtime and harvest resume their wonted sway. But how altered are they all! The sun and the moon have changed their size, their brilliancy, and their colour; new planets stud the sky; new comets wheel around the sun; and only the more distant stars retain their positions unaltered. The year has changed its length; seasons and climate are revolutionized; zones formerly frigid or tropical have become temperate; and those temperate, torrid. The old vegetation, blighted by drought or nipped by unwonted frost, withers away, and new trees and plants take its place. The fauna change with the flora; birds and animals migrate; while whole races of men follow their example, or adapt themselves with difficulty to their altered climates. But scarcely are they settled down to their new circumstances ere a similar change again takes place, and they are whirled off to perform an equally brief circuit around yet another sun. And so on they go in their restless career—

"It may be for years, and it may be for ever,"

unless a favouring chance carries their planet very near to one of its suns, and thus enables that orb to establish an indisputable sway over it, and secure it as a permanent satellite.

The second class of stars to which we alluded—the periodical and temporary stars—are much rarer phenomena than those which we have just been considering, while their actual nature is altogether unknown to us. There are on record about six or eight instances in which bright stars have suddenly appeared in parts of the heaven where previously there was none, and after continuing to shine with varying brilliancy for a few months or years, have been again utterly extinguished. In one case, at least, it is believed that a star of this kind has reappeared several times at intervals of about one hundred and fifty years—a fact which, if true, would seem to indicate some periodicity in the causes of its appearances and disappearances. In several cases of a somewhat similar kind this periodicity is unquestionably to be found. A good many stars undergo regular increases and diminutions of brilliancy, the period of some being two or three days, of others as many months, and of others several years. Some of them, at stated intervals, disappear for a short time altogether. Various theories have been suggested to account for these phenomena. Some astronomers suppose that the stars in question have large dark planets or companion suns revolving round them, which at intervals interpose between them and us, and cut off the whole or a part of their light. Others attribute their varying brilliancy to dark spots and patches upon their surfaces. The temporary stars some suppose to have been altogether annihilated, or to have had their sources of light and heat exhausted. Others suppose them to revolve in very long orbits like the comets, and only to become visible when at the parts of their course nearest to the earth. All these hypotheses are possible, but hypotheses it is to be feared they will ever remain. Nothing but actual observation could tell us which is the correct one, and the bodies in question are so distant that evidence of this kind we can never hope to obtain.

Of the physical constitution of the stars we know but little. Analogy tells us that they are bodies of the same character, and probably of much the same magnitude, as our own sun. Recent spectrum analysis goes further, and shows us from an examination of their light that the substances which exist most plentifully in the sun's atmosphere, such as sodium, are also to be met with largely among the stars. More information about them than this we have not much hope of attaining to. There is no reasonable probability of our ever having telescopes powerful enough to give us further revelations of the nature of the stars. To our present instruments they appear simply as specks of light of no visible dimensions, and differing only in brightness. According to these varying degrees of brilliancy the stars are classed—the brightest being styled of the first magnitude, the next of the second magnitude, and so on through the telescopic stars down to the fifteenth. But this term must not be misunderstood. None of them have any perceptible magnitude whatever; even Sirius, the brightest, presents no marked disc like the planets; he is strictly a mathematical point of light—position without magnitude. How much the stars differ from each other in actual size and inherent brilliancy, and how far their gradations of apparent brightness are due simply to their different distances from us, is a question which it is absolutely impossible to answer with certainty in more than two or three cases. The tiny orb, which is only revealed to us by the most powerful telescopes, is perhaps a not less glorious sun than Sirius or Procyon, although buried at such a depth in the abysses of space as to be altogether invisible to the unaided eye.

The first speculations as to the distribution of the stars in space were made by Sir William Herschel. They were founded on what was confessedly an hypothesis, and therefore did not profess to give a result more than approximately true. Later observations have weakened Herschel's hypothesis and caused his theory to be modified, but as considerable weight must still be attached to it, we shall proceed to give it in its original form, and then mention the circumstances which have led to its modification.

We have seen that the varying degrees of brightness in the stars are due to one or more of the following causes—difference of distance, difference of size, or difference of illuminating power. Doubtless all these causes actually exist and produce their respective effects; but let us see which will most readily account for the observed results. Suppose one star A to appear a hundred times as bright to us as another B. If they are equal in size and distance, A's absolute illuminating power must be a hundred times greater than B's. If they are equally distant and equally brilliant, A's apparent magnitude must be a hundred times greater than B's, and therefore his radius ten times, and his volume a thousand times greater. But, lastly, if they are equally brilliant and equally large, B must be ten times further away than A. Thus the difference between A and B may be due either to A's being a thousand times larger, a hundred times more luminous, or only ten times nearer. In Herschel's time there was no reason for supposing the stars to vary more in size or brilliancy than in distance, and as variations in the latter accounted far the most readily for the observed differences, they were clearly, by all the laws of probability, the most likely to furnish the true explanation.

Herschel acted upon this assumption.* He proceeded actually to compare the light emanating from the different stars, and calculated from this their probable relative distances. This was done without much difficulty, and he next set himself the great task of discovering from these data the way in which the stars are distributed through space, the configuration of the great stellar universe, and the position which our sun occupies in it. The labour required for this was immense. It involved a careful examination of every part of the sky, both in the northern and southern hemispheres, and a tabling of the number of stars in them arranged in order of magnitude. He patiently directed his telescope by turns to the different quarters of the heavens, and calculated first the number of the larger stars which were to be found in them. The result of this showed

---

* We are not aware that he has anywhere stated the argument in the form given above, but there can be no doubt that we have correctly stated the train of reasoning which must have passed through his mind.

that the first three or four magnitudes were distributed about equally over the whole sky; and he accordingly inferred that, to a certain distance at least, the stars were grouped pretty uniformly all round us. But then came a sudden break. When he counted those next in order, he found that, except in one portion of the sky, there were scarcely any; and when he arrived at the telescopic stars—those namely which are invisible to the naked eye—there were none at all, except in that great luminous belt which spans the whole firmament, and which is known by the name of the Milky Way. The inference from these facts was obvious. In most directions the stars came very speedily to an end, but in one circle all round us they seem to extend almost to infinity. We all know the appearance presented to the naked eye by the Milky Way—a white fleecy background, dotted all over with bright and distinct stars. When the telescope is turned upon it, we get a step further; some of the white background is in its turn resolved into separate stars, but another indistinct layer rises up behind them in turn. Higher and higher telescopic powers were attained, but still with the same result; the astronomer's eye penetrated further and further into the depths of space, but still the dim white background of star-dust filled the field of the glass. At length, however, by some optical improvements of Herschel's own devising, he succeeded in considerably increasing the efficiency of his telescopes, and was rewarded by finding the last layer of star-dust completely resolved into distinct and separate orbs. Background there was now none; clear and bright the last stars shone out from the deep black void of the midnight sky. The astronomer laid down his glass; the furthest limits of our universe had been sounded, and its bounds assigned it in every direction. Laying down the telescope, Herschel took up the compasses, and proceeded to map on paper the results of his long and patient search. The conclusion he arrived at was, that the starry universe formed a roundish but irregular disc, with a deep cleft at one side extending nearly down to the sun, which occupies pretty much the centre of the disc. Thus viewed from above or below, the appearance presented would be circular, while laterally it would be that figured in the diagram. *S* is the sun, and

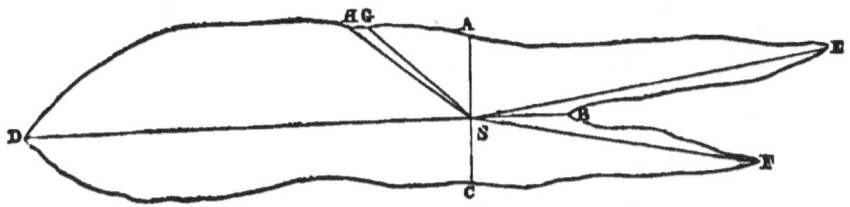

if we look in any of the directions *SA*, *SB*, *SC*, the range of stars which we see is a very brief one; but looking along *SD*, or any other direction in a plane through it perpendicular to that of the paper, we have a much further vista. These directions accordingly correspond to the Milky Way in the heavens. In one part the Milky Way splits up into two branches, separated by a short interval from each other. These two branches are marked in the figure by the lines *SE*, *SF*. The constellations are wedges cut out of this great star-disc. Thus the Great Bear, for example, lies between the lines SG, SH, and therefore contains no very small stars. The Swan, on the other hand, lies along SD, and is hence enriched by a brilliant background of star-dust. Herschel calculated that the number of stars in this enormous cluster is certainly not less than five-and-a-half millions, and is probably one or two millions more.

Such is Herschel's theory, and it is in every respect worthy of the genius and originality of its author. It proceeds on what we have found to be *à priori* the most probable hypothesis—namely, that the different apparent sizes of the stars are mainly due to variations of distance. But no doubt the other possible causes, differences in actual size or brilliancy, must also operate to some extent in the same direction; and in not a few cases we are bound to admit that they present the more probable explanation. There are dotted up and down over the heavens many rich clusters of stars, generally roundish in form, and with comparatively few stars in their immediate neighbourhood. These clusters comprehend stars of every degree of brightness, the faintest being the most numerous, and on the hypothesis of equal magnitude they would imply the existence of vast assemblages of stars, streaming far out into space, and each forming a sort of isolated cone. On the other hand, the appearance might be equally explained by supposing the clusters to be globular in form, their component stars, although differing so much in brightness, being all comparatively near together. Such an arrangement is so much more simple and likely than the other, that the chances in its favour more than counterbalance the *à priori* probability of equal magnitude; and we can scarcely doubt that in these cases the stars differ from each other in size rather than in distance. Herschel himself, in his later years, observed some of these cases, and accepted the explanation given above. Mr. Proctor argues that by doing so he virtually abandoned altogether his system of star-gauging, and gave up his cloven disc. But we cannot think that Herschel's language anywhere warrants this. No doubt the established fact that some stars are much smaller than others, weakens to a certain extent a theory based upon the idea of general equality, but it by no means upsets it. The indubitable fact remains that if two stars be taken at random, one of which is brighter than the other, the probable reason is that it is the nearer rather than the larger. In spite of all exceptions, this remains, and it is the back-bone of Herschel's speculations. And we certainly think that if he had abandoned his cloven disc theory, which he justly regarded as one of his most important achievements, he would have published the fact explicitly, instead of leaving it to be deduced inferentially from a stray sentence here and another there. And we think, therefore, that he adhered in the main to his theory of the general form of the stellar universe, and most subsequent astronomers have not shown much disposition to question it.

Before passing on, we must remark that the star-clusters mentioned above must present scenes of rare magnificence to the dwellers upon one of their planets. The soft sweet glory of our nightly sky would pale to nothing compared with the dazzling effulgence that encircles them. Bright stars are massed round them with a lavishness many thousand times greater than in the neighbourhood of our solar system. Indeed, instead of having a moon and an ocean of stars to rule the night, they will have an ocean of minor suns; and the softer light of moons, and stars of other systems, would be lost in their overwhelming brilliancy. Even by day myriads of bright orbs would contest for precedence with the primary sun; and at night, if such a term can be used at all, their combined rays would scarcely allow his absence to be noticed.

Nor are these star-clusters the greatest marvels of the Milky Way. In many places it is dotted with white spots, of which the telescope can make absolutely nothing. It was long taken for granted that they were clusters of stars like the rest, and that more powerful instruments would in time prove them to be such. But our new and magical ally, the spectroscope, has revealed to us their true nature. It shows that they consist not of solid, but of purely gaseous matter. In fact they appear as vast oceans of flaming gas, doubtless much resembling what we have described as the condition of the solar envelope, but hanging altogether isolated in space, while they spread their huge billows over countless millions of miles. In others we see the work of condensation already begun, as their central parts show traces of solid, or at least of liquid matter. In fact they realize and confirm Laplace's magnificent conception of the original state of our own system, a void chaotic mass, containing in it the germs of all the stars that lighten our midnight sky. If ages and ages of time are given them, their transformation will doubtless be effected in turn, and they too will split up into their countless myriads of suns. Perhaps, indeed, these youngest members of our system may be spared when the older heavens have passed away, and we may look to them for the new heavens and the new earth wherein dwelleth righteousness.

Herschel's labours completed and his results in the main granted, a harder problem still remains behind. The relative distances of the stars have been computed, the farthest bounds of the known universe have been pierced, its figure determined, and its limits assigned it in every direction. But of the absolute dimensions of this great system, astronomers in Herschel's time knew nothing. They had estimated that the farthest stars were probably about five hundred times more distant from us than the nearest ones. But the distance of even the nearest was a sealed mystery. It was known that it could be measured only by millions of millions of miles; but how many of these great units it contained they could not tell. The way in which the distance of the nearer heavenly bodies is found is very simple. When a land surveyor wishes to ascertain the distance of an inaccessible object, he measures what is called a base-line; and making an observation first from one end of this and then from the other, the displacement in the apparent position of the object gives him its distance from either station. And this is the method pursued with the sun and moon. They are observed simultaneously from two distant points of the earth's surface, and from their consequent displacement—or parallax, as it is called in scientific parlance—their distance is readily found. But no such plan avails us with the fixed stars. The distance of any two stations on the surface of our globe is as nothing compared with the enormous space which separates us from them. But the earth's motion in its orbit comes to our aid, and gives us two standpoints immeasurably farther apart from each other than its own two poles. Let us carefully observe one of the stars now, and then wait till six months have elapsed. The earth's revolution about the sun has brought us to a station two hundred million miles away from that of our first observation. And here surely with such an enormous base-line for our observations the difficulty will be easily solved—the star will appear to have shifted to quite a new part of the heavens. But no—to an ordinary telescope no change whatever is visible. One of the chief arguments of the old astronomers against the Copernican system was founded upon this: if the earth revolved in an orbit of such magnitude, the stars should appear in altogether different positions at different seasons of the year. Copernicus, with a little hesitation, gave the true reply—the stars must be at such a distance from us that our orbit is but as a speck in comparison with it. The astronomers laughed this to scorn; it was impossible to believe that the works of creation should have such vast extent as this explanation would involve. But they were attempting to limit the power of the Almighty. In the eternity of God a thousand years appear as one day; to His infinitude a million

million miles are but a single span. Even the distance they thought so impossibly great, we, with the new light of science, know to be but an infinitesimal fraction of the whole dimensions of the universe.

From the days of Copernicus down to the present time, telescopes have steadily been increasing in power and efficiency. Astronomers were well aware that the problem of finding the stellar parallax was only an instrumental difficulty; the stars must suffer some displacement according to the season of the year, and only a sufficiently good telescope in the hands of a sufficiently skilful and accurate observer was required to determine it. By comparing the stellar light with the solar, they had arrived at a rough idea of the probable distance and parallax of some of the stars, and had found reason to think that the parallactic angle was not so small as to make its detection a hopeless task. Several generations of astronomers, however, passed away, and left this, one of the great objects of their life, unfulfilled. The great glory of discovering stellar parallax is shared equally by a Scottish and a Prussian astronomer—Henderson of Edinburgh and Bessel of Köningsberg—who made at the same time, nearly forty years ago, independent observations of two different stars. The extreme difficulty of the problem will be seen when we state that the displacement found by Bessel, that of a star in the neck of the Swan, is only an angle of a third of a second, or less than a five-thousandth part of the apparent diameter of the sun. We must remember that every astronomical observation is subject to a host of errors. The most perfect telescope ever set up has a score of imperfections in construction and adjustment, and these have to be carefully calculated from repeated observations, and allowed for by difficult mathematical processes. There are also many astronomical sources of error, such as the finite velocity with which light is propagated, and the refraction of its rays by the earth's atmosphere. All these causes produce a far greater displacement in the star than its actual parallax, and the successful elimination of them all, and determination of the small residual angle, is justly regarded as one of the greatest triumphs of human skill and ingenuity. The parallax of these stars having been found, their distances were given at once by a simple trigonometrical formula. The result is, that the nearest star is two hundred thousand times farther from the sun than the earth is,—in other words, the distance of the sun from its nearest neighbour in the great stellar cluster is twenty millions of millions of miles. It follows that the full dimensions of that great cluster from end to end must be at least twenty thousand billion miles.

One problem more, the last and the loftiest, yet remains to be solved, before we can say that we have completely mastered the system of the universe. We have calculated the dimensions of the great stellar cluster, we have determined its configuration, we have estimated the number of orbs which it contains. The question yet remains whether the stars are really fixed, as their popular name supposes, or whether they, like all the minor bodies we have considered, have their own special orbits and revolutions. Satellites circle round their primaries, planets wheel in obedience to the behest of their parent suns, comets under the same potent spell wing their fiery flight through space. And are there no fixed centres amid all this ceaseless motion, no spots on which the wearied imagination may settle, and contemplate from a solid and stable standpoint the workings of the great mechanism around? Science answers, there is none! Wherever there is matter there must be gravitation. The greatest and most glorious orbs of heaven are not less fully bound by that all-pervading law than the lightest speck of sea-foam or the filmy texture of the comets. The sun himself, upon whose majestic court hundreds of bright attendants wait, is subjected in turn to the influence of his mighty brethren, and rolls at their bidding along his appointed course.

We have seen that the motion of the earth in its orbit causes a displacement in the apparent positions of the stars. This displacement, however, is only a periodical and temporary one; as the seasons circle round, the earth returns to the spot from whence he set out, and the stars resume their old positions. The fact that some of them had a distinct and separate motion, indicating a permanent change of their position relatively to the sun, was first discovered by Edmund Halley. Some observations of the three brilliant stars—Sirius, Arcturus, and Aldebaran—made by the old Egyptian astronomers, had fortunately been handed down to his time, and on looking over them he perceived that these stars must have shifted their positions since that early time, by a small but well-marked amount. This indicated that either these stars, or the sun, or probably both, must have changed their places by many million miles since these old records were penned by the philosophers of Alexandria. Other astronomers followed in Halley's track, and by the beginning of this century the proper motions, as they are called, of more than a hundred stars had been determined, chiefly by comparing them with Tycho Brahe's catalogue, made out two hundred years before. These proper motions showed great differences in amount and in direction, and no attempt was made to reconcile and systematize them until the subject was taken up by the bold and speculative genius of Sir William Herschel, who revelled in difficulties, and whose daring and ambitious spirit always selected the loftiest and apparently most hopeless themes. He succeeded in evoking order out of apparent confusion and chaos, and announced his discovery of the fact, that the sun, with all his gorgeous following, is sweeping majestically through space in the direction of the constellation Hercules. It was not till fifty years afterwards that another astronomer was found bold enough to grapple with this mighty theme. It was then taken up by some of the leading astronomers of Russia, with the advantage of half a century's additional observations, and Herschel's results were confirmed in the fullest manner possible. The direction in which the earth is moving is now known beyond the possibility of a doubt. His velocity, however, has been variously estimated at from thirty million to a hundred million miles per annum.

Of course the stellar proper motions we have been speaking of are all lateral ones,— at right angles, that is, to the lines joining us to the respective stars. The telescope could never tell us whether the stars have any motion of recess from or approach towards us, unless that motion were so great and long continued as to affect their apparent brightness. But that wonderful modern instrument, the spectroscope, comes here again most unexpectedly to our aid. The way in which it does so is this. The sun's light, as all our readers are aware, is not homogeneous, but compounded of all the colours into which we see it resolved by the prism, or by the exquisite touch of Nature herself in the rainbow.* Now the fundamental distinction between the different coloured rays, and that which enables them to be thus separated from each other, is that the pulsations of either of which they consist all take place with different degrees of rapidity. As the higher notes of the musical scale correspond to more frequent vibrations of the air, so the acuter, or violet, colours are due to more rapid undulations of the ether. The rapidity of these undulations is almost inconceivable, varying from four to eight hundred million million pulsations per second. They can, however, be reckoned with the utmost accuracy, and every shade of colour is as well known and as distinctly identified as every note in music. Now on analyzing, by the spectroscope, the light emanating from Sirius, Dr. Huggins found that all its rays were pulsating with

---

* And, indeed, of other colours which our eyes are not capable of appreciating. There are rays below the red ones, which produce the sensation of heat, though not of light; while those above the violet, while they fall unavailing on the retina, produce the chief effect on the still more sensitive photographic plate.

less than their normal rate. The red wavelets are issuing from the star at the rate of four hundred million million per second, and yet they reach us diminished in number by some forty thousand million per second. The inference from this is obvious. It can only be explained on the hypothesis that the source of light is itself regreding from us; and a simple proportion with the velocity of light establishes that the distance between the sun and Sirius is increasing by twenty miles per second. Other stars have been observed in the same way; some are approaching us, and some receding from us, with velocities reaching as high as fifty miles per second. It is only to the brightest stars, however, that the spectroscope can at present be applied, and no attempt can yet be made to form any general inference from the various results.

The proper motions of the stars are of course due partly to our change of position in space and partly to their own. What the great centre of all this universal motion is we are at present unable to determine. Mädler, of Dorpat, is the only astronomer who has had the boldness to attempt this lofty theme. By studying Herschel's diagram of the stellar system, and combining it with the known direction of our sun's motion, he was led to believe that the centre of that system must be situated in or near the constellation Taurus. A careful examination of all the stars in that quarter of the heavens made him finally fix upon Alcyone, the central orb of the Pleiades, as being the object of his search. His speculations are doubtless very premature; the data upon which they are founded are slight and partially uncertain, on account of the extreme slowness of the motion from which they are deduced. In fact it is probable that many generations must pass away before a sufficiently long course of observation can either confirm or disprove the conclusions at which he arrived. If his theory be correct, the sweet influences of the Pleiades must be potent influences indeed. Holding their eternal court unmoved in the centre of the heavens, they send out their resistless influence to the farthest confines of space, and bend into stately curves around them the most distant bodies of the universe, some of whose grand orbits cannot be traversed in less than five hundred million years.

OTHER UNIVERSES.

THE astronomer has now completed his investigation of the great stellar system of which our sun forms a member. The figure of that system has been defined, its dimensions calculated, and its motions traced out and analyzed. This was the consummation to which, until very recent periods, astronomers of all ages had been accustomed to look as the great goal to which their science tended, though a goal which even the most sanguine of them scarcely hoped that it would ever actually reach. And now that it has been so fully attained, can the astronomer sit down and rest on his laurels and boast that he has fathomed the remotest depths of the universe of God? Not so. While with slow and toilsome steps he has been creeping up to his first goal, he has at the same time been seeing another gradually emerging from the obscurity in front of him, and now that the former is reached, it is but to see the latter standing clearly out in the distance, more hopelessly inaccessible than the other had ever seemed to be. For when we stand on the remotest orb of the Milky Way, the telescope reveals new marvels to our gaze, and opens up fresh and undreamt of regions for scientific research. Not yet are the wonders of creation exhausted. Had it been so, had these really been the uttermost bounds of God's created works, we should still have pronounced them well worthy in magnificence and grandeur of the Omnipotence which called them into being. Let us think for a moment on what a scale of inconceivable magnitude the universe thus far is built. The orbit of our earth is two hundred million miles in diameter, but so insignificant is this vast distance compared with the great gulf which separates us from the fixed stars, that to all except the very most powerful telescopes those stars seem to occupy exactly the same positions in the sky when viewed from two opposite points of our course.

Try a still farther flight,—pass over twenty millions of millions of miles. We have reached the nearest of the stars, and taking our stand on one of its planets, and waiting till evening falls, we look eagerly abroad to mark the altered aspect of the heavens. Here surely, where we have put such an overwhelming distance between us and our former position, the face of the sky will be no longer recognizable—the old heavens will have passed away from over our head, as well as the old earth from beneath our feet. But no,—as the stars one by one steal out from the darkness they group themselves into their old well-known configurations. There is the Little Bear with its pole-star, and the Great Bear with its pointers; there are the bands of Orion and the sweet influences of the Pleiades; there are Mazzaroth and Arcturus, just as they appeared to Job five thousand years ago, and sixty billion miles away. Vast as is the space we have traversed, it is not a thousandth part of that which separates the two most distant stars of the system, and hence we need not wonder that the change we have found is no greater than that which comes over the distant landscape as the traveller advances a score or two of yards along his way. Let us then pursue our journey still further. Sun after sun beams upon us with its brilliant band of planets and comets,—sun after sun pales and lessens in the distance as we leave it behind in our flight; and gradually a change creeps over the face of the heavens. The general figures of the constellations remain the same, but those behind contract their dimensions and shrink more closely together, while those in front are opening out and growing larger and brighter. At length we near the farthest confines of the Milky Way. Very few and very scattered are the stars which still remain in front of us. We can number them all with ease. And now but three are left before us,—but two,—but one. That one is reached in turn. We pass to the further side and look forth into the mysterious abyss which lies beyond. Before, behind, to the right, to the left—whichever way we turn our gaze, it meets with nought but the blackness of darkness—the deep gloom of the midnight sky is unbroken by the gleam of a single star. Onward still we wing our daring flight; the last resting-place is abandoned, the last oasis left behind, and we adventure forth into the trackless wastes of space. One by one the planets of this last sun are passed in our course; now and then a comet overtakes us, and blazes swiftly past into the depths beyond; but if we look onwards, we see that even it soon pauses in its reckless flight, and wheels back on rapid wing to less solitary and untrodden regions. The sun itself dwindles down to a star, and takes its place among a cluster of others which come forth from behind and around it as its paling light permits them to become visible. And soon this cluster too fades, till all distinction of stars in it is lost, and nothing is left but a dim white patch of light, ere long to be blotted out in turn, as it seems to be swallowed up by the surrounding darkness. All created works are left behind, and we stand alone, face to face, with the infinitude of God,—alone where mortal footstep has never trod, where presence there has never been, save that of the ever omnipresent Creator and the spirits which pass and repass, ascending and descending the ladder of vision which bridges the chasm between heaven and earth, as they go and come, ministering to the heirs of salvation.

But suppose that our vision is now quickened by telescopic aid. We turn the glass in the direction from which we have just come to get a last look of the universe we are leaving behind us. And surely enough the little white patch steals out again from the darkness in the centre of the field of view. But what is that faint film of light that clouds the outer edge of the circle? Turn the full power of the instrument upon it, and it brightens into a white patch exactly similar to the former. Move the telescope round, and another, and another, meets the eye. Direct it to any new quarter of the heavens, and the sight presented is the same. The whole sky is mottled with these flecks of white. Thick they are as the motes that dance in the sunbeam, close as the stars that stud the firmament, innumerable as the grains of sand upon the shore. In aspect they exactly resemble the dim and distant appearance presented to view by the system which we have just left,—so exactly, that when once the glass has been turned away from it, we find it impossible, on turning back, to pick it out from the multitudes that surround it. Let us choose out one of the nearest and brightest of these, and wing our flight towards it. As we approach it, we might think that we were but returning to the system we had left. The white patch widens and brightens, stars emerge from it by thousands and tens of thousands, till it fills the whole firmament with a blaze of splendour, surpassing by many-fold the brilliancy of our own nocturnal sky. For the telescope teaches us that while each of these objects is a system of stars, probably not inferior in glory to that of which we form a part, many of them must surpass it in magnificence at least a thousand-fold.*

It would be hopeless to attempt expressing in ordinary language the vast distance at which these clusters of stars are situated from us. If we were to reckon it in miles, or even in millions of miles, figures would pile upon figures, till in their number all definite idea of their value was lost. We must choose another unit to measure these infinitudes of space—a unit compared with which the dimensions of our own solar system shrink into absolute nothingness. The velocity of light is such that it would flash fifteen times from pole to pole of our earth between

---

* The gaseous nebulæ described in the last chapter were originally supposed to belong to this category of external star-clusters; but though they have been struck out of the list, vast numbers still remain. The spectroscope shows that they are not gaseous, and as they are altogether irresoluble into separate stars, we learn that they must be situated far beyond the confines of the Milky Way.

two beats of the pendulum. It bridges the huge chasm that separates us from the sun in little more than eight minutes. But the light that shows us these faint star-clusters had been travelling with this frightful velocity for more than two million years since it left its distant source. We see them to-day in the fields of our telescopes, not as they are now, but as they were countless ages before the creation of man upon the earth. What they are now, who can tell? A system which might appear to us gaseous may have been long ago resolved into a cluster of stars; while one apparently composed of active suns may have exhausted its energies and burnt itself out ages ago.

And what we were when their light started on its mission towards us, God alone knows. A fiery globe of molten rock—a thin cloud of vapour without form and void—or, it may be, not yet in existence at all, unseen and undreamt of save in the eternal counsels of the Creator. Not till the rays had well-nigh completed their flight were the progenitors of those for whose eyes they were destined first formed upon the earth. The six thousand years of man are as nothing compared with their long journey. Two hundred generations have come and gone since Adam walked in Paradise, but if each of these generations had been told over two hundred fold, the antiquity of man would not have rivalled the hoary age of these tiny waves of light. So small are the undulations of ether, that forty thousand of them follow each other within the space of a single inch, so impalpable that they beat upon our eyeballs in countless millions and with incalculable velocity without injuring their delicate surface; and yet so infinitely strong, when guided by their Maker's hand, that they have steered their unerring course for millions of billions of miles, and reached their destination unaltered and unenfeebled.

Of a truth "things small and great," the infinitesimal and the infinite, "bless the Lord; they praise Him and magnify Him for ever." What overwhelming force in these words of

God when read by the light of His works:— "When I consider Thy heavens, the work of Thy fingers, the moon and the stars which Thou hast ordained; what is man that Thou art mindful of him, and the son of man that Thou visitest him?" And what unspeakable preciousness in these:—"Thus saith the Lord, the heaven is My throne, and the earth is My footstool; but to this man will I look, even to him that is poor and of a contrite spirit and that trembleth at My word."

And now let us go one step further, and ask ourselves where these magnificent creations, rising above each other in the scale of magnitude and grandeur, are to have an end. First we had planets with their attendant satellites, then suns with their accompanying planets, then a great cluster consisting of many million suns, and now this vast system composed of thousands of similar clusters. How many steps more we might go in this ascending scale before we reached the climax it is impossible to say. The system of clusters which we have above described may be itself but a unit in a yet greater and more gorgeous whole, and that whole in turn an insignificant fraction of a creation grander yet. But wherever the end may be, to us in our present state it has already come. Further than we have now reached, our finite powers of observation can never hope to attain. A veil of impenetrable obscurity is drawn over all that lies beyond. The Almighty has interposed His stern fiat before the advancing flood of human science, which would fain overspread all creation with its triumphant billows. "Hitherto shalt thou come but no further, and here shall thy proud waves be stayed." The glories that lie beyond are among those things which eye hath not seen, which ear hath not heard, and which it hath not entered into the heart of man to conceive. But though we cannot trace the steps in the ascending scale of creation, we may soar past them in imagination, and ask what the great climax will be. God himself is infinite, but His works must be finite. Suns, clusters, and systems may rise above each other in almost endless succession, but at length some one great system must be reached, whose members, circling round and round in harmony among themselves, must include within their vast limits all the works of the Creator. And what is the mighty centre around which all these motions take place, the one fixed spot in the universe about which all else is in rapid and ceaseless revolution? What can be the worthy centre of this magnificence, the glory compared with which all others sink into the shade? there is indeed a glory that excelleth, a glory such that, in the Apostle's words, even "that which was made glorious hath no glory by reason of the glory that excelleth." But this is a glory uncreate, a glory that shines with no borrowed splendour; it is the glory of the Godhead. Men speak much of heaven as consisting in the felt nearness and presence of God, and hence of its being a state rather than a place. But they forget that while God himself is infinite, the human nature of our Lord and Saviour cannot be so, and hence that there must be some one spot dignified above all others by a special Shechinah—a special manifestation of the glory of the Godhead—that spot where the seer of Patmos beheld a throne set in heaven, and One that sat upon the throne, and in the midst of it a Lamb as it had been slain. And if we ask again what can be the fitting centre of all the gorgeous systems which the science of astronomy reveals to our astonished gaze, what answer *shall* we, what answer *can* we, give but one? Surely we must say with the patriarch, "THIS IN NONE OTHER THAN THE HOUSE OF GOD, THIS IS THE GATE OF HEAVEN."

THE END.

W. METCALFE AND SON, PRINTERS, CAMBRIDGE.

July 1890.

A Catalogue

OF

Educational Books

PUBLISHED BY

Macmillan & Co.

BEDFORD STREET, STRAND, LONDON

CONTENTS

	PAGE
CLASSICS—	
ELEMENTARY CLASSICS	2
CLASSICAL SERIES	4
CLASSICAL LIBRARY; Texts, Commentaries, Translations	6
GRAMMAR, COMPOSITION, AND PHILOLOGY	9
ANTIQUITIES, ANCIENT HISTORY, AND PHILOSOPHY	12
MODERN LANGUAGES AND LITERATURE—	
ENGLISH	13
FRENCH	18
GERMAN	19
MODERN GREEK	20
ITALIAN	20
SPANISH	21
MATHEMATICS—	
ARITHMETIC	21
BOOK-KEEPING	22
ALGEBRA	22
EUCLID AND PURE GEOMETRY	23
GEOMETRICAL DRAWING	24
MENSURATION	24
TRIGONOMETRY	24
ANALYTICAL GEOMETRY	25
PROBLEMS AND QUESTIONS IN MATHEMATICS	26
HIGHER PURE MATHEMATICS	26
MECHANICS	27

	PAGE
PHYSICS	29
ASTRONOMY	31
HISTORICAL	32
NATURAL SCIENCES—	
CHEMISTRY	32
PHYSICAL GEOGRAPHY, GEOLOGY, AND MINERALOGY	34
BIOLOGY	34
MEDICINE	37
HUMAN SCIENCES—	
MENTAL AND MORAL PHILOSOPHY	38
POLITICAL ECONOMY	39
LAW AND POLITICS	40
ANTHROPOLOGY	41
EDUCATION	41
TECHNICAL KNOWLEDGE—	
CIVIL AND MECHANICAL ENGINEERING	42
MILITARY AND NAVAL SCIENCE	43
AGRICULTURE	43
DOMESTIC ECONOMY	44
BOOK-KEEPING	44
GEOGRAPHY	44
HISTORY	45
ART	48
DIVINITY	49

A

CLASSICS.

Elementary Classics; Classical Series; Classical Library, (1) Texts, (2) Translations; Grammar, Composition, and Philology; Antiquities, Ancient History, and Philosophy.

ELEMENTARY CLASSICS.

18mo, Eighteenpence each.

The following contain Introductions, Notes, and Vocabularies, and in some cases **Exercises.**

ACCIDENCE, LATIN, AND EXERCISES ARRANGED FOR BEGINNERS.—By W. WELCH, M.A., and C. G. DUFFIELD, M.A.
AESCHYLUS.—PROMETHEUS VINCTUS. By Rev. H. M. STEPHENSON, M.A.
ARRIAN.—SELECTIONS. With Exercises. By Rev. JOHN BOND, M.A., and Rev. A. S. WALPOLE, M.A.
AULUS GELLIUS, STORIES FROM.—Adapted for Beginners. With Exercises. By Rev. G. H. NALL, M.A., Assistant Master at Westminster.
CÆSAR.—THE HELVETIAN WAR. Being Selections from Book I. of The Gallic War. Adapted for Beginners. With Exercises. By W. WELCH, M.A., and C. G. DUFFIELD, M.A.
THE INVASION OF BRITAIN. Being Selections from Books IV. and V. of The Gallic War. Adapted for Beginners. With Exercises. By W. WELCH, M.A., and C. G. DUFFIELD, M.A.
THE GALLIC WAR. BOOK I. By Rev. A. S. WALPOLE, MA.
BOOKS II. AND III. By the Rev. W. G. RUTHERFORD, M.A., LL.D.
BOOK IV. By CLEMENT BRYANS, M.A., Assistant Master at Dulwich College.
BOOK V. By C. COLBECK, M.A., Assistant Master at Harrow.
BOOK VI. By the same Editor.
SCENES FROM BOOKS V. AND VI. By the same Editor.
BOOK VII. By Rev. J. BOND, M.A., and Rev. A. S. WALPOLE, M.A.
CICERO.—DE SENECTUTE. By E. S. SHUCKBURGH, M.A.
DE AMICITIA. By the same Editor.
STORIES OF ROMAN HISTORY. Adapted for Beginners. With Exercises. By Rev. G. E. JEANS, M.A., and A. V. JONES, M A.
EURIPIDES.—ALCESTIS. By M. A. BAYFIELD, M.A.
MEDEA. By the same Editor. [In the Press.
HECUBA. By Rev. J. BOND, M.A., and Rev. A. S. WALPOLE, M.A.
EUTROPIUS.—Adapted for Beginners. With Exercises. By W. WELCH, M.A. and C. G. DUFFIELD, M.A.
HOMER.—ILIAD. BOOK I. By Rev. J. BOND, M.A., and Rev. A.S. WALPOLE, M.A.
BOOK XVIII. By S. R. JAMES, M.A., Assistant-Master at Eton.
ODYSSEY. BOOK I. By Rev. J. BOND, M.A., and Rev. A. S. WALPOLE, M.A.
HORACE.—ODES. BOOKS I.—IV. By T. E. PAGE, M.A., Assistant Master at the Charterhouse. Each 1s. 6d.

LIVY.—BOOK I. By H. M. STEPHENSON, M.A.
  BOOK XXI. Adapted from Mr. Capes's Edition. By J. E. MELHUISH, M.A.
  BOOK XXII. By the same. *[Shortly.*
  THE HANNIBALIAN WAR. Being part of the XXI. and XXII. BOOKS OF LIVY adapted for Beginners. By G. C. MACAULAY, M.A.
  THE SIEGE OF SYRACUSE. Being part of the XXIV. and XXV. BOOKS OF LIVY, adapted for Beginners. With Exercises. By G. RICHARDS, M.A., and Rev. A. S. WALPOLE, M.A.
  LEGENDS OF ANCIENT ROME. Adapted for Beginners. With Exercises. By H. WILKINSON, M.A.
LUCIAN.—EXTRACTS FROM LUCIAN. With Exercises. By Rev. J. BOND, M.A., and Rev. A. S. WALPOLE, M.A.
NEPOS.—SELECTIONS ILLUSTRATIVE OF GREEK AND ROMAN HISTORY. With Exercises. By G. S. FARNELL, M.A.
OVID.—SELECTIONS. By E. S. SHUCKBURGH, M.A.
  EASY SELECTIONS FROM OVID IN ELEGIAC VERSE. With Exercises. By H. WILKINSON, M.A.
  STORIES FROM THE METAMORPHOSES. With Exercises. By Rev. J. BOND, M.A., and Rev. A. S. WALPOLE, M.A.
PHÆDRUS—SELECT FABLES. Adapted for Beginners. With Exercises. By Rev. A. S. WALPOLE, M.A.
THUCYDIDES.—THE RISE OF THE ATHENIAN EMPIRE. BOOK I. Chs. 89-117 and 228-238. With Exercises. By F. H. COLSON, M.A.
VIRGIL.—SELECTIONS. By E. S. SHUCKBURGH, M.A.
  GEORGICS. BOOK I. By T. E. PAGE, M.A.
  BOOK II. By Rev. J. H. SKRINE, M.A.
  ÆNEID. BOOK I. By Rev. A. S. WALPOLE, M.A.
  BOOK II. By T. E. PAGE, M.A.
  BOOK III. By T. E. PAGE, M.A.
  BOOK IV. By Rev. H. M. STEPHENSON, M.A.
  BOOK V. By Rev. A. CALVERT, M.A.
  BOOK VI. By T. E. PAGE, M.A.
  BOOK VII. By Rev. A. CALVERT, M.A.
  BOOK VIII. By Rev. A. CALVERT, M.A. *[In preparation.*
  BOOK IX. By Rev. H. M. STEPHENSON, M.A.
  BOOK X. By S. G. OWEN, M.A. *[In preparation.*
XENOPHON.—ANABASIS. BOOK I. By Rev. A. S. WALPOLE, M.A.
  BOOK I. With Exercises. By E. A. WELLS, M.A.
  BOOK II. By Rev. A. S. WALPOLE, M.A.
  BOOK III. By Rev. G. H. NALL. *[In preparation.*
  SELECTIONS FROM BOOK IV. With Exercises. By Rev. E. D. STONE, M.A.
  BOOK IV. By the same Editor. *[In preparation.*
  SELECTIONS FROM THE CYROPÆDIA. With Exercises. By A. H. COOKE, M.A., Fellow and Lecturer of King's College, Cambridge.

The following contain Introductions and Notes, but no Vocabulary:—

CICERO.—SELECT LETTERS. By Rev. G. E. JEANS, M.A.
HERODOTUS.—SELECTIONS FROM BOOKS VII. AND VIII. THE EXPEDITION OF XERXES. By A. H. COOKE, M.A.
HORACE.—SELECTIONS FROM THE SATIRES AND EPISTLES. By Rev. W. J. V. BAKER, M.A.
  SELECT EPODES AND ARS POETICA. By H. A. DALTON, M.A., Assistant Master at Winchester.
PLATO.—EUTHYPHRO AND MENEXENUS. By C. E. GRAVES, M.A., Classical Lecturer at St. John's College, Cambridge.
TERENCE.—SCENES FROM THE ANDRIA. By F. W. CORNISH, M.A., Assistant Master at Eton

4 CLASSICS

THE GREEK ELEGIAC POETS.—FROM CALLINUS TO CALLIMACHUS. Selected by Rev. HERBERT KYNASTON, D.D.
THUCYDIDES.—BOOK IV. CHS. 1-41. THE CAPTURE OF SPHACTERIA. By C. E. GRAVES, M.A.

CLASSICAL SERIES FOR COLLEGES AND SCHOOLS.
Fcap. 8vo.

ÆSCHINES.—IN CTESIPHONTEM. By Rev. T. GWATKIN, M.A., and E. S. SHUCKBURGH, M.A. [In the Press.
ÆSCHYLUS.—PERSÆ. By A. O. PRICKARD, M.A., Fellow and Tutor of New College, Oxford. With Map. 8s. 6d.
SEVEN AGAINST THEBES. SCHOOL EDITION. By A. W. VERRALL, Litt.D., Fellow of Trinity College, Cambridge, and M. A. BAYFIELD, M.A., Headmaster's Assistant at Malvern College. 8s. 6d.
ANDOCIDES.—DE MYSTERIIS. By W. J. HICKIE, M.A. 2s. 6d.
ATTIC ORATORS.—Selections from ANTIPHON, ANDOCIDES, LYSIAS, ISOCRATES, AND ISAEUS. By R. C. JEBB, Litt.D., Regius Professor of Greek in the University of Cambridge. 6s.
CÆSAR.—THE GALLIC WAR. By Rev. JOHN BOND, M.A., and Rev. A. S. WALPOLE, M.A. With Maps. 6s.
CATULLUS.—SELECT POEMS. Edited by F. P. SIMPSON, B.A. 5s. The Text of this Edition is carefully expurgated for School use.
CICERO.—THE CATILINE ORATIONS. By A. S. WILKINS, Litt.D., Professor of Latin in the Owens College, Victoria University, Manchester. 3s. 6d.
 PRO LEGE MANILIA. By Prof. A. S. WILKINS, Litt.D. 2s. 6d.
 THE SECOND PHILIPPIC ORATION. By JOHN E. B. MAYOR, M.A., Professor of Latin in the University of Cambridge. 5s.
 PRO ROSCIO AMERINO. By E. H. DONKIN, M.A. 4s. 6d.
 PRO P. SESTIO. By Rev. H. A. HOLDEN, Litt.D. 5s.
DEMOSTHENES.—DE CORONA. By B. DRAKE, M.A. 7th Edition, revised by E. S. SHUCKBURGH, M.A. 4s. 6d.
 ADVERSUS LEPTINEM. By Rev. J. R. KING, M.A., Fellow and Tutor of Oriel College, Oxford. 4s. 6d.
 THE FIRST PHILIPPIC. By Rev. T. GWATKIN, M.A. 2s. 6d.
 IN MIDIAM. By Prof. A. S. WILKINS, Litt.D., and HERMAN HAGER, Ph.D., of the Owens College, Victoria University, Manchester. [In preparation.
EURIPIDES.—HIPPOLYTUS. By Rev. J. P. MAHAFFY, D.D., Fellow of Trinity College, and Professor of Ancient History in the University of Dublin, and J. B. BURY, M.A., Fellow of Trinity College, Dublin. 3s. 6d.
 MEDEA. By A. W. VERRALL, Litt.D., Fellow of Trinity College, Cambridge. 8s. 6d.
 IPHIGENIA IN TAURIS. By E. B. ENGLAND, M.A. 4s. 6d.
 ION. By M. A. BAYFIELD, M.A., Headmaster's Assistant at Malvern College. 3s. 6d.
 BACCHAE. By R. Y. TYRRELL, M.A., Regius Professor of Greek in the University of Dublin. [In preparation.
HERODOTUS.—BOOK III. By G. C. MACAULAY, M.A. [In the Press.
 BOOK V. By J. STRACHAN, M.A., Professor of Greek in the Owens College, Victoria University, Manchester. [In preparation.
 BOOK VI. By the same. [In the Press.
 BOOKS VII. and VIII. By Mrs. MONTAGU BUTLER. [In the Press.
HESIOD.—THE WORKS AND DAYS. By W. T. LENDRUM, M.A., Assistant Master at Dulwich College. [In preparation.
HOMER.—ILIAD. BOOKS I., IX., XI., XVI.—XXIV. THE STORY OF ACHILLES. By the late J. H. PRATT, M.A., and WALTER LEAF, Litt.D., Fellows of Trinity College, Cambridge. 6s.

ODYSSEY. BOOK IX. By Prof. JOHN E. B. MAYOR. 2s. 6d.
ODYSSEY. BOOKS XXI.–XXIV. THE TRIUMPH OF ODYSSEUS By S. G. HAMILTON, B.A., Fellow of Hertford College, Oxford. 3s. 6d.
HORACE.—THE ODES. By T. E. PAGE, M.A., Assistant Master at the Charterhouse. 6s. (BOOKS I., II., III., and IV. separately, 2s. each).
THE SATIRES. By ARTHUR PALMER, M.A., Professor of Latin in the University of Dublin. 6s.
THE EPISTLES AND ARS POETICA. By A. S. WILKINS, Litt.D., Professor of Latin in the Owens College, Victoria University, Manchester. 6s.
ISAEOS.—THE ORATIONS. By WILLIAM RIDGEWAY, M.A., Professor of Greek in Queen's College, Cork. [In preparation.
JUVENAL.—THIRTEEN SATIRES. By E. G. HARDY, M.A. 5s. The Text is carefully expurgated for School use.
SELECT SATIRES. By Prof. JOHN E. B. MAYOR. X. and XI. 3s. 6d. XII.–XVI. 4s. 6d.
LIVY. BOOKS II. and III. By Rev. H. M. STEPHENSON, M.A. 5s.
BOOKS XXI. and XXII. By Rev. W. W. CAPES, M.A. With Maps. 5s.
BOOKS XXIII. and XXIV. By G. C. MACAULAY, M.A. With Maps. 5s.
THE LAST TWO KINGS OF MACEDON. EXTRACTS FROM THE FOURTH AND FIFTH DECADES OF LIVY. By F. H. RAWLINS, M.A., Assistant Master at Eton. With Maps. 3s. 6d.
THE SUBJUGATION OF ITALY. SELECTIONS FROM THE FIRST DECADE. By G. E. MARINDIN, M.A. [In preparation.
LUCRETIUS.—BOOKS I.–III. By J. H. WARBURTON LEE, M.A., Assistant Master at Rossall. 4s. 6d.
LYSIAS.—SELECT ORATIONS. By E. S. SHUCKBURGH, M.A. 6s.
MARTIAL.—SELECT EPIGRAMS. By Rev. H. M. STEPHENSON, M.A. 6s. 6d.
OVID.—FASTI. By G. H. HALLAM, M.A., Assistant Master at Harrow. With Maps. 5s.
HEROIDUM EPISTULÆ XIII. By E. S. SHUCKBURGH, M.A. 4s. 6d.
METAMORPHOSES. BOOKS I.–III. By C. SIMMONS, M.A. [In preparation.
BOOKS XIII. and XIV. By the same Editor. 4s. 6d.
PLATO.—LACHES. By M. T. TATHAM, M.A. 2s. 6d.
THE REPUBLIC. BOOKS I.–V. By T. H. WARREN, M.A., President of Magdalen College, Oxford. 6s.
PLAUTUS.—MILES GLORIOSUS. By R. W. TYRRELL, M.A., Regius Professor of Greek in the University of Dublin. 2d Ed., revised. 5s.
AMPHITRUO. By ARTHUR PALMER, M.A., Professor of Latin in the University of Dublin. 5s.
PLINY.—LETTERS. BOOKS I. and II. By J. COWAN, M.A., Assistant Master at the Manchester Grammar School. 5s.
LETTERS. BOOK III. By Prof. JOHN E. B. MAYOR. With Life of Pliny by G. H. RENDALL, M.A. 5s.
PLUTARCH.—LIFE OF THEMISTOKLES. By Rev. H. A. HOLDEN, Litt.D. 5s.
LIVES OF GALBA AND OTHO. By E. G. HARDY, M.A. 6s.
POLYBIUS.—THE HISTORY OF THE ACHÆAN LEAGUE AS CONTAINED IN THE REMAINS OF POLYBIUS. By W. W. CAPES, M.A. 6s. 6d.
PROPERTIUS.—SELECT POEMS. By Prof. J. P. POSTGATE, Litt.D., Fellow of Trinity College, Cambridge. 2d Ed., revised. 6s.
SALLUST.—CATILINA and JUGURTHA. By C. MERIVALE, D.D., Dean of Ely. 4s. 6d. Or separately, 2s. 6d. each.
BELLUM CATULINÆ. By A. M. COOK, M.A., Assistant Master at St. Paul's School. 4s. 6d.
JUGURTHA. By the same Editor. [In preparation.
TACITUS.—THE ANNALS. BOOKS I. and II. By J. S. REID, Litt.D.
[In preparation.
THE ANNALS. BOOK VI. By A. J. CHURCH, M.A., and W. J. BRODRIBB, M.A. 2s. 6d.

THE HISTORIES. BOOKS I. and II. By A. D. GODLEY, M.A., Fellow of Magdalen College, Oxford. 5s. BOOKS III.-V. By the same. 5s.
AGRICOLA and GERMANIA. By A. J. CHURCH, M.A., and W. J. BRODRIBB, M.A. 3s. 6d. Or separately, 2s. each.
TERENCE.—HAUTON TIMORUMENOS. By E. S. SHUCKBURGH, M.A. 3s. With Translation. 4s. 6d.
PHORMIO. By Rev. JOHN BOND, M.A., and Rev. A. S. WALPOLE, M.A. 4s. 6d.
THUCYDIDES.—BOOK I. By C. BRYANS, M.A. [In preparation.
BOOK II. By E. C. MARCHANT, M.A., Assistant Master at St. Paul's School.
[In preparation.
BOOK III. By C. BRYANS. [In preparation.
BOOK IV. By C. E. GRAVES, M.A., Classical Lecturer at St. John's College, Cambridge. 5s.
BOOK V. By the same Editor. [In the Press.
BOOKS VI. AND VII. THE SICILIAN EXPEDITION. By Rev. PERCIVAL FROST, M.A. With Map. 5s.
BOOK VIII. By Prof. T. G. TUCKER, M.A. [In preparation.
TIBULLUS.—SELECT POEMS. By Prof. J. P. POSTGATE, Litt.D. [In preparation.
VIRGIL.—ÆNEID. BOOKS II. AND III. THE NARRATIVE OF ÆNEAS. By E. W. HOWSON, M.A., Assistant Master at Harrow. 3s.
XENOPHON.—THE ANABASIS. BOOKS I.-IV. By Profs. W. W. GOODWIN and J. W. WHITE. Adapted to Goodwin's Greek Grammar. With Map. 5s.
HELLENICA. BOOKS I. AND II. By H. HAILSTONE, B.A. With Map. 4s. 6d.
CYROPÆDIA. BOOKS VII. AND VIII. By A. GOODWIN, M.A., Professor of Classics in University College, London. 5s.
MEMORABILIA SOCRATIS. By A. R. CLUER, B.A., Balliol College, Oxford. 6s.
HIERO. By Rev H. A. HOLDEN, Litt.D., LL.D. 3s. 6d.
OECONOMICUS. By the same. With Lexicon. 6s.

CLASSICAL LIBRARY.

Texts, Edited with Introductions and Notes, for the use of Advanced Students; Commentaries and Translations.

ÆSCHYLUS.—THE SUPPLICES. A Revised Text, with Translation. By T. G. TUCKER, M.A., Professor of Classical Philology in the University of Melbourne. 8vo. 10s. 6d.
THE SEVEN AGAINST THEBES. With Translation. By A. W. VERRALL, Litt.D., Fellow of Trinity College, Cambridge. 8vo. 7s. 6d.
AGAMEMNON. With Translation. By A W. VERRALL, Litt.D. 8vo. 12s.
AGAMEMNON, CHOEPHORŒ, AND EUMENIDES. By A. O. PRICKARD, M.A., Fellow and Tutor of New College, Oxford. 8vo. [In preparation.
THE EUMENIDES. With Verse Translation. By BERNARD DRAKE, M.A. 8vo. 5s.
ANTONINUS, MARCUS AURELIUS.—BOOK IV. OF THE MEDITATIONS. With Translation. By HASTINGS CROSSLEY, M.A. 8vo. 6s.
ARISTOTLE.—THE METAPHYSICS. BOOK I. Translated by a Cambridge Graduate. 8vo. 5s.
THE POLITICS. By R. D. HICKS, M.A., Fellow of Trinity College, Cambridge. 8vo. [In the Press.
THE POLITICS. Translated by Rev. J. E. C. WELLDON, M.A., Headmaster of Harrow. Cr. 8vo. 10s. 6d.
THE RHETORIC. Translated by the same. Cr. 8vo. 7s. 6d.
AN INTRODUCTION TO ARISTOTLE'S RHETORIC. With Analysis, Notes, and Appendices. By E. M. COPE, Fellow and late Tutor of Trinity College, Cambridge. 8vo. 14s.

CLASSICAL LIBRARY

THE ETHICS. Translated by Rev. J. E. C. WELLDON, M.A. Cr. 8vo.
  [*In preparation.*
THE SOPHISTICI ELENCHI. With Translation. By E. POSTE, M.A., Fellow of Oriel College, Oxford. 8vo. 8s. 6d.
ARISTOPHANES.—THE BIRDS. Translated into English Verse. By B. H. KENNEDY, D.D. Cr. 8vo. 6s. Help Notes to the Same, for the Use of Students. 1s. 6d.
ATTIC ORATORS.—FROM ANTIPHON TO ISAEOS. By R. C. JEBB, Litt.D., Regius Professor of Greek in the University of Cambridge. 2 vols. 8vo. 25s.
BABRIUS.—With Lexicon. By Rev. W. G. RUTHERFORD, M.A., LL.D., Headmaster of Westminster. 8vo. 12s. 6d.
CICERO.—THE ACADEMICA. By J. S. REID, Litt.D., Fellow of Caius College, Cambridge. 8vo. 15s.
THE ACADEMICS. Translated by the same. 8vo. 5s. 6d.
SELECT LETTERS. After the Edition of ALBERT WATSON, M.A. Translated by G. E. JEANS, M.A., Fellow of Hertford College, Oxford. Cr. 8vo. 10s. 6d.
EURIPIDES.—MEDEA. Edited by A. W. VERRALL, Litt.D. 8vo. 7s. 6d.
IPHIGENIA IN AULIS. Edited by E. B. ENGLAND, M.A. 8vo. [*In the Press.*
INTRODUCTION TO THE STUDY OF EURIPIDES. By Professor J. P. MAHAFFY. Fcap. 8vo. 1s. 6d. (*Classical Writers*).
HERODOTUS.—BOOKS I.-III. THE ANCIENT EMPIRES OF THE EAST. Edited by A. H. SAYCE, Deputy-Professor of Comparative Philology, Oxford. 8vo. 16s.
BOOKS IV.-IX. Edited by R. W. MACAN, M.A., Lecturer in Ancient History at Brasenose College, Oxford. 8vo. [*In preparation.*
THE HISTORY. Translated by G. C. MACAULAY, M.A. 2 vols. Cr. 8vo. 18s.
HOMER.—THE ILIAD. By WALTER LEAF, Litt.D. 8vo. Books I.-XII. 14s. Books XIII.-XXIV. 14s.
THE ILIAD. Translated into English Prose by ANDREW LANG, M.A., WALTER LEAF, Litt.D., and ERNEST MYERS, M.A. Cr. 8vo. 12s. 6d.
THE ODYSSEY. Done into English by S. H. BUTCHER, M.A., Professor of Greek in the University of Edinburgh, and ANDREW LANG, M.A. Cr. 8vo. 6s.
INTRODUCTION TO THE STUDY OF HOMER. By the Right Hon. W. E. GLADSTONE. 18mo. 1s. (*Literature Primers.*)
HOMERIC DICTIONARY. Translated from the German of Dr. G. AUTENRIETH by R. P. KEEP, Ph.D. Illustrated. Cr. 8vo. 6s.
HORACE.—Translated by J. LONSDALE, M.A., and S. LEE, M.A. Gl. 8vo. 3s. 6d.
STUDIES, LITERARY AND HISTORICAL, IN THE ODES OF HORACE. By A. W. VERRALL, Litt.D. 8vo. 8s. 6d.
JUVENAL.—THIRTEEN SATIRES OF JUVENAL. By JOHN E. B. MAYOR, M.A., Professor of Latin in the University of Cambridge. Cr. 8vo. 2 vols. 10s. 6d. each. Vol. I. 10s. 6d. Vol. II. 10s. 6d.
THIRTEEN SATIRES. Translated by ALEX. LEEPER, M.A., LL.D., Warden of Trinity College, Melbourne. Cr. 8vo. 3s. 6d.
KTESIAS.—THE FRAGMENTS OF THE PERSIKA OF KTESIAS. By JOHN GILMORE, M.A. 8vo. 8s. 6d.
LIVY.—BOOKS I.-IV. Translated by Rev. H. M. STEPHENSON, M.A.
  [*In preparation.*
BOOKS XXI.-XXV. Translated by A. J. CHURCH, M.A., and W. J. BRODRIBB, M.A. Cr. 8vo. 7s. 6d.
INTRODUCTION TO THE STUDY OF LIVY. By Rev. W. W. CAPES, M.A. Fcap. 8vo. 1s. 6d. (*Classical Writers.*)
MARTIAL.—BOOKS I. AND II. OF THE EPIGRAMS. By Prof. JOHN E. B. MAYOR, M.A. 8vo. [*In the Press.*
PAUSANIAS.—DESCRIPTION OF GREECE. Translated with Commentary by J. G. FRAZER, M.A., Fellow of Trinity College, Cambridge.
  [*In preparation.*

PHRYNICHUS.—THE NEW PHRYNICHUS; being a Revised Text of the Ecloga of the Grammarian Phrynichus. With Introduction and Commentary by Rev. W. G. RUTHERFORD, M.A., LL.D., Headmaster of Westminster. 8vo. 18s.

PINDAR.—THE EXTANT ODES OF PINDAR. Translated by ERNEST MYERS, M.A. Cr. 8vo. 5s.

THE OLYMPIAN AND PYTHIAN ODES. Edited, with an Introductory Essay, by BASIL GILDERSLEEVE, Professor of Greek in the Johns Hopkins University, U.S.A. Cr. 8vo. 7s. 6d.

THE NEMEAN ODES. By J. B. BURY, M.A., Fellow of Trinity College, Dublin. 8vo. [*In the Press.*

PLATO.—PHÆDO. By R. D. ARCHER-HIND, M.A., Fellow of Trinity College, Cambridge. 8vo. 8s. 6d.

PHÆDO. By W. D. GEDDES, LL.D., Principal of the University of Aberdeen. 8vo. 8s. 6d.

TIMAEUS. With Translation. By R. D. ARCHER-HIND, M.A. 8vo. 16s.

THE REPUBLIC OF PLATO. Translated by J. LL. DAVIES, M.A., and D. J VAUGHAN, M.A. 18mo. 4s. 6d.

EUTHYPHRO, APOLOGY, CRITO, AND PHÆDO. Translated by F. J. CHURCH. 18mo. 4s. 6d.

PHÆDRUS, LYSIS, AND PROTAGORAS. Translated by J. WRIGHT, M.A. 18mo. 4s. 6d.

PLAUTUS.—THE MOSTELLARIA. By WILLIAM RAMSAY, M.A. Edited by G. G. RAMSAY, M.A., Professor of Humanity in the University of Glasgow 8vo. 14s.

PLINY.—CORRESPONDENCE WITH TRAJAN. C. Plinii Caecilii Secundi Epistulæ ad Traianum Imperatorem cum Eiusdem Responsis. By E. G. HARDY, M.A. 8vo. 10s. 6d.

POLYBIUS.—THE HISTORIES OF POLYBIUS. Translated by E. S. SHUCKBURGH, M.A. 2 vols. Cr. 8vo. 24s.

SALLUST.—CATILINE AND JUGURTHA. Translated by A. W. POLLARD, B.A. Cr. 8vo. 6s. THE CATILINE (separately). 3s.

SOPHOCLES—ŒDIPUS THE KING. Translated into English Verse by E. D. A. MORSHEAD, M.A., Assistant Master at Winchester. Fcap. 8vo. 3s. 6d.

TACITUS.—THE ANNALS. By G. O. HOLBROOKE, M.A., Professor of Latin in Trinity College, Hartford, U.S.A. With Maps. 8vo. 16s.

THE ANNALS. Translated by A. J. CHURCH, M.A., and W. J. BRODRIBB, M.A. With Maps. Cr. 8vo. 7s. 6d.

THE HISTORIES. By Rev. W. A. SPOONER, M.A., Fellow of New College, Oxford. 8vo. [*In the Press.*

THE HISTORY. Translated by A. J. CHURCH, M.A., and W. J. BRODRIBB, M.A. With Map. Cr. 8vo. 6s.

THE AGRICOLA AND GERMANY, WITH THE DIALOGUE ON ORATORY. Translated by A. J. CHURCH, M.A., and W. J. BRODRIBB, M.A. With Maps. Cr. 8vo. 4s. 6d.

INTRODUCTION TO THE STUDY OF TACITUS. By A. J. CHURCH, M.A., and W. J. BRODRIBB, M.A. Fcap. 8vo. 1s. 6d. (*Classical Writers.*)

THEOCRITUS, BION, AND MOSCHUS. Translated by A. LANG, M.A. 18mo 4s. 6d.

*** Also an Edition on Large Paper. Cr. 8vo. 9s.

THUCYDIDES.—BOOK IV. A Revision of the Text, Illustrating the Principal Causes of Corruption in the Manuscripts of this Author. By Rev. W. G. RUTHERFORD, M.A., LL.D., Headmaster of Westminster. 8vo. 7s. 6d.

BOOK VIII. By H. C. GOODHART, M.A., Fellow of Trinity College, Cambridge. [*In the Press.*

VIRGIL.—Translated by J. LONSDALE, M.A., and S. LEE, M.A. Gl. 8vo. 3s. 6d.

THE ÆNEID. Translated by J. W. MACKAIL, M.A., Fellow of Balliol College, Oxford. Cr. 8vo. 7s. 6d.

XENOPHON.—Translated by H. G. DAKYNS, M.A. In four vols. Vol. I., containing "The Anabasis" and Books I. and II. of "The Hellenica." Cr. 8vo 10s. 6d. [Vol. II. *in the Press*

GRAMMAR, COMPOSITION, & PHILOLOGY.

BELCHER.—SHORT EXERCISES IN LATIN PROSE COMPOSITION AND EXAMINATION PAPERS IN LATIN GRAMMAR. Part I. By Rev. H. BELCHER, LL.D., Rector of the High School, Dunedin, N.Z. 18mo. 1s. 6d. KEY, for Teachers only. 18mo. 3s. 6d.
Part II., On the Syntax of Sentences, with an Appendix, including EXERCISES IN LATIN IDIOMS, etc. 18mo. 2s. KEY, for Teachers only. 18mo. 3s.

BLACKIE.—GREEK AND ENGLISH DIALOGUES FOR USE IN SCHOOLS AND COLLEGES. By JOHN STUART BLACKIE, Emeritus Professor of Greek in the University of Edinburgh. New Edition. Fcap. 8vo. 2s. 6d.

BRYANS.—LATIN PROSE EXERCISES BASED UPON CAESAR'S GALLIC WAR. With a Classification of Cæsar's Chief Phrases and Grammatical Notes on Cæsar's Usages. By CLEMENT BRYANS, M.A., Assistant Master at Dulwich College. Ex. fcap. 8vo. 2s. 6d. KEY, for Teachers only. 4s. 6d.
GREEK PROSE EXERCISES based upon Thucydides. By the same.
[*In preparation.*

COOKSON.—A LATIN SYNTAX. By CHRISTOPHER COOKSON, M.A., Assistant Master at St. Paul's School. 8vo. [*In preparation.*

CORNELL UNIVERSITY STUDIES IN CLASSICAL PHILOLOGY. Edited by I. FLAGG, W. G. HALE, and B. I. WHEELER. I. The *CUM*-Constructions: their History and Functions. By W. G. HALE. Part 1. Critical. 1s. 8d. nett. Part 2. Constructive. 3s. 4d. nett. II. Analogy and the Scope of its Application in Language. By B. I. WHEELER. 1s. 3d. nett.

EICKE.—FIRST LESSONS IN LATIN. By K. M. EICKE, B.A., Assistant Master at Oundle School. Gl. 8vo. 2s. 6d.

ENGLAND.—EXERCISES ON LATIN SYNTAX AND IDIOM. ARRANGED WITH REFERENCE TO ROBY'S SCHOOL LATIN GRAMMAR. By E. B. ENGLAND, Assistant Lecturer at the Owens College, Victoria University, Manchester. Cr. 8vo. 2s. 6d. KEY, for Teachers only. 2s. 6d.

GILES.—A MANUAL OF GREEK AND LATIN PHILOLOGY. By P. GILES, M.A., Fellow of Gonville and Caius College, Cambridge. Cr. 8vo.
[*In the Press.*

GOODWIN.—Works by W. W. GOODWIN, LL.D., D.C.L., Professor of Greek in Harvard University, U.S.A.
SYNTAX OF THE MOODS AND TENSES OF THE GREEK VERB. New Ed., revised and enlarged. 8vo. 14s.
A GREEK GRAMMAR. Cr. 8vo. 6s.
A GREEK GRAMMAR FOR SCHOOLS. Cr. 8vo. 3s. 6d.

GREENWOOD.—THE ELEMENTS OF GREEK GRAMMAR. Adapted to the System of Crude Forms. By J. G. GREENWOOD, sometime Principal of the Owens College, Manchester. Cr. 8vo. 5s. 6d.

HADLEY AND ALLEN.—A GREEK GRAMMAR FOR SCHOOLS AND COLLEGES. By JAMES HADLEY, late Professor in Yale College. Revised and in part rewritten by F. DE F. ALLEN, Professor in Harvard College. Cr. 8vo. 6s.

HODGSON.—MYTHOLOGY FOR LATIN VERSIFICATION. A brief sketch of the Fables of the Ancients, prepared to be rendered into Latin Verse for Schools. By F. HODGSON, B.D., late Provost of Eton. New Ed., revised by F. C. HODGSON, M.A. 18mo. 3s.

JACKSON.—FIRST STEPS TO GREEK PROSE COMPOSITION. By BLOMFIELD JACKSON, M.A., Assistant Master at King's College School. 18mo. 1s. 6d. KEY, for Teachers only. 18mo. 3s. 6d.
SECOND STEPS TO GREEK PROSE COMPOSITION, with Miscellaneous Idioms, Aids to Accentuation, and Examination Papers in Greek Scholarship. By the same. 18mo. 2s. 6d. KEY, for Teachers only. 18mo. 3s. 6d.

KYNASTON.—EXERCISES IN THE COMPOSITION OF GREEK IAMBIC VERSE by Translations from English Dramatists. By Rev. H. KYNASTON, D.D., Professor of Classics in the University of Durham. With Vocabulary Ex. fcap. 8vo. 5s.
KEY, for Teachers only. Ex. fcap. 8vo. 4s. 6d.

CLASSICS

LUPTON.—AN INTRODUCTION TO LATIN ELEGIAC VERSE COMPOSITION. By J. H. LUPTON, Sur-Master of St. Paul's School. Gl. 8vo. 2s. 6d.
KEY TO PART II. (XXV.—C.) Gl. 8vo. 3s. 6d.
AN INTRODUCTION TO LATIN LYRIC VERSE COMPOSITION. By the same. Gl. 8vo. 3s. KEY, for Teachers only. Gl. 8vo. 4s. 6d.
MACKIE.—PARALLEL PASSAGES FOR TRANSLATION INTO GREEK AND ENGLISH. With Indexes. By Rev. ELLIS C. MACKIE, M.A., Classical Master at Heversham Grammar School. Gl. 8vo. 4s. 6d.
MACMILLAN.—FIRST LATIN GRAMMAR. By M. C. MACMILLAN, M.A. Fcap. 8vo. 1s. 6d.
MACMILLAN'S GREEK COURSE.—Edited by Rev. W. G. RUTHERFORD, M.A., LL.D., Headmaster of Westminster. Gl. 8vo.
FIRST GREEK GRAMMAR—ACCIDENCE. By the Editor. 2s.
FIRST GREEK GRAMMAR—SYNTAX. By the same. 2s.
ACCIDENCE AND SYNTAX. In one volume. 3s. 6d.
EASY EXERCISES IN GREEK ACCIDENCE. By H. G. UNDERHILL, M.A., Assistant Master at St. Paul's Preparatory School. 2s.
A SECOND GREEK EXERCISE BOOK. By Rev. W. A. HEARD, M.A., Headmaster of Fettes College, Edinburgh. 2s. 6d.
MANUAL OF GREEK ACCIDENCE. By the Editor. [*In preparation.*
MANUAL OF GREEK SYNTAX. By the Editor. [*In preparation.*
ELEMENTARY GREEK COMPOSITION. By the Editor. [*In preparation.*
MACMILLAN'S GREEK READER.—STORIES AND LEGENDS. A First Greek Reader, with Notes, Vocabulary, and Exercises. By F. H. COLSON, M.A., Headmaster of Plymouth College. Gl. 8vo. 3s.
MACMILLAN'S LATIN COURSE.—By A. M. COOK, M.A., Assistant Master at St. Paul's School. First Part. Gl. 8vo. 3s. 6d. Second Part. 2s. 6d.
[*Third Part in preparation.*
MACMILLAN'S SHORTER LATIN COURSE.—By A. M. COOK, M.A. Being an abridgment of "Macmillan's Latin Course," First Part. Gl. 8vo. 1s. 6d.
MACMILLAN'S LATIN READER.—A LATIN READER FOR THE LOWER FORMS IN SCHOOLS. By H. J. HARDY, M.A., Assistant Master at Winchester. Gl. 8vo. 2s. 6d.
MARSHALL.—A TABLE OF IRREGULAR GREEK VERBS, classified according to the arrangement of Curtius's Greek Grammar. By J. M. MARSHALL, M.A., Headmaster of the Grammar School, Durham. 8vo. 1s.
MAYOR.—FIRST GREEK READER. By Prof. JOHN E. B. MAYOR, M.A., Fellow of St. John's College, Cambridge. Fcap. 8vo. 4s. 6d.
MAYOR.—GREEK FOR BEGINNERS.—By Rev. J. B. MAYOR, M.A., late Professor of Classical Literature in King's College, London. Part I., with Vocabulary, 1s. 6d. Parts II. and III., with Vocabulary and Index. Fcap. 8vo. 3s. 6d. Complete in one Vol. 4s. 6d.
NIXON.—PARALLEL EXTRACTS, Arranged for Translation into English and Latin, with Notes on Idioms. By J. E. NIXON, M.A., Fellow and Classical Lecturer, King's College, Cambridge. Part I.—Historical and Epistolary. Cr. 8vo. 3s. 6d.
PROSE EXTRACTS, Arranged for Translation into English and Latin, with General and Special Prefaces on Style and Idiom. By the same. I. Oratorical. II. Historical. III. Philosophical. IV. Anecdotes and Letters. 2d Ed. enlarged to 280 pp. Cr. 8vo. 4s. 6d.
SELECTIONS FROM PROSE EXTRACTS, including Easy Anecdotes and Letters and Notes and Hints. By the same. 120 pp. 3s.
Translations of about 70 Extracts can be supplied to Schoolmasters (2s. 6d.), on application to the Author: and about 40 similarly of "Parallel Extracts," 1s. 6d. post free.
PANTIN.—A FIRST LATIN VERSE BOOK. By W. E. P. PANTIN, M.A., Assistant Master at St. Paul's School. Gl. 8vo. 1s. 6d.
PEILE.—A PRIMER OF PHILOLOGY. By J. PEILE, Litt. D., Master of Christ's College, Cambridge. 18mo. 1s.

GRAMMAR, COMPOSITION, AND PHILOLOGY 11

POSTGATE.—SERMO LATINUS. A short Guide to Latin Prose Composition. By Prof. J. P. POSTGATE, Litt.D., Fellow of Trinity College, Cambridge. Gl. 8vo. 2s. 6d. KEY to "Selected Passages." Gl. 8vo. 3s. 6d.

POSTGATE AND VINCE.—A DICTIONARY OF LATIN ETYMOLOGY. By J. P. POSTGATE and C. A. VINCE. [*In preparation.*

POTTS.—HINTS TOWARDS LATIN PROSE COMPOSITION. By A. W. POTTS, M.A., LL.D., late Fellow of St. John's College, Cambridge. Ex. fcap. 8vo. 3s.

PASSAGES FOR TRANSLATION INTO LATIN PROSE. Edited with Notes and References to the above. Ex. fcap. 8vo. 2s. 6d. KEY, for Teachers only. 2s. 6d.

PRESTON.—EXERCISES IN LATIN VERSE OF VARIOUS KINDS. By Rev. G. PRESTON. Gl. 8vo. 2s. 6d. KEY, for Teachers only. Gl. 8vo. 5s.

REID.—A GRAMMAR OF TACITUS. By J. S. REID, Litt. D., Fellow of Caius College, Cambridge. [*In the Press.*

A GRAMMAR OF VIRGIL. By the same. [*In preparation.*

ROBY.—Works by H. J. ROBY, M.A., late Fellow of St. John's College, Cambridge.

A GRAMMAR OF THE LATIN LANGUAGE, from Plautus to Suetonius. Part I. Sounds, Inflexions, Word-formation, Appendices. Cr. 8vo. 9s. Part II. Syntax, Prepositions, etc. 10s. 6d.

SCHOOL LATIN GRAMMAR. Cr. 8vo. 5s.

RUSH.—SYNTHETIC LATIN DELECTUS. With Notes and Vocabulary. By E. RUSH, B.A. Ex. fcap. 8vo. 2s. 6d.

RUST.—FIRST STEPS TO LATIN PROSE COMPOSITION. By Rev. G. RUST, M.A. 18mo. 1s. 6d. KEY, for Teachers only. By W. M. YATES. 18mo. 3s. 6d.

RUTHERFORD.—Works by the Rev. W. G. RUTHERFORD, M.A., LL.D., Headmaster of Westminster.

REX LEX. A Short Digest of the principal Relations between the Latin, Greek, and Anglo-Saxon Sounds. 8vo. [*In preparation.*

THE NEW PHRYNICHUS; being a Revised Text of the Ecloga of the Grammarian Phrynichus. With Introduction and Commentary. 8vo. 18s. (See also *Macmillan's Greek Course.*)

SHUCKBURGH.—PASSAGES FROM LATIN AUTHORS FOR TRANSLATION INTO ENGLISH. Selected with a view to the needs of Candidates for the Cambridge Local, and Public Schools' Examinations. By E. S. SHUCKBURGH, M.A. Cr. 8vo. 2s.

SIMPSON.—LATIN PROSE AFTER THE BEST AUTHORS: Cæsarian Prose. By F. P. SIMPSON, B.A. Ex. fcap. 8vo. 2s. 6d. KEY, for Teachers only. Ex. fcap. 8vo. 5s.

STRACHAN AND WILKINS.—ANALECTA. Selected Passages for Translation. By J. S. STRACHAN, M.A., Professor of Greek, and A. S. WILKINS, Litt. D., Professor of Latin in the Owens College, Manchester. Cr. 8vo. 5s.

THRING.—Works by the Rev. E. THRING, M.A., late Headmaster of Uppingham.

A LATIN GRADUAL. A First Latin Construing Book for Beginners. With Coloured Sentence Maps. Fcap. 8vo. 2s. 6d.

A MANUAL OF MOOD CONSTRUCTIONS. Fcap. 8vo. 1s. 6d.

WELCH AND DUFFIELD.—LATIN ACCIDENCE AND EXERCISES ARRANGED FOR BEGINNERS. By W. WELCH and C. G. DUFFIELD, Assistant Masters at Cranleigh School. 18mo. 1s. 6d.

WHITE.—FIRST LESSONS IN GREEK. Adapted to GOODWIN'S GREEK GRAMMAR, and designed as an introduction to the ANABASIS OF XENOPHON. By JOHN WILLIAMS WHITE, Assistant-Professor of Greek in Harvard University, U.S.A. Cr. 8vo. 4s. 6d.

WRIGHT.—Works by J. WRIGHT, M.A., late Headmaster of Sutton Coldfield School.

A HELP TO LATIN GRAMMAR; or, the Form and Use of Words in Latin, with Progressive Exercises. Cr. 8vo. 4s. 6d.

THE SEVEN KINGS OF ROME. An Easy Narrative, abridged from the First Book of Livy by the omission of Difficult Passages; being a First Latin Reading Book, with Grammatical Notes and Vocabulary. Fcap. 8vo. 3s. 6d.

FIRST LATIN STEPS; OR, AN INTRODUCTION BY A SERIES OF EXAMPLES TO THE STUDY OF THE LATIN LANGUAGE. Cr. 8vo. 3s.
ATTIC PRIMER. Arranged for the Use of Beginners. Ex. fcap. 8vo. 2s. 6d.
A COMPLETE LATIN COURSE, comprising Rules with Examples, Exercises, both Latin and English, on each Rule, and Vocabularies. Cr. 8vo. 2s. 6d.

ANTIQUITIES, ANCIENT HISTORY, AND PHILOSOPHY.

ARNOLD.—A HANDBOOK OF LATIN EPIGRAPHY. By W. T. ARNOLD, M.A. [In preparation.
THE ROMAN SYSTEM OF PROVINCIAL ADMINISTRATION TO THE ACCESSION OF CONSTANTINE THE GREAT. By the same. Cr. 8vo. 6s.
ARNOLD.—THE SECOND PUNIC WAR. Being Chapters from THE HISTORY OF ROME by the late THOMAS ARNOLD, D.D., Headmaster of Rugby. Edited, with Notes, by W. T. ARNOLD, M.A. With 8 Maps. Cr. 8vo. 8s. 6d.
BEESLY.—STORIES FROM THE HISTORY OF ROME. By Mrs. BEESLY. Fcap. 8vo. 2s. 6d.
BURN.—ROMAN LITERATURE IN RELATION TO ROMAN ART. By Rev. ROBERT BURN, M.A., late Fellow of Trinity College, Cambridge. Illustrated. Ex. cr. 8vo. 14s.
BURY.—A HISTORY OF THE LATER ROMAN EMPIRE FROM ARCADIUS TO IRENE, A.D. 395-800. By J. B. BURY, M.A., Fellow of Trinity College, Dublin. 2 vols. 8vo. 32s.
CLASSICAL WRITERS.—Edited by JOHN RICHARD GREEN, M.A., LL.D. Fcap. 8vo. 1s. 6d. each.
SOPHOCLES. By Prof. L. CAMPBELL, M.A.
EURIPIDES. By Prof. MAHAFFY, D.D.
DEMOSTHENES. By Prof. S. H. BUTCHER, M.A.
VIRGIL. By Prof. NETTLESHIP, M.A.
LIVY. By Rev. W. W. CAPES, M.A.
TACITUS. By Prof. A. J. CHURCH, M.A., and W. J. BRODRIBB, M.A.
MILTON. By Rev. STOPFORD A. BROOKE, M.A.
FREEMAN.—Works by EDWARD A. FREEMAN, D.C.L., LL.D., Regius Professor of Modern History in the University of Oxford.
HISTORY OF ROME. (Historical Course for Schools.) 18mo. [In preparation.
HISTORY OF GREECE. (Historical Course for Schools.) 18mo. [In preparation.
A SCHOOL HISTORY OF ROME. Cr. 8vo. [In preparation.
HISTORICAL ESSAYS. Second Series. [Greek and Roman History.] 8vo. 10s. 6d.
FYFFE.—A SCHOOL HISTORY OF GREECE. By C. A. FYFFE, M.A. Cr. 8vo. [In preparation.
GARDNER.—SAMOS AND SAMIAN COINS. An Essay. By PERCY GARDNER, Litt.D., Professor of Archæology in the University of Oxford. With Illustrations. 8vo. 7s. 6d.
GEDDES.—THE PROBLEM OF THE HOMERIC POEMS. By W. D. GEDDES Principal of the University of Aberdeen. 8vo. 14s.
GLADSTONE.—Works by the Rt. Hon. W. E. GLADSTONE, M.P.
THE TIME AND PLACE OF HOMER. Cr. 8vo. 6s. 6d.
A PRIMER OF HOMER. 18mo. 1s.
GOW.—A COMPANION TO SCHOOL CLASSICS. By JAMES GOW, Litt.D., Master of the High School, Nottingham. With Illustrations. 2d Ed., revised. Cr. 8vo. 6s.
HARRISON AND VERRALL.—MYTHOLOGY AND MONUMENTS OF ANCIENT ATHENS. Translation of a portion of the "Attica" of Pausanias. By MARGARET DE G. VERRALL. With Introductory Essay and Archæological Commentary by JANE E. HARRISON. With Illustrations and Plans. Cr. 8vo. 16s.

ANCIENT HISTORY AND PHILOSOPHY 13

JEBB.—Works by R. C. JEBB, Litt.D., Professor of Greek in the University of Cambridge.
THE ATTIC ORATORS FROM ANTIPHON TO ISAEOS. 2 vols. 8vo. 25s.
A PRIMER OF GREEK LITERATURE. 18mo. 1s.
(See also *Classical Series.*)
KIEPERT.—MANUAL OF ANCIENT GEOGRAPHY. By Dr. H KIEPERT. Cr. 8vo. 5s.
LANCIANI.—ANCIENT ROME IN THE LIGHT OF RECENT DISCOVERIES.—By RODOLFO LANCIANI, Professor of Archæology in the University of Rome. Illustrated. 4to. 24s.
MAHAFFY.—Works by J. P. MAHAFFY, D.D., Fellow of Trinity College, Dublin, and Professor of Ancient History in the University of Dublin.
SOCIAL LIFE IN GREECE; from Homer to Menander. Cr. 8vo. 9s.
GREEK LIFE AND THOUGHT; from the Age of Alexander to the Roman Conquest. Cr. 8vo. 12s. 6d.
THE GREEK WORLD UNDER ROMAN SWAY. From Plutarch to Polybius. Cr. 8vo. [*In the Press.*
RAMBLES AND STUDIES IN GREECE. With Illustrations. With Map. Cr. 8vo. 10s. 6d.
A HISTORY OF CLASSICAL GREEK LITERATURE. In 2 vols. Cr. 8vo. Vol. I. The Poets, with an Appendix on Homer by Prof. SAYCE. 9s. Vol. II. The Prose Writers. In two parts.
A PRIMER OF GREEK ANTIQUITIES. With Illustrations. 18mo. 1s.
EURIPIDES. 18mo. 1s. 6d. (*Classical Writers.*)
MAYOR.—BIBLIOGRAPHICAL CLUE TO LATIN LITERATURE. Edited after HÜBNER. With large Additions. By Prof. JOHN E. B. MAYOR. Cr. 8vo. 10s. 6d.
NEWTON.—ESSAYS IN ART AND ARCHÆOLOGY. By Sir CHARLES NEWTON, K.C.B., D.C.L. 8vo. 12s. 6d.
SAYCE.—THE ANCIENT EMPIRES OF THE EAST. By A. H. SAYCE, M.A., Deputy-Professor of Comparative Philology, Oxford. Cr. 8vo. 6s.
SHUCKBURGH.—A SCHOOL HISTORY OF ROME. By E. S. SHUCKBURGH, M.A. Cr. 8vo. [*In preparation.*
STEWART.—THE TALE OF TROY. Done into English by AUBREY STEWART. Gl. 8vo. 3s. 6d.
WALDSTEIN.—CATALOGUE OF CASTS IN THE MUSEUM OF CLASSICAL ARCHÆOLOGY, CAMBRIDGE. By CHARLES WALDSTEIN, University Reader in Classical Archæology. Cr. 8vo. 1s. 6d.
*** Also an Edition on Large Paper, small 4to. 5s.
WILKINS.—Works by Prof. WILKINS, Litt.D., LL.D.
A PRIMER OF ROMAN ANTIQUITIES. Illustrated. 18mo. 1s.
A PRIMER OF ROMAN LITERATURE. 18mo. 1s.
WILKINS AND ARNOLD.—A MANUAL OF ROMAN ANTIQUITIES. By Prof. A. S. WILKINS, Litt.D., and W. T. ARNOLD, M.A. Cr. 8vo. Illustrated.
[*In preparation.*

MODERN LANGUAGES AND LITERATURE.

English; French; German; Modern Greek; Italian; Spanish.

ENGLISH.

ABBOTT.—A SHAKESPEARIAN GRAMMAR An Attempt to Illustrate some of the Differences between Elizabethan and Modern English. By the Rev. E. A. ABBOTT, D.D., formerly Headmaster of the City of London School. Ex. fcap. 8vo. 6s.
BACON.—ESSAYS. With Introduction and Notes, by F. G. SELBY, M.A., Professor of Logic and Moral Philosophy, Deccan College, Poona. Gl. 8vo. 3s. 6d.

14 MODERN LANGUAGES AND LITERATURE

BURKE.—REFLECTIONS ON THE FRENCH REVOLUTION. By the same. Gl. 8vo. [*In July.*

BROOKE.—PRIMER OF ENGLISH LITERATURE. By Rev. STOPFORD A. BROOKE, M.A. 18mo. 1s.

EARLY ENGLISH LITERATURE. By the same. 2 vols. 8vo. [*In preparation.*

BUTLER.—HUDIBRAS. With Introduction and Notes, by ALFRED MILNES, M.A. Ex. fcap. 8vo. Part I. 3s. 6d. Parts II. and III. 4s. 6d.

CAMPBELL.—SELECTIONS. With Introduction and Notes, by CECIL M. BARROW, M.A., Principal and Professor of English and Classics, Doveton College, Madras. Gl. 8vo. [*In preparation.*

COWPER.—THE TASK: an Epistle to Joseph Hill, Esq.; TIROCINIUM, or a Review of the Schools; and THE HISTORY OF JOHN GILPIN. Edited, with Notes, by W. BENHAM, B.D. Gl. 8vo. 1s. (*Globe Readings from Standard Authors.*)

THE TASK. With Introduction and Notes, by F. J. ROWE, M.A., and W. T. WEBB, M.A., Professors of English Literature, Presidency College, Calcutta. [*In preparation.*

DOWDEN.—SHAKESPERE. By Prof. DOWDEN. 18mo. 1s.

DRYDEN.—SELECT PROSE WORKS. Edited, with Introduction and Notes, by Prof. C. D. YONGE. Fcap. 8vo. 2s. 6d.

GLOBE READERS. For Standards I.-VI. Edited by A. F. MURISON. Illustrated. Gl. 8vo.

Primer I. (48 pp.)	3d.	Book III. (232 pp.)	1s. 3d.
Primer II. (48 pp.)	3d.	Book IV. (328 pp.)	1s. 9d.
Book I. (96 pp.)	6d.	Book V. (416 pp.)	2s.
Book II. (136 pp.)	9d.	Book VI. (448 pp.)	2s. 6d.

*__THE SHORTER GLOBE READERS.__—Illustrated. Gl. 8vo.

Primer I. (48 pp.)	3d.	Standard III. (178 pp.)	1s.
Primer II. (48 pp.)	3d.	Standard IV. (182 pp.)	1s.
Standard I. (92 pp.)	6d.	Standard V. (216 pp.)	1s. 3d.
Standard II. (124 pp.)	9d.	Standard VI. (228 pp.)	1s. 6d.

* This Series has been abridged from "The Globe Readers" to meet the demand for smaller reading books.

GOLDSMITH.—THE TRAVELLER, or a Prospect of Society; and the DESERTED VILLAGE. With Notes, Philological and Explanatory, by J. W. HALES, M.A. Cr. 8vo. 6d.

THE VICAR OF WAKEFIELD. With a Memoir of Goldsmith, by Prof. MASSON. Gl. 8vo. 1s. (*Globe Readings from Standard Authors.*)

SELECT ESSAYS. With Introduction and Notes, by Prof. C. D. YONGE. Fcap. 8vo. 2s. 6d.

THE TRAVELLER AND THE DESERTED VILLAGE. With Introduction and Notes. By A. BARRETT, B.A., Professor of English Literature, Elphinstone College, Bombay. Gl. 8vo. 1s. 6d.

THE VICAR OF WAKEFIELD. With Introduction and Notes. By H. LITTLEDALE, B.A., Professor of History and English Literature, Baroda College. Gl. 8vo. [*In preparation.*

GOSSE.—A HISTORY OF EIGHTEENTH CENTURY LITERATURE (1660-1780). By EDMUND GOSSE, M.A. Cr. 8vo. 7s. 6d.

GRAY.—POEMS. With Introduction and Notes, by JOHN BRADSHAW, LL.D. Gl. 8vo. [*In preparation.*

HALES.—LONGER ENGLISH POEMS. With Notes, Philological and Explanatory, and an Introduction on the Teaching of English, by J. W. HALES, M.A., Professor of English Literature at King's College, London. Ex. fcap. 8vo. 4s. 6d.

HELPS.—ESSAYS WRITTEN IN THE INTERVALS OF BUSINESS. With Introduction and Notes, by F. J. ROWE, M.A., and W. T. WEBB, M.A., Gl. 8vo. 2s. 6d.

JOHNSON.—LIVES OF THE POETS. The Six Chief Lives (Milton, Dryden, Swift, Addison, Pope, Gray), with Macaulay's "Life of Johnson." With Preface and Notes by MATTHEW ARNOLD. Cr. 8vo. 4s. 6d.

ENGLISH

LAMB.—TALES FROM SHAKSPEARE. With Preface by the Rev. CANON AINGER, M.A., LL.D. Gl. 8vo. 2s. (*Globe Readings from Standard Authors.*)

LITERATURE PRIMERS.—Edited by JOHN RICHARD GREEN, LL.D. 18mo. 1s. each.

    ENGLISH GRAMMAR. By Rev. R. MORRIS, LL.D.
    ENGLISH GRAMMAR EXERCISES. By R. MORRIS, LL.D., and H. C. BOWEN, M.A.
    EXERCISES ON MORRIS'S PRIMER OF ENGLISH GRAMMAR. By J. WETHERELL, M.A.
    ENGLISH COMPOSITION. By Professor NICHOL.
    QUESTIONS AND EXERCISES ON ENGLISH COMPOSITION By Prof. NICHOL and W. S. M'CORMICK.
    ENGLISH LITERATURE. By STOPFORD BROOKE, M.A.
    SHAKSPERE. By Professor DOWDEN.
    THE CHILDREN'S TREASURY OF LYRICAL POETRY. Selected and arranged with Notes by FRANCIS TURNER PALGRAVE. In Two Parts. 1s. each.
    PHILOLOGY. By J. PEILE, Litt.D.
    ROMAN LITERATURE. By Prof. A. S. WILKINS, Litt.D.
    GREEK LITERATURE. By Prof. JEBB, Litt.D.
    HOMER. By the Rt. Hon. W. E. GLADSTONE, M.P.

A HISTORY OF ENGLISH LITERATURE IN FOUR VOLUMES. Cr. 8vo.
    EARLY ENGLISH LITERATURE. By STOPFORD BROOKE, M.A. [*In preparation.*
    ELIZABETHAN LITERATURE. (1560-1665.) By GEORGE SAINTSBURY. 7s. 6d.
    EIGHTEENTH CENTURY LITERATURE. (1660-1780.) By EDMUND GOSSE, M.A. 7s. 6d.
    THE MODERN PERIOD. By Prof. DOWDEN. [*In preparation.*

MACMILLAN'S READING BOOKS.
    PRIMER. 18mo. 48 pp. 2d.
    BOOK I. for Standard I. 96 pp. 4d.
    BOOK II. for Standard II. 144 pp. 5d.
    BOOK III. for Standard III. 160 pp. 6d.
    BOOK IV. for Standard IV. 176 pp. 8d.
    BOOK V. for Standard V. 380 pp. 1s.
    BOOK VI. for Standard VI. Cr. 8vo. 430 pp. 2s.

Book VI. is fitted for Higher Classes, and as an Introduction to English Literature.

MACMILLAN'S COPY BOOKS.—1. Large Post 4to. Price 4d. each. 2. Post Oblong. Price 2d. each.

1. INITIATORY EXERCISES AND SHORT LETTERS.
2. WORDS CONSISTING OF SHORT LETTERS.
*3. LONG LETTERS. With Words containing Long Letters—Figures.
*4. WORDS CONTAINING LONG LETTERS.
4a. PRACTISING AND REVISING COPY-BOOK. For Nos. 1 to 4.
*5. CAPITALS AND SHORT HALF-TEXT. Words beginning with a Capital.
*6. HALF-TEXT WORDS beginning with Capitals—Figures.
*7. SMALL-HAND AND HALF-TEXT. With Capitals and Figures.
*8. SMALL-HAND AND HALF-TEXT. With Capitals and Figures.
8a. PRACTISING AND REVISING COPY-BOOK. For Nos. 5 to 8.
*9. SMALL-HAND SINGLE HEADLINES—Figures.
10. SMALL-HAND SINGLE HEADLINES—Figures.
11. SMALL-HAND DOUBLE HEADLINES—Figures.
12. COMMERCIAL AND ARITHMETICAL EXAMPLES, &c.
12a. PRACTISING AND REVISING COPY-BOOK. For Nos. 8 to 12.

* *These numbers may be had with Goodman's Patent Sliding Copies.* Large Post 4to. Price 6d. each.

MARTIN.—THE POET'S HOUR: Poetry selected and arranged for Children. By FRANCES MARTIN. 18mo. 2s. 6d.
    SPRING-TIME WITH THE POETS. By the same. 18mo. 3s. 6d.

16 MODERN LANGUAGES AND LITERATURE

MILTON.—PARADISE LOST. Books I. and II. With Introduction and Notes, by MICHAEL MACMILLAN, B.A., Professor of Logic and Moral Philosophy, Elphinstone College, Bombay. Gl. 8vo. 2s. 6d. Or separately, 1s. 6d. each.
L'ALLEGRO, IL PENSEROSO, LYCIDAS, ARCADES, SONNETS, &c. With Introduction and Notes, by W. BELL, M.A., Professor of Philosophy and Logic, Government College, Lahore. Gl. 8vo. 2s.
COMUS. By the same. Gl. 8vo. 1s. 6d.
SAMSON AGONISTES. By H. M. PERCIVAL, M.A., Professor of English Literature, Presidency College, Calcutta. Gl. 8vo. 2s. 6d.
INTRODUCTION TO THE STUDY OF MILTON. By STOPFORD BROOKE, M.A. Fcap. 8vo. 1s. 6d. (*Classical Writers.*)
MORLEY.—ON THE STUDY OF LITERATURE. Address to the Students of the London Society for the Extension of University Teaching, delivered at the Mansion House, February 26, 1887. By JOHN MORLEY. Gl. 8vo, cloth. 1s. 6d.
  * *Also a Popular Edition in Pamphlet form for Distribution, price 2d.*
APHORISMS. Address delivered before the Philosophical Society of Edinburgh, November 11, 1887. By the same. Gl. 8vo. 1s. 6d.
MORRIS.—Works by the Rev. R. MORRIS, LL.D.
PRIMER OF ENGLISH GRAMMAR. 18mo. 1s.
ELEMENTARY LESSONS IN HISTORICAL ENGLISH GRAMMAR, containing Accidence and Word Formation. 18mo. 2s. 6d.
HISTORICAL OUTLINES OF ENGLISH ACCIDENCE, comprising Chapters on the History and Development of the Language, and on Word Formation. Ex. fcap. 8vo. 6s.
MORRIS AND KELLNER.—HISTORICAL OUTLINES OF ENGLISH SYNTAX. By Rev. R. MORRIS and Dr. L. KELLNER. [*In preparation.*
NICHOL.—A SHORT HISTORY OF ENGLISH LITERATURE. By Prof. JOHN NICHOL. Gl. 8vo. [*In preparation.*
OLIPHANT.—THE OLD AND MIDDLE ENGLISH. By T. L. KINGTON OLIPHANT. New Ed., revised and enlarged, of "The Sources of Standard English." Gl. 8vo. 9s.
THE NEW ENGLISH. By the same. 2 vols. Cr. 8vo. 21s.
PALGRAVE.—THE CHILDREN'S TREASURY OF LYRICAL POETRY. Selected and arranged, with Notes, by FRANCIS T. PALGRAVE. 18mo. 2s. 6d. Also in Two Parts. 1s. each.
PATMORE.—THE CHILDREN'S GARLAND FROM THE BEST POETS. Selected and arranged by COVENTRY PATMORE. Gl. 8vo. 2s. (*Globe Readings from Standard Authors.*)
PLUTARCH.—Being a Selection from the Lives which illustrate Shakespeare. North's Translation. Edited, with Introductions, Notes, Index of Names, and Glossarial Index, by Prof. W. W. SKEAT, Litt.D. Cr. 8vo. 6s.
RANSOME.—SHORT STUDIES OF SHAKESPEARE'S PLOTS. By CYRIL RANSOME, Professor of Modern History and Literature, Yorkshire College, Leeds. Cr. 8vo. 3s. 6d.
RYLAND.—CHRONOLOGICAL OUTLINES OF ENGLISH LITERATURE. By F. RYLAND, M.A. Cr. 8vo. [*In the Press.*
SAINTSBURY.—A HISTORY OF ELIZABETHAN LITERATURE. 1560-1665. By GEORGE SAINTSBURY. Cr. 8vo. 7s. 6d.
SCOTT.—LAY OF THE LAST MINSTREL, and THE LADY OF THE LAKE. Edited, with Introduction and Notes, by FRANCIS TURNER PALGRAVE. Gl. 8vo. 1s. (*Globe Readings from Standard Authors.*)
THE LAY OF THE LAST MINSTREL. With Introduction and Notes, by G. H. STUART, M.A., Professor of English Literature, Presidency College, Madras. Gl. 8vo. Cantos I. to III. 1s. 6d. Introduction and Canto I. 9d.
MARMION, and THE LORD OF THE ISLES. By F. T. PALGRAVE. Gl. 8vo. 1s. (*Globe Readings from Standard Authors.*)
MARMION. With Introduction and Notes, by MICHAEL MACMILLAN, B.A. Gl. 8vo. 3s. 6d.
THE LADY OF THE LAKE. By G. H. STUART, M.A. [*In the Press.*

ENGLISH

ROKEBY. With Introduction and Notes, by MICHAEL MACMILLAN, B.A. Gl. 8vo. 3s. 6d.
SHAKESPEARE.—A SHAKESPEARIAN GRAMMAR. By Rev. E. A. ABBOTT, D.D. Gl. 8vo. 6s.
A SHAKESPEARE MANUAL. By F. G. FLEAY, M.A. 2d Ed. Ex. fcap. 8vo. 4s. 6d.
PRIMER OF SHAKSPERE. By Prof. DOWDEN. 18mo. 1s.
SHORT STUDIES OF SHAKESPEARE'S PLOTS. By CYRIL RANSOME, M.A. Cr. 8vo. 3s. 6d.
THE TEMPEST. With Introduction and Notes, by K. DEIGHTON, late Principal of Agra College. Gl. 8vo. 1s. 6d.
MUCH ADO ABOUT NOTHING. By the same. Gl. 8vo. 2s.
THE MERCHANT OF VENICE. By the same. Gl. 8vo. 1s. 6d.
TWELFTH NIGHT. By the same. Gl. 8vo. 1s. 6d.
THE WINTER'S TALE. By the same. Gl. 8vo. 2s. 6d.
RICHARD II. By the same. Gl. 8vo. [In August.
KING JOHN. By the same. Gl. 8vo. [In preparation.
HENRY V. By the same. Gl. 8vo. 2s.
RICHARD III. By C. H. TAWNEY, M.A., Principal and Professor of English Literature, Presidency College, Calcutta. Gl. 8vo. 2s. 6d.
JULIUS CÆSAR. By K. DEIGHTON. Gl. 8vo. 2s.
MACBETH. By the same. Gl. 8vo. 1s. 6d.
OTHELLO. By the same. Gl. 8vo. 2s. 6d.
CYMBELINE. By the same. Gl. 8vo. 2s. 6d.
SONNENSCHEIN AND MEIKLEJOHN.—THE ENGLISH METHOD OF TEACHING TO READ. By A. SONNENSCHEIN and J. M. D. MEIKLEJOHN, M.A. Fcap. 8vo.

COMPRISING:

THE NURSERY BOOK, containing all the Two-Letter Words in the Language. 1d. (Also in Large Type on Sheets for School Walls. 5s.)
THE FIRST COURSE, consisting of Short Vowels with Single Consonants. 7d.
THE SECOND COURSE, with Combinations and Bridges, consisting of Short Vowels with Double Consonants. 7d.
THE THIRD AND FOURTH COURSES, consisting of Long Vowels, and all the Double Vowels in the Language. 7d.

SOUTHEY.—LIFE OF NELSON. With Introduction and Notes, by MICHAEL MACMILLAN, B.A. Gl. 8vo. 3s. 6d.
TAYLOR.—WORDS AND PLACES; or, Etymological Illustrations of History, Ethnology, and Geography. By Rev. ISAAC TAYLOR, Litt.D. With Maps. Gl. 8vo. 6s.
TENNYSON.—THE COLLECTED WORKS OF LORD TENNYSON. An Edition for Schools. In Four Parts. Cr. 8vo. 2s. 6d. each.
TENNYSON FOR THE YOUNG. Edited, with Notes for the Use of Schools, by the Rev. ALFRED AINGER, LL.D., Canon of Bristol. [In preparation.
SELECTIONS FROM TENNYSON. With Introduction and Notes, by F. J. ROWE, M.A., and W. T. WEBB, M.A. Gl. 8vo. 8s. 6d.
This selection contains:—Recollections of the Arabian Nights, The Lady of Shalott, Oenone, The Lotos Eaters, Ulysses, Tithonus, Morte d'Arthur, Sir Galahad, Dora, Ode on the Death of the Duke of Wellington, and The Revenge.
THRING.—THE ELEMENTS OF GRAMMAR TAUGHT IN ENGLISH. By EDWARD THRING, M.A. With Questions. 4th Ed. 18mo. 2s.
VAUGHAN.—WORDS FROM THE POETS. By C. M. VAUGHAN. 18mo. 1s.
WARD.—THE ENGLISH POETS. Selections, with Critical Introductions by various Writers and a General Introduction by MATTHEW ARNOLD. Edited by T. H. WARD, M.A. 4 Vols. Vol. I. CHAUCER TO DONNE.—Vol. II. BEN JONSON TO DRYDEN.—Vol. III. ADDISON TO BLAKE.—Vol. IV. WORDSWORTH TO ROSSETTI. Cr. 8vo. Each 7s. 6d.

B

18 MODERN LANGUAGES AND LITERATURE

**WETHERELL.—EXERCISES ON MORRIS'S PRIMER OF ENGLISH GRAM-
MAR.** By JOHN WETHERELL, M.A., Headmaster of Towcester Grammar
School. 18mo. 1s.
WOODS.—A FIRST POETRY BOOK. By M. A. WOODS, Head Mistress of the
Clifton High School for Girls. Fcap. 8vo. 2s. 6d.
A SECOND POETRY BOOK By the same. In two Parts. 2s. 6d. each.
A THIRD POETRY BOOK. By the same. 4s. 6d.
WORDSWORTH.—SELECTIONS. With Introduction and Notes, by WILLIAM
WORDSWORTH, B.A., Principal and Professor of History and Political Economy,
Elphinstone College, Bombay Gl. 8vo. [*In preparation.*
YONGE.—A BOOK OF GOLDEN DEEDS. By CHARLOTTE M. YONGE. Gl.
8vo. 2s.
THE ABRIDGED BOOK OF GOLDEN DEEDS. 18mo. 1s.

FRENCH.

BEAUMARCHAIS.—LE BARBIER DE SEVILLE. With Introduction and
Notes. By L. P. BLOUET. Fcap. 8vo. 3s. 6d.
BOWEN.—FIRST LESSONS IN FRENCH. By H. COURTHOPE BOWEN, M.A.
Ex. fcap. 8vo. 1s.
BREYMANN.—Works by HERMANN BREYMANN, Ph.D., Professor of Philology in
the University of Munich.
A FRENCH GRAMMAR BASED ON PHILOLOGICAL PRINCIPLES. Ex.
fcap. 8vo. 4s. 6d.
FIRST FRENCH EXERCISE BOOK. Ex. fcap. 8vo. 4s. 6d.
SECOND FRENCH EXERCISE BOOK. Ex. fcap. 8vo. 2s. 6d.
FASNACHT.—Works by G. E. FASNACHT, late Assistant Master at Westminster.
THE ORGANIC METHOD OF STUDYING LANGUAGES. Ex. fcap. 8vo. I.
French. 3s. 6d.
A SYNTHETIC FRENCH GRAMMAR FOR SCHOOLS. Cr. 8vo. 3s. 6d.
**GRAMMAR AND GLOSSARY OF THE FRENCH LANGUAGE OF THE
SEVENTEENTH CENTURY.** Cr. 8vo. [*In preparation.*
MACMILLAN'S PRIMARY SERIES OF FRENCH READING BOOKS.—Edited by
G. E. FASNACHT. With Illustrations, Notes, Vocabularies, and Exercises.
Gl. 8vo.
CORNAZ—NOS ENFANTS ET LEURS AMIS. By EDITH HARVEY. 1s. 6d.
**DE MAISTRE—LA JEUNE SIBÉRIENNE ET LE LÉPREUX DE LA CITÉ
D'AOSTE.** By STEPHANE BARLET, B.Sc. &c. 1s. 6d.
FLORIAN—FABLES. By Rev. CHARLES YELD, M.A., Headmaster of University
School, Nottingham. 1s. 6d.
LA FONTAINE—A SELECTION OF FABLES. By L. M. MORIARTY, B.A.,
Assistant Master at Harrow. 2s. 6d.
MOLESWORTH—FRENCH LIFE IN LETTERS. By Mrs. MOLESWORTH.
1s. 6d.
PERRAULT—CONTES DE FÉES. By G. E. FASNACHT. 1s. 6d.
MACMILLAN'S PROGRESSIVE FRENCH COURSE.—By G. E. FASNACHT. Ex.
fcp. 8vo.
FIRST YEAR, containing Easy Lessons on the Regular Accidence. 1s.
SECOND YEAR, containing an Elementary Grammar with copious Exercises,
Notes, and Vocabularies. 2s.
THIRD YEAR, containing a Systematic Syntax, and Lessons in Composition.
2s. 6d.
**THE TEACHER'S COMPANION TO MACMILLAN'S PROGRESSIVE FRENCH
COURSE.** With Copious Notes, Hints for Different Renderings, Synonyms,
Philological Remarks, etc. By G. E. FASNACHT. Ex. fcap. 8vo. Each Year
4s. 6d.
MACMILLAN'S FRENCH COMPOSITION.—By G. E. FASNACHT. Ex. fcap.
8vo. Part I. Elementary. 2s. 6d. Part II. Advanced. [*In the Press.*
**THE TEACHER'S COMPANION TO MACMILLAN'S COURSE OF FRENCH
COMPOSITION.** By G. E. FASNACHT. Part I. Ex. fcap. 8vo. 4s. 6d.

MACMILLAN'S PROGRESSIVE FRENCH READERS. By G. E. FASNACHT. Ex. fcap. 8vo.
  FIRST YEAR, containing Tales, Historical Extracts, Letters, Dialogues, Ballads, Nursery Songs, etc., with Two Vocabularies: (1) in the order of subjects; (2) in alphabetical order. With Imitative Exercises. 2s. 6d.
  SECOND YEAR, containing Fiction in Prose and Verse, Historical and Descriptive Extracts, Essays, Letters, Dialogues, etc. With Imitative Exercises. 2s. 6d.
MACMILLAN'S FOREIGN SCHOOL CLASSICS. Edited by G. E. FASNACHT. 18mo.
  CORNEILLE—LE CID. By G. E. FASNACHT. 1s.
  DUMAS—LES DEMOISELLES DE ST. CYR. By VICTOR OGER, Lecturer at University College, Liverpool. 1s. 6d.
  LA FONTAINE'S FABLES. Books I.—VI. By L. M. MORIARTY, B.A., Assistant Master at Harrow. [*In preparation.*
  MOLIÈRE—L'AVARE. By the same. 1s.
  MOLIÈRE—LE BOURGEOIS GENTILHOMME. By the same. 1s. 6d.
  MOLIÈRE—LES FEMMES SAVANTES. By G. E. FASNACHT. 1s.
  MOLIÈRE—LE MISANTHROPE. By the same. 1s.
  MOLIÈRE—LE MÉDECIN MALGRE LUI. By the same. 1s.
  RACINE—BRITANICUS. By E. PELLISSIER, M.A., Assistant Master at Clifton College. 2s.
  FRENCH READINGS FROM ROMAN HISTORY. Selected from various Authors, by C. COLBECK, M.A., Assistant Master at Harrow. 4s. 6d.
  SAND, GEORGE—LA MARE AU DIABLE. By W. E. RUSSELL, M.A., Assistant Master at Haileybury. 1s.
  SANDEAU, JULES—MADEMOISELLE DE LA SEIGLIERE. By H. C. STEEL, Assistant Master at Winchester. 1s. 6d.
  THIERS'S HISTORY OF THE EGYPTIAN EXPEDITION. By Rev. H. A. BULL, M.A., Assistant Master at Wellington. [*In preparation.*
  VOLTAIRE—CHARLES XII. By G. E. FASNACHT. 3s. 6d.
MASSON.—A COMPENDIOUS DICTIONARY OF THE FRENCH LANGUAGE. Adapted from the Dictionaries of Professor A. ELWALL. By GUSTAVE MASSON. Cr. 8vo. 6s.
MOLIERE.—LE MALADE IMAGINAIRE. With Introduction and Notes, by F TARVER, M.A., Assistant Master at Eton. Fcap. 8vo. 2s. 6d.
PELLISSIER.—FRENCH ROOTS AND THEIR FAMILIES. A Synthetic Vocabulary, based upon Derivations. By E. PELLISSIER, M.A., Assistant Master at Clifton College. Gl. 8vo. 6s.

GERMAN.

HUSS.—A SYSTEM OF ORAL INSTRUCTION IN GERMAN, by means of Progressive Illustrations and Applications of the leading Rules of Grammar. By H. C. O. HUSS, Ph.D. Cr. 8vo. 5s.
MACMILLAN'S PROGRESSIVE GERMAN COURSE. By G. E. FASNACHT. Ex. fcp. 8vo.
  FIRST YEAR. Easy lessons and Rules on the Regular Accidence. 1s. 6d.
  SECOND YEAR. Conversational Lessons in Systematic Accidence and Elementary Syntax. With Philological Illustrations and Etymological Vocabulary. 3s. 6d.
  THIRD YEAR. [*In the Press.*
  TEACHER'S COMPANION TO MACMILLAN'S PROGRESSIVE GERMAN COURSE. With copious Notes, Hints for Different Renderings, Synonyms, Philological Remarks, etc. By G. E. FASNACHT. Ex. fcap. 8vo. FIRST YEAR. 4s. 6d. SECOND YEAR. 4s. 6d.
MACMILLAN'S PROGRESSIVE GERMAN READERS. By G. E. FASNACHT. Ex. fcap. 8vo.
  FIRST YEAR, containing an Introduction to the German order of Words, with Copious Examples, extracts from German Authors in Prose and Poetry; Notes, and Vocabularies. 2s. 6d.

MACMILLAN'S PRIMARY SERIES OF GERMAN READING BOOKS. Edited by G. E. FASNACHT. With Notes, Vocabularies and Exercises. Gl. 8vo.
GRIMM—KINDER UND HAUSMÄRCHEN. By G. E. FASNACHT. 2s. 6d.
HAUFF—DIE KARAVANE. By HERMAN HAGER, Ph.D., Lecturer in the Owens College, Manchester. 3s.
SCHMID, CHR. VON—H. VON EICHENFELS. By G. E. FASNACHT. 2s. 6d.
MACMILLAN'S FOREIGN SCHOOL CLASSICS.—Edited by G. E. FASNACHT. 18mo.
FREYTAG (G.).—DOKTOR LUTHER. By F. STORR, M.A., Headmaster of the Modern Side, Merchant Taylors' School. [*In preparation.*
GOETHE—GÖTZ VON BERLICHINGEN. By H. A. BULL, M.A., Assistant Master at Wellington. 2s.
GOETHE—FAUST. PART I., followed by an Appendix on PART II. By JANE LEE, Lecturer in German Literature at Newnham College, Cambridge. 4s. 6d.
HEINE—SELECTIONS FROM THE REISEBILDER AND OTHER PROSE WORKS. By C. COLBECK, M.A., Assistant Master at Harrow. 2s. 6d.
LESSING—MINNA VON BARNHELM. By JAMES SIME, M.A. [*In preparation.*
SCHILLER—SELECTIONS FROM SCHILLER'S LYRICAL POEMS. With a Memoir of Schiller. By E. J. TURNER, B.A., and E. D. A. MORSHEAD, M.A. Assistant Masters at Winchester. 2s. 6d.
SCHILLER—DIE JUNGFRAU VON ORLEANS. By JOSEPH GOSTWICK. 2s. 6d.
SCHILLER—MARIA STUART. By C. SHELDON, D.Lit., of the Royal Academical Institution, Belfast. 2s. 6d.
SCHILLER—WILHELM TELL. By G. E. FASNACHT. 2s. 6d.
SCHILLER—WALLENSTEIN. Part I. DAS LAGER. By H. B. COTTERILL, M.A. 2s.
UHLAND—SELECT BALLADS. Adapted as a First Easy Reading Book for Beginners. With Vocabulary. By G. E. FASNACHT. 1s.
PYLODET.—NEW GUIDE TO GERMAN CONVERSATION ; containing an Alphabetical List of nearly 800 Familiar Words; followed by Exercises, Vocabulary of Words in frequent use, Familiar Phrases and Dialogues, a Sketch of German Literature, Idiomatic Expressions, etc. By L. PYLODET. 18mo. 2s. 6d.
WHITNEY.—A COMPENDIOUS GERMAN GRAMMAR. By W. D. WHITNEY, Professor of Sanskrit and Instructor in Modern Languages in Yale College. Cr. 8vo. 4s. 6d.
A GERMAN READER IN PROSE AND VERSE. By the Same. With Notes and Vocabulary. Cr. 8vo. 5s.
WHITNEY AND EDGREN.—A COMPENDIOUS GERMAN AND ENGLISH DICTIONARY, with Notation of Correspondences and Brief Etymologies. By Prof. W. D. WHITNEY, assisted by A. H. EDGREN. Cr. 8vo. 7s. 6d.
THE GERMAN-ENGLISH PART, separately, 5s.

MODERN GREEK.

VINCENT AND DICKSON.—HANDBOOK TO MODERN GREEK. By Sir EDGAR VINCENT, K.C.M.G., and T. G. DICKSON, M.A. With Appendix on the relation of Modern and Classical Greek by Prof. JEBB. Cr. 8vo. 6s.

ITALIAN.

DANTE.—THE PURGATORY OF DANTE. With Translation and Notes, by A. J. BUTLER, M.A. Cr. 8vo. 12s. 6d.
THE PARADISO OF DANTE. With Translation and Notes, by the Same. Cr. 8vo. 12s. 6d.
READINGS ON THE PURGATORIO OF DANTE. Chiefly based on the Commentary of Benvenuto Da Imola. By the Hon. W. WARREN VERNON, M.A. With an Introduction by the Very Rev the DEAN OF ST. PAUL'S. 2 vols. Cr. 8vo. 24s.

SPANISH 21

SPANISH.

CALDERON.—FOUR PLAYS OF CALDERON. With Introduction and Notes. By NORMAN MACCOLL, M.A. Cr. 8vo. 14s.
The four plays here given are *El Principe Constante, La Vida es Sueno, El Alcalde de Zalamea,* and *El Escondido y La Tapada.*

MATHEMATICS.

Arithmetic, Book-keeping, Algebra, Euclid and Pure Geometry, Geometrical Drawing, Mensuration, Trigonometry, Analytical Geometry (Plane and Solid), Problems and Questions in Mathematics, Higher Pure Mathematics, Mechanics (Statics, Dynamics, Hydrostatics, Hydrodynamics: see also Physics), Physics (Sound, Light, Heat, Electricity, Elasticity, Attractions, &c.), Astronomy, Historical.

ARITHMETIC.

ALDIS.—THE GREAT GIANT ARITHMOS. A most Elementary Arithmetic for Children. By MARY STEADMAN ALDIS. Illustrated. Gl. 8vo. 2s. 6d.

ARMY PRELIMINARY EXAMINATION, SPECIMENS OF PAPERS SET AT THE, 1882-89.—With Answers to the Mathematical Questions. Subjects: Arithmetic, Algebra, Euclid, Geometrical Drawing, Geography, French, English Dictation. Cr. 8vo. 3s. 6d.

BRADSHAW.—A COURSE OF EASY ARITHMETICAL EXAMPLES FOR BEGINNERS. By J. G. BRADSHAW, B.A., Assistant Master at Clifton College. Gl. 8vo. 2s. With Answers, 2s. 6d.

BROOKSMITH.—ARITHMETIC IN THEORY AND PRACTICE. By J. BROOKSMITH, M.A. Cr. 8vo. 4s. 6d.

BROOKSMITH.—ARITHMETIC FOR BEGINNERS. By J. and E. J. BROOKSMITH. Gl. 8vo. 1s. 6d.

CANDLER.—HELP TO ARITHMETIC. Designed for the use of Schools. By H. CANDLER, Mathematical Master of Uppingham School. 2d Ed. Ex. fcap. 8vo. 2s. 6d.

DALTON.—RULES AND EXAMPLES IN ARITHMETIC. By the Rev. T. DALTON, M.A., Assistant Master at Eton. New Ed., with Answers. 18mo. 2s. 6d.

GOYEN—HIGHER ARITHMETIC AND ELEMENTARY MENSURATION. By P. GOYEN, Inspector of Schools, Dunedin, New Zealand. Cr. 8vo. 5s.

HALL AND KNIGHT.—ARITHMETICAL EXERCISES AND EXAMINATION PAPERS. With an Appendix containing Questions in LOGARITHMS and MENSURATION. By H. S. HALL, M.A., Master of the Military and Engineering Side, Clifton College, and S. R. KNIGHT, B.A. Gl. 8vo. 2s. 6d.

LOCK.—Works by Rev. J. B. LOCK, M.A., Senior Fellow, Assistant Tutor and Lecturer in Gonville and Caius College, Cambridge.

ARITHMETIC FOR SCHOOLS. With Answers and 1000 additional Examples for Exercise. 3d Ed., revised. Gl. 8vo. 4s. 6d. Or in Two Parts:— Part I. Up to and including Practice. 2s. Part II. With 1000 additional Examples for Exercise. 3s. KEY. Cr. 8vo. 10s. 6d.

ARITHMETIC FOR BEGINNERS. A School Class-Book of Commercial Arithmetic. Gl. 8vo. 2s. 6d. KEY. Cr. 8vo. 8s. 6d.

A SHILLING CLASS-BOOK OF ARITHMETIC, ADAPTED FOR USE IN ELEMENTARY SCHOOLS. 18mo. 1s. With Answers 1s. 6d. [*In July.*

MATHEMATICS

PEDLEY.—EXERCISES IN ARITHMETIC for the Use of Schools. Containing more than 7000 original Examples. By SAMUEL PEDLEY. Cr. 8vo. 5s. Also in Two Parts, 2s. 6d. each.

SMITH.—Works by Rev. BARNARD SMITH, M.A., late Fellow and Senior Bursar of St. Peter's College, Cambridge.
ARITHMETIC AND ALGEBRA, in their Principles and Application; with numerous systematically arranged Examples taken from the Cambridge Examination Papers, with especial reference to the Ordinary Examination for the B.A. Degree. New Ed., carefully revised. Cr. 8vo. 10s. 6d.
ARITHMETIC FOR SCHOOLS. Cr. 8vo. 4s. 6d. KEY. Cr. 8vo. 4s. 6d.
EXERCISES IN ARITHMETIC. Cr. 8vo. 2s. With Answers, 2s. 6d. Answers separately, 6d.
SCHOOL CLASS-BOOK OF ARITHMETIC. 18mo. 3s. Or separately, in Three Parts, 1s. each. KEYS. Parts I., II., and III., 2s. 6d. each.
SHILLING BOOK OF ARITHMETIC. 18mo. Or separately, Part I., 2d.; Part II., 3d.; Part III., 7d. Answers, 6d. KEY. 18mo. 4s. 6d.
THE SAME, with Answers. 18mo, cloth. 1s. 6d.
EXAMINATION PAPERS IN ARITHMETIC. 18mo. 1s. 6d. The Same, with Answers. 18mo. 2s. Answers, 6d. KEY. 18mo. 4s. 6d.
THE METRIC SYSTEM OF ARITHMETIC, ITS PRINCIPLES AND APPLICATIONS, with Numerous Examples. 18mo. 3d.
A CHART OF THE METRIC SYSTEM, on a Sheet, size 42 in. by 34 in. on Roller. 3s. 6d. Also a Small Chart on a Card. Price 1d.
EASY LESSONS IN ARITHMETIC, combining Exercises in Reading, Writing, Spelling, and Dictation. Part I. Cr. 8vo. 9d.
EXAMINATION CARDS IN ARITHMETIC. With Answers and Hints.
Standards I. and II., in box, 1s. Standards III., IV., and V., in boxes, 1s. each. Standard VI. in Two Parts, in boxes, 1s. each.
A and B papers, of nearly the same difficulty, are given so as to prevent copying, and the colours of the A and B papers differ in each Standard, and from those of every other Standard, so that a master or mistress can see at a glance whether the children have the proper papers.

BOOK-KEEPING.

THORNTON.—FIRST LESSONS IN BOOK-KEEPING. By J. THORNTON. Cr. 8vo. 2s. 6d. KEY. Oblong 4to. 10s. 6d.
PRIMER OF BOOK-KEEPING. 18mo. 1s. KEY. [*Immediately.*

ALGEBRA.

DALTON.—RULES AND EXAMPLES IN ALGEBRA. By Rev. T. DALTON, Assistant Master at Eton. Part I. 18mo. 2s. KEY. Cr. 8vo. 7s. 6d. Part II. 18mo. 2s. 6d.

HALL AND KNIGHT.—Works by H. S. HALL, M.A., Master of the Military and Engineering Side, Clifton College, and S. R. KNIGHT, B.A.
ELEMENTARY ALGEBRA FOR SCHOOLS. 5th Ed., revised and corrected. Gl. 8vo, bound in maroon coloured cloth, 3s. 6d.; with Answers, bound in green coloured cloth, 4s. 6d. [KEY. *In the Press.*
ALGEBRAICAL EXERCISES AND EXAMINATION PAPERS. To accompany ELEMENTARY ALGEBRA. 2d Ed., revised. Gl. 8vo. 2s. 6d.
HIGHER ALGEBRA. 3d Ed. Cr. 8vo. 7s. 6d. KEY. Cr. 8vo. 10s. 6d.

JONES AND CHEYNE.—ALGEBRAICAL EXERCISES. Progressively Arranged. By Rev. C. A. JONES and C. H. CHEYNE, M.A., late Mathematical Masters at Westminster School. 18mo. 2s. 6d.
KEY. By Rev. W. FAILES, M.A., Mathematical Master at Westminster School. Cr. 8vo. 7s. 6d.

EUCLID AND PURE GEOMETRY

SMITH.—ARITHMETIC AND ALGEBRA, in their Principles and Application; with numerous systematically arranged Examples taken from the Cambridge Examination Papers, with especial reference to the Ordinary Examination for the B.A. Degree. By Rev. BARNARD SMITH, M.A. New Edition, carefully revised. Cr. 8vo. 10s. 6d.

SMITH.—Works by CHARLES SMITH, M.A., Master of Sidney Sussex College, Cambridge.
ELEMENTARY ALGEBRA. 2d Ed., revised. Gl. 8vo. 4s. 6d.
A TREATISE ON ALGEBRA. Cr. 8vo. 7s. 6d. KEY. Cr. 8vo. 10s. 6d.

TODHUNTER.—Works by ISAAC TODHUNTER, F.R.S.
ALGEBRA FOR BEGINNERS. 18mo. 2s. 6d. KEY. Cr. 8vo. 6s. 6d.
ALGEBRA FOR COLLEGES AND SCHOOLS. Cr. 8vo. 7s. 6d. KEY. Cr. 8vo. 10s. 6d.

EUCLID AND PURE GEOMETRY.

COCKSHOTT AND WALTERS.—A TREATISE ON GEOMETRICAL CONICS. In accordance with the Syllabus of the Association for the Improvement of Geometrical Teaching. By A. COCKSHOTT, M.A., Assistant Master at Eton; and Rev. F. B. WALTERS, M.A., Principal of King William's College, Isle of Man. Cr. 8vo. 5s.

CONSTABLE.—GEOMETRICAL EXERCISES FOR BEGINNERS. By SAMUEL CONSTABLE. Cr. 8vo. 3s. 6d.

CUTHBERTSON.—EUCLIDIAN GEOMETRY. By FRANCIS CUTHBERTSON, M.A., LL.D. Ex. fcap. 8vo. 4s. 6d.

DAY.—PROPERTIES OF CONIC SECTIONS PROVED GEOMETRICALLY. By Rev. H. G. DAY, M.A. Part I. The Ellipse, with an ample collection of Problems. Cr. 8vo. 3s. 6d.

DODGSON.—Works by CHARLES L. DODGSON, M.A., Student and late Mathematical Lecturer, Christ Church, Oxford.
EUCLID, BOOKS I. AND II. 6th Ed., with words substituted for the Algebraical Symbols used in the 1st Ed. Cr. 8vo. 2s.
EUCLID AND HIS MODERN RIVALS. 2d Ed. Cr. 8vo. 6s.
CURIOSA MATHEMATICA. Part I. A New Theory of Parallels. 2d Ed. Cr. 8vo. 2s.

DREW.—GEOMETRICAL TREATISE ON CONIC SECTIONS. By W. H. DREW, M.A. New Ed., enlarged. Cr. 8vo. 5s.

DUPUIS.—ELEMENTARY SYNTHETIC GEOMETRY OF THE POINT, LINE, AND CIRCLE IN THE PLANE. By N. F. DUPUIS, M.A., Professor of Pure Mathematics in the University of Queen's College, Kingston, Canada. Gl. 8vo. 4s. 6d.

HALL AND STEVENS.—A TEXT-BOOK OF EUCLID'S ELEMENTS. Including Alternative Proofs, together with additional Theorems and Exercises, classified and arranged. By H. S. HALL, M.A., and F. H. STEVENS, M.A., Masters of the Military and Engineering Side, Clifton College. Gl. 8vo. Book I., 1s.; Books I. and II., 1s. 6d.; Books I.-IV., 3s.; Books III.-VI., 3s.; Books I.-VI. and XI., 4s. 6d.; Book XI., 1s. [KEY. *In preparation.*

HALSTED.—THE ELEMENTS OF GEOMETRY By G. B. HALSTED, Professor of Pure and Applied Mathematics in the University of Texas. 8vo. 12s. 6d.

LOCK.—EUCLID FOR BEGINNERS. Being an Introduction to existing Text-books. By Rev. J. B. LOCK, M.A. [*In the Press.*

MAULT.—NATURAL GEOMETRY: an Introduction to the Logical Study of Mathematics. For Schools and Technical Classes. With Explanatory Models based upon the Tachymetrical works of Ed. Lagout. By A. MAULT. 18mo. 1s. Models to Illustrate the above, in Box, 12s. 6d.

MILNE AND DAVIS.—GEOMETRICAL CONICS. Part I. The Parabola. By Rev. J. J. MILNE, M.A., and R. F. DAVIS, M.A. Cr. 8vo. [*In the Press.*

SYLLABUS OF PLANE GEOMETRY (corresponding to Euclid, Books I.-VI.)— Prepared by the Association for the Improvement of Geometrical Teaching. Cr. 8vo. 1s.

MATHEMATICS

SYLLABUS OF MODERN PLANE GEOMETRY.—Prepared by the Association for the Improvement of Geometrical Teaching. Cr. 8vo. Sewed. 1s.

TODHUNTER.—THE ELEMENTS OF EUCLID. By I. Todhunter, F.R.S. 18mo. 3s. 6d. KEY. Cr. 8vo. 6s. 6d.

WILSON.—Works by Rev. J. M. Wilson, M.A., Head Master of Clifton College.
 ELEMENTARY GEOMETRY. BOOKS I.-V. Containing the Subjects of Euclid's first Six Books. Following the Syllabus of the Geometrical Association. Ex. fcap. 8vo. 4s. 6d.
 SOLID GEOMETRY AND CONIC SECTIONS. With Appendices on Transversals and Harmonic Division. Ex. fcap. 8vo. 3s. 6d.

GEOMETRICAL DRAWING.

EAGLES.—CONSTRUCTIVE GEOMETRY OF PLANE CURVES. By T. H. Eagles, M.A., Instructor in Geometrical Drawing and Lecturer in Architecture at the Royal Indian Engineering College, Cooper's Hill. Cr. 8vo. 12s.

EDGAR AND PRITCHARD.—NOTE-BOOK ON PRACTICAL SOLID OR DESCRIPTIVE GEOMETRY. Containing Problems with help for Solutions. By J. H. Edgar and G. S. Pritchard. 4th Ed., revised by A. Meeze. Gl. 8vo. 4s. 6d.

KITCHENER.—A GEOMETRICAL NOTE-BOOK. Containing Easy Problems in Geometrical Drawing preparatory to the Study of Geometry. For the Use of Schools. By F. E. Kitchener, M.A., Head Master of the Newcastle-under-Lyme High School. 4to. 2s.

MILLAR.—ELEMENTS OF DESCRIPTIVE GEOMETRY. By J. B. Millar, Civil Engineer, Lecturer on Engineering in the Victoria University, Manchester. 2d Ed. Cr. 8vo. 6s.

PLANT.—GEOMETRICAL DRAWING. By E. C. Plant. Globe 8vo.
[*In preparation.*

MENSURATION.

STEVENS.—ELEMENTARY MENSURATION. With Exercises on the Mensuration of Plane and Solid Figures. By F. H. Stevens, M.A. Gl. 8vo.
[*In preparation.*

TEBAY.—ELEMENTARY MENSURATION FOR SCHOOLS. By S. Tebay. Ex. fcap. 8vo. 3s. 6d.

TODHUNTER.—MENSURATION FOR BEGINNERS. By Isaac Todhunter, F.R.S. 18mo. 2s. 6d. KEY. By Rev. Fr. L. McCarthy. Cr. 8vo. 7s. 6d.

TRIGONOMETRY.

BEASLEY.—AN ELEMENTARY TREATISE ON PLANE TRIGONOMETRY. With Examples. By R. D. Beasley, M.A. 9th Ed., revised and enlarged. Cr. 8vo. 3s. 6d.

BOTTOMLEY.—FOUR-FIGURE MATHEMATICAL TABLES. Comprising Logarithmic and Trigonometrical Tables, and Tables of Squares, Square Roots, and Reciprocals. By J. T. Bottomley, M.A., Lecturer in Natural Philosophy in the University of Glasgow. 8vo. 2s. 6d.

HAYWARD.—THE ALGEBRA OF CO-PLANAR VECTORS AND TRIGONOMETRY. By R. B. Hayward, M.A., F.R.S., Assistant Master at Harrow.
[*In preparation.*

JOHNSON.—A TREATISE ON TRIGONOMETRY. By W. E. Johnson, M.A. late Scholar and Assistant Mathematical Lecturer at King's College, Cambridge. Cr. 8vo. 8s. 6d.

LOCK.—Works by Rev. J. B. Lock, M.A., Senior Fellow, Assistant Tutor and Lecturer in Gonville and Caius College, Cambridge.
 TRIGONOMETRY FOR BEGINNERS, as far as the Solution of Triangles. 3d Ed. Gl. 8vo. 2s. 6d. KEY. Cr. 8vo. 6s. 6d.
 ELEMENTARY TRIGONOMETRY. 6th Ed. (in this edition the chapter on logarithms has been carefully revised). Gl. 8vo. 4s. 6d. KEY. Cr. 8vo. 8s. 6d.

HIGHER TRIGONOMETRY. 5th Ed. Gl. 8vo. 4s. 6d. Both Parts complete in One Volume. Gl. 8vo. 7s. 6d.

M'CLELLAND AND PRESTON.—A TREATISE ON SPHERICAL TRIGONOMETRY. With applications to Spherical Geometry and numerous Examples. By W. J. M'CLELLAND, M.A., Principal of the Incorporated Society's School, Santry, Dublin, and T. PRESTON, M.A. Cr. 8vo. 8s. 6d., or: Part I. To the End of Solution of Triangles, 4s. 6d. Part II., 5s.

PALMER.—TEXT-BOOK OF PRACTICAL LOGARITHMS AND TRIGONOMETRY. By J. H. PALMER, Headmaster, R.N., H.M.S. *Cambridge*, Devonport. Gl. 8vo. 4s. 6d.

SNOWBALL.—THE ELEMENTS OF PLANE AND SPHERICAL TRIGONOMETRY. By J. C. SNOWBALL. 14th Ed. Cr. 8vo. 7s. 6d.

TODHUNTER.—Works by ISAAC TODHUNTER, F.R.S.
TRIGONOMETRY FOR BEGINNERS. 18mo. 2s. 6d. KEY. Cr. 8vo. 8s. 6d.
PLANE TRIGONOMETRY. Cr. 8vo. 5s. KEY. Cr. 8vo. 10s. 6d.
A TREATISE ON SPHERICAL TRIGONOMETRY. Cr. 8vo. 4s. 6d.

WOLSTENHOLME.—EXAMPLES FOR PRACTICE IN THE USE OF SEVEN-FIGURE LOGARITHMS. By JOSEPH WOLSTENHOLME, D.Sc., late Professor of Mathematics in the Royal Indian Engineering Coll., Cooper's Hill. 8vo. 5s.

ANALYTICAL GEOMETRY (Plane and Solid).

DYER.—EXERCISES IN ANALYTICAL GEOMETRY. By J. M. DYER, M.A., Assistant Master at Eton. Illustrated. Cr. 8vo. 4s. 6d.

FERRERS.—AN ELEMENTARY TREATISE ON TRILINEAR CO-ORDINATES, the Method of Reciprocal Polars, and the Theory of Projectors. By the Rev. N. M. FERRERS, D.D., F.R.S., Master of Gonville and Caius College, Cambridge. 4th Ed., revised. Cr. 8vo. 6s. 6d.

FROST.—Works by PERCIVAL FROST, D.Sc., F.R.S., Fellow and Mathematical Lecturer at King's College, Cambridge.
AN ELEMENTARY TREATISE ON CURVE TRACING. 8vo. 12s.
SOLID GEOMETRY. 3d Ed. Demy 8vo. 16s.
HINTS FOR THE SOLUTION OF PROBLEMS in the Third Edition of SOLID GEOMETRY. 8vo. 8s. 6d.

HAYWARD.—THE ELEMENTS OF SOLID GEOMETRY. By R. B. HAYWARD, M.A., F.R.S. Gl. 8vo. [*In the Press.*

JOHNSON.—CURVE TRACING IN CARTESIAN CO-ORDINATES. By W. WOOLSEY JOHNSON, Professor of Mathematics at the U.S. Naval Academy, Annapolis, Maryland. Cr. 8vo. 4s. 6d.

PUCKLE.—AN ELEMENTARY TREATISE ON CONIC SECTIONS AND ALGEBRAIC GEOMETRY. With Numerous Examples and Hints for their Solution. By G. H. PUCKLE, M.A. 5th Ed., revised and enlarged. Cr. 8vo. 7s. 6d.

SMITH.—Works by CHARLES SMITH, M.A., Master of Sidney Sussex College, Cambridge.
CONIC SECTIONS. 7th Ed. Cr. 8vo. 7s. 6d.
SOLUTIONS TO CONIC SECTIONS. Cr. 8vo. 10s. 6d.
AN ELEMENTARY TREATISE ON SOLID GEOMETRY. 2d Ed. Cr. 8vo. 9s. 6d.

TODHUNTER.—Works by ISAAC TODHUNTER, F.R.S.
PLANE CO-ORDINATE GEOMETRY, as applied to the Straight Line and the Conic Sections. Cr. 8vo. 7s. 6d.
KEY. By C. W. BOURNE, M.A., Headmaster of King's College School. Cr. 8vo. 10s. 6d.
EXAMPLES OF ANALYTICAL GEOMETRY OF THREE DIMENSIONS. New Ed., revised. Cr. 8vo. 4s.

PROBLEMS AND QUESTIONS IN MATHEMATICS.

ARMY PRELIMINARY EXAMINATION, 1882-1889, Specimens of Papers set at the. With Answers to the Mathematical Questions. Subjects: Arithmetic, Algebra, Euclid, Geometrical Drawing, Geography, French, English Dictation. Cr. 8vo. 3s. 6d.

CAMBRIDGE SENATE-HOUSE PROBLEMS AND RIDERS, WITH SOLUTIONS:—
1875—PROBLEMS AND RIDERS. By A. G. GREENHILL, F.R.S. Cr. 8vo. 8s. 6d.
1878—SOLUTIONS OF SENATE-HOUSE PROBLEMS. By the Mathematical Moderators and Examiners. Edited by J. W. L. GLAISHER, F.R.S., Fellow of Trinity College, Cambridge. 12s.

CHRISTIE.—A COLLECTION OF ELEMENTARY TEST-QUESTIONS IN PURE AND MIXED MATHEMATICS; with Answers and Appendices on Synthetic Division, and on the Solution of Numerical Equations by Horner's Method. By JAMES R. CHRISTIE, F.R.S. Cr. 8vo. 8s. 6d.

MILNE.—Works by Rev. JOHN J. MILNE, Private Tutor.
WEEKLY PROBLEM PAPERS. With Notes intended for the use of Students preparing for Mathematical Scholarships, and for Junior Members of the Universities who are reading for Mathematical Honours. Pott 8vo. 4s. 6d.
SOLUTIONS TO WEEKLY PROBLEM PAPERS. Cr. 8vo. 10s. 6d.
COMPANION TO WEEKLY PROBLEM PAPERS. Cr. 8vo. 10s. 6d.

SANDHURST MATHEMATICAL PAPERS, for admission into the Royal Military College, 1881-1889. Edited by E. J. BROOKSMITH, B.A., Instructor in Mathematics at the Royal Military Academy, Woolwich. Cr. 8vo. [In the Press.

WOOLWICH MATHEMATICAL PAPERS, for Admission into the Royal Military Academy, Woolwich, 1880-1888 inclusive. Edited by E. J. BROOKSMITH, B.A. Cr. 8vo. 6s.

WOLSTENHOLME.—Works by JOSEPH WOLSTENHOLME, D.Sc., late Professor of Mathematics in the Royal Engineering Coll. Cooper's Hill.
MATHEMATICAL PROBLEMS, on Subjects included in the First and Second Divisions of the Schedule of Subjects for the Cambridge Mathematical Tripos Examination. New Ed., greatly enlarged. 8vo. 18s.
EXAMPLES FOR PRACTICE IN THE USE OF SEVEN-FIGURE LOGARITHMS. 8vo. 5s.

HIGHER PURE MATHEMATICS.

AIRY.—Works by Sir G. B. AIRY, K.C.B., formerly Astronomer-Royal.
ELEMENTARY TREATISE ON PARTIAL DIFFERENTIAL EQUATIONS. With Diagrams. 2d Ed. Cr. 8vo. 5s. 6d.
ON THE ALGEBRAICAL AND NUMERICAL THEORY OF ERRORS OF OBSERVATIONS AND THE COMBINATION OF OBSERVATIONS. 2d. Ed., revised. Cr. 8vo. 6s. 6d.

BOOLE.—THE CALCULUS OF FINITE DIFFERENCES. By G. BOOLE. 3d Ed., revised by J. F. MOULTON, Q.C. Cr. 8vo. 10s. 6d.

CARLL—A TREATISE ON THE CALCULUS OF VARIATIONS. By LEWIS B. CARLL. Arranged with the purpose of Introducing, as well as Illustrating, its Principles to the Reader by means of Problems, and Designed to present in all Important Particulars a Complete View of the Present State of the Science. 8vo. 21s.

EDWARDS.—THE DIFFERENTIAL CALCULUS. By JOSEPH EDWARDS, M.A., With Applications and numerous Examples. Cr. 8vo. 10s. 6d.

FERRERS.—AN ELEMENTARY TREATISE ON SPHERICAL HARMONICS, AND SUBJECTS CONNECTED WITH THEM. By Rev. N. M. FERRERS, D.D., F.R.S., Master of Gonville and Caius College, Cambridge. Cr. 8vo. 7s. 6d.

FORSYTH.—A TREATISE ON DIFFERENTIAL EQUATIONS. By ANDREW RUSSELL FORSYTH, F.R.S., Fellow and Assistant Tutor of Trinity College, Cambridge. 2d Ed. 8vo. 14s.

FROST.—AN ELEMENTARY TREATISE ON CURVE TRACING. By PERCIVAL FROST, M.A., D.Sc. 8vo. 12s.

GREENHILL.—DIFFERENTIAL AND INTEGRAL CALCULUS. By A. G. GREENHILL, Professor of Mathematics to the Senior Class of Artillery Officers, Woolwich. Cr. 8vo. 7s. 6d.

JOHNSON.—Works by WILLIAM WOOLSEY JOHNSON, Professor of Mathematics at the U.S. Naval Academy, Annapolis, Maryland.
  INTEGRAL CALCULUS, an Elementary Treatise on the; Founded on the Method of Rates or Fluxions. 8vo. 9s.
  CURVE TRACING IN CARTESIAN CO-ORDINATES. Cr. 8vo. 4s. 6d.
  A TREATISE ON ORDINARY AND DIFFERENTIAL EQUATIONS. Ex. cr. 8vo. 15s.

KELLAND AND TAIT.—INTRODUCTION TO QUATERNIONS, with numerous examples. By P. KELLAND and P. G. TAIT, Professors in the Department of Mathematics in the University of Edinburgh. 2d Ed. Cr. 8vo. 7s. 6d.

KEMPE.—HOW TO DRAW A STRAIGHT LINE: a Lecture on Linkages. By A. B. KEMPE. Illustrated. Cr. 8vo. 1s. 6d.

KNOX.—DIFFERENTIAL CALCULUS FOR BEGINNERS. By ALEXANDER KNOX. Fcap. 8vo. 8s. 6d.

MERRIMAN.—A TEXT-BOOK OF THE METHOD OF LEAST SQUARES. By MANSFIELD MERRIMAN, Professor of Civil Engineering at Lehigh University, U.S.A. 8vo. 8s. 6d.

MUIR.—Works by THOS. MUIR, Mathematical Master in the High School of Glasgow.
  A TREATISE ON THE THEORY OF DETERMINANTS. With graduated sets of Examples. Cr. 8vo. 7s. 6d.
  THE THEORY OF DETERMINANTS IN THE HISTORICAL ORDER OF ITS DEVELOPMENT. Part I. Determinants in General. Leibnitz (1693) to Cayley (1841). 8vo. 10s. 6d.

RICE AND JOHNSON.—DIFFERENTIAL CALCULUS, an Elementary Treatise on the; Founded on the Method of Rates or Fluxions. By J. M. RICE, Professor of Mathematics in the United States Navy, and W. W. JOHNSON, Professor of Mathematics at the United States Naval Academy. 3d Ed., revised and corrected. 8vo. 18s. Abridged Ed. 9s.

TODHUNTER.—Works by ISAAC TODHUNTER, F.R.S.
  AN ELEMENTARY TREATISE ON THE THEORY OF EQUATIONS. Cr. 8vo. 7s. 6d.
  A TREATISE ON THE DIFFERENTIAL CALCULUS. Cr. 8vo. 10s. 6d. KEY. Cr. 8vo. 10s. 6d.
  A TREATISE ON THE INTEGRAL CALCULUS AND ITS APPLICATIONS. Cr. 8vo. 10s. 6d. KEY. Cr 8vo. 10s. 6d.
  A HISTORY OF THE MATHEMATICAL THEORY OF PROBABILITY, from the time of Pascal to that of Laplace. 8vo. 18s.
  AN ELEMENTARY TREATISE ON LAPLACE'S, LAME'S, AND BESSEL'S FUNCTIONS. Cr. 8vo. 10s. 6d.

MECHANICS: Statics, Dynamics, Hydrostatics, Hydrodynamics. (See also Physics.)

ALEXANDER AND THOMSON.—ELEMENTARY APPLIED MECHANICS. By Prof. T. ALEXANDER, and A. W. THOMSON. Part II. Transverse Stress. Cr. 8vo. 10s. 6d.

BALL.—EXPERIMENTAL MECHANICS. A Course of Lectures delivered at the Royal College of Science for Ireland. By Sir R. S. BALL, F.R.S. 2d Ed. Illustrated. Cr. 8vo. 6s.

MATHEMATICS

CHISHOLM.—THE SCIENCE OF WEIGHING AND MEASURING, AND THE STANDARDS OF MEASURE AND WEIGHT. By H. W. CHISHOLM, Warden of the Standards. Illustrated. Cr. 8vo. 4s. 6d.

CLARKE.—A TABLE OF SPECIFIC GRAVITY FOR SOLIDS AND LIQUIDS. (Constants of Nature: Part I.) New Ed., revised and enlarged. By F. W. CLARKE, Chief Chemist, U.S. Geological Survey. 8vo. 12s. 6d. (Published for the Smithsonian Institution, Washington, U.S.A.)

CLIFFORD.—THE ELEMENTS OF DYNAMIC. An Introduction to the Study of Motion and Rest in Solid and Fluid Bodies. By W. K. CLIFFORD. Part I.—Kinematic. Cr. 8vo. Books I—III. 7s. 6d.; Book IV. and Appendix, 6s.

COTTERILL.—APPLIED MECHANICS: an Elementary General Introduction to the Theory of Structures and Machines. By J. H. COTTERILL, F.R.S., Professor of Applied Mechanics in the Royal Naval College, Greenwich. 8vo. 18s.

COTTERILL AND SLADE.—ELEMENTARY MANUAL OF APPLIED MECHANICS. By Prof. J. H. COTTERILL and J. H. SLADE. Cr. 8vo. [*In the Press.*

DYNAMICS, SYLLABUS OF ELEMENTARY. Part I. Linear Dynamics. With an Appendix on the Meanings of the Symbols in Physical Equations. Prepared by the Association for the Improvement of Geometrical Teaching. 4to. 1s.

GANGUILLET AND KUTTER.—A GENERAL FORMULA FOR THE UNIFORM FLOW OF WATER IN RIVERS AND OTHER CHANNELS. By E. GANGUILLET and W. R. KUTTER, Engineers in Berne, Switzerland. Translated from the German, with numerous Additions, including Tables and Diagrams, and the Elements of over 1200 Gaugings of Rivers, Small Channels, and Pipes in English Measure, by RUDOLPH HERING, Assoc. Am. Soc. C.E., M. Inst. C.E., and JOHN C. TRAUTWINE Jun., Assoc. Am. Soc. C.E., Assoc. Inst. C.E. 8vo. 17s.

GREAVES.—Works by JOHN GREAVES, M.A., Fellow and Mathematical Lecturer at Christ's College, Cambridge.

STATICS FOR BEGINNERS. Gl. 8vo. 3s. 6d.

A TREATISE ON ELEMENTARY STATICS. 2d Ed. Cr. 8vo. 6s. 6d.

HICKS.—ELEMENTARY DYNAMICS OF PARTICLES AND SOLIDS. By W. M. HICKS, Principal and Professor of Mathematics and Physics, Firth College, Sheffield. Cr. 8vo. 6s. 6d.

JELLETT.—A TREATISE ON THE THEORY OF FRICTION. By JOHN H. JELLETT, B.D., late Provost of Trinity College, Dublin. 8vo. 8s. 6d.

KENNEDY.—THE MECHANICS OF MACHINERY. By A. B. W. KENNEDY, F.R.S. Illustrated. Cr. 8vo. 12s. 6d.

LOCK.—Works by Rev. J. B. LOCK, M.A.

ELEMENTARY STATICS. 2d Ed. Gl. 8vo. 4s. 6d.

DYNAMICS FOR BEGINNERS. 3d Ed. Gl. 8vo. 4s. 6d.

MACGREGOR.—KINEMATICS AND DYNAMICS. An Elementary Treatise. By J. G. MACGREGOR, D.Sc., Munro Professor of Physics in Dalhousie College, Halifax, Nova Scotia. Illustrated. Cr. 8vo. 10s. 6d.

PARKINSON.—AN ELEMENTARY TREATISE ON MECHANICS. By S. PARKINSON, D.D., F.R.S., late Tutor and Prælector of St. John's College, Cambridge. 6th Ed., revised. Cr. 8vo. 9s. 6d.

PIRIE.—LESSONS ON RIGID DYNAMICS. By Rev. G. PIRIE, M.A., Professor of Mathematics in the University of Aberdeen. Cr. 8vo. 6s.

REULEAUX.—THE KINEMATICS OF MACHINERY. Outlines of a Theory of Machines. By Prof. F. REULEAUX. Translated and Edited by Prof. A. B. W. KENNEDY, F.R.S. Illustrated. 8vo. 21s.

ROUTH.—Works by EDWARD JOHN ROUTH, D.Sc., LL.D., F.R.S., Hon. Fellow of St. Peter's College, Cambridge.

A TREATISE ON THE DYNAMICS OF THE SYSTEM OF RIGID BODIES. With numerous Examples. Fourth and enlarged Edition. Two Vols. 8vo. Vol. I.—Elementary Parts. 14s. Vol. II.—The Advanced Parts. 14s.

STABILITY OF A GIVEN STATE OF MOTION, PARTICULARLY STEADY MOTION. Adams Prize Essay for 1877. 8vo. 8s. 6d.

SANDERSON.—HYDROSTATICS FOR BEGINNERS. By F. W. SANDERSON, M.A., Assistant Master at Dulwich College. Gl. 8vo. 4s. 6d.

PHYSICS

TAIT AND STEELE.—A TREATISE ON DYNAMICS OF A PARTICLE. By Professor TAIT, M.A., and W. J. STEELE, B.A. 6th Ed., revised. Cr. 8vo. 12s.
TODHUNTER.—Works by ISAAC TODHUNTER, F.R.S.
MECHANICS FOR BEGINNERS. 18mo. 4s. 6d. KEY. Cr. 8vo. 6s. 6d.
A TREATISE ON ANALYTICAL STATICS. 5th Ed. Edited by Prof. J. D. EVERETT, F.R.S. Cr. 8vo. 10s. 6d.

PHYSICS: Sound, Light, Heat, Electricity, Elasticity, Attractions, etc. (See also Mechanics.)

AIRY.—Works by Sir G. B. AIRY, K.C.B., formerly Astronomer-Royal.
ON SOUND AND ATMOSPHERIC VIBRATIONS. With the Mathematical Elements of Music. 2d Ed., revised and enlarged. Cr. 8vo. 9s.
A TREATISE ON MAGNETISM. Cr. 8vo. 9s. 6d.
GRAVITATION: an Elementary Explanation of the Principal Perturbations in the Solar System. 2d Ed. Cr. 8vo. 7s. 6d.
CLAUSIUS.—MECHANICAL THEORY OF HEAT. By R. CLAUSIUS. Translated by W. R. BROWNE, M.A. Cr. 8vo. 10s. 6d.
CUMMING.—AN INTRODUCTION TO THE THEORY OF ELECTRICITY. By LINNÆUS CUMMING, M.A., Assistant Master at Rugby. Illustrated. Cr. 8vo. 8s. 6d.
DANIELL.—A TEXT-BOOK OF THE PRINCIPLES OF PHYSICS. By ALFRED DANIELL, D.Sc. Illustrated. 2d Ed., revised and enlarged. 8vo. 21s.
DAY.—ELECTRIC LIGHT ARITHMETIC. By R. E. DAY, Evening Lecturer in Experimental Physics at King's College, London. Pott 8vo. 2s.
EVERETT.—UNITS AND PHYSICAL CONSTANTS. By J. D. EVERETT, F.R.S., Professor of Natural Philosophy, Queen's College, Belfast. 2d Ed. Ex. fcap. 8vo. 5s.
FERRERS.—AN ELEMENTARY TREATISE ON SPHERICAL HARMONICS, and Subjects connected with them. By Rev. N. M. FERRERS, D.D., F.R.S., Master of Gonville and Caius College, Cambridge. Cr. 8vo. 7s. 6d.
FESSENDEN.—A SCHOOL CLASS-BOOK OF PHYSICS. By C. FESSENDEN. Illustrated. Fcp. 8vo. [In the Press.
GRAY.—THE THEORY AND PRACTICE OF ABSOLUTE MEASUREMENTS IN ELECTRICITY AND MAGNETISM. By A. GRAY, F.R.S.E., Professor of Physics in the University College of North Wales. Two Vols. Cr. 8vo. Vol. I. 12s. 6d. [Vol. II. In the Press.
ABSOLUTE MEASUREMENTS IN ELECTRICITY AND MAGNETISM. 2d Ed., revised and greatly enlarged. Fcap. 8vo. 5s. 6d.
IBBETSON.—THE MATHEMATICAL THEORY OF PERFECTLY ELASTIC SOLIDS, with a Short Account of Viscous Fluids. By W. J. IBBETSON, late Senior Scholar of Clare College, Cambridge. 8vo. 21s.
JONES.—EXAMPLES IN PHYSICS. By D. E. JONES, B.Sc., Professor of Physics in the University College of Wales, Aberystwyth. Fcap. 8vo. 3s. 6d.
SOUND, LIGHT, AND HEAT. An Elementary Text-Book. With Illustrations. Fcap. 8vo. [In the Press.
LODGE.—MODERN VIEWS OF ELECTRICITY. By OLIVER J. LODGE, F.R.S., Professor of Experimental Physics in University College, Liverpool. Illustrated. Cr. 8vo. 6s. 6d.
LOEWY.—Works by B. LOEWY, Examiner in Experimental Physics to the College of Preceptors.
QUESTIONS AND EXAMPLES ON EXPERIMENTAL PHYSICS: Sound, Light, Heat, Electricity, and Magnetism. Fcap. 8vo. 2s.
A GRADUATED COURSE OF NATURAL SCIENCE FOR ELEMENTARY AND TECHNICAL SCHOOLS AND COLLEGES. In Three Parts. Part I. FIRST YEAR'S COURSE. Gl. 8vo. 2s.
LUPTON.—NUMERICAL TABLES AND CONSTANTS IN ELEMENTARY SCIENCE. By S. LUPTON, M.A., late Assistant Master at Harrow. Ex. fcap. 8vo. 2s. 6d.

MATHEMATICS

MACFARLANE.—PHYSICAL ARITHMETIC. By A. MACFARLANE, D.Sc., late Examiner in Mathematics at the University of Edinburgh. Cr. 8vo. 7s. 6d.

MAYER.—SOUND: a Series of Simple, Entertaining, and Inexpensive Experiments in the Phenomena of Sound. By A. M. MAYER, Professor of Physics in the Stevens Institute of Technology. Illustrated. Cr. 8vo. 3s. 6d.

MAYER AND BARNARD.—LIGHT: a Series of Simple, Entertaining, and Inexpensive Experiments in the Phenomena of Light. By A. M. MAYER and C. BARNARD. Illustrated. Cr. 8vo. 2s. 6d.

MOLLOY.—GLEANINGS IN SCIENCE: Popular Lectures on Scientific Subjects. By the Rev. GERALD MOLLOY, D.Sc., Rector of the Catholic University of Ireland. 8vo. 7s. 6d.

NEWTON.—PRINCIPIA. Edited by Prof. Sir W. THOMSON and Prof. BLACKBURNE. 4to. 31s. 6d.

THE FIRST THREE SECTIONS OF NEWTON'S PRINCIPIA. With Notes and Illustrations. Also a Collection of Problems, principally intended as Examples of Newton's Methods. By P. FROST, M.A., D.Sc. 3d. Ed. 8vo. 12s.

PARKINSON.—A TREATISE ON OPTICS. By S. PARKINSON, D.D., F.R.S., late Tutor and Prælector of St. John's College, Cambridge. 4th Ed., revised and enlarged. Cr. 8vo. 10s. 6d.

PEABODY.—THERMODYNAMICS OF THE STEAM-ENGINE AND OTHER HEAT-ENGINES. By CECIL H. PEABODY, Associate Professor of Steam Engineering, Massachusetts Institute of Technology. 8vo. 21s.

PERRY. — STEAM: an Elementary Treatise. By JOHN PERRY, Professor of Mechanical Engineering and Applied Mechanics at the Technical College, Finsbury. 18mo. 4s. 6d.

PRESTON.—A TREATISE ON THE THEORY OF LIGHT. By THOMAS PRESTON, M.A. Illustrated. 8vo. [*In the Press.*

RAYLEIGH.—THE THEORY OF SOUND. By Lord Rayleigh, F.R.S. 8vo. Vol. I. 12s. 6d. Vol. II. 12s. 6d. [Vol. III. *In the Press.*

SHANN.—AN ELEMENTARY TREATISE ON HEAT, IN RELATION TO STEAM AND THE STEAM-ENGINE. By G. SHANN, M.A. Illustrated. Cr. 8vo. 4s. 6d.

SPOTTISWOODE.—POLARISATION OF LIGHT. By the late W. SPOTTISWOODE, F.R.S. Illustrated. Cr. 8vo. 3s. 6d.

STEWART.—Works by BALFOUR STEWART, F.R.S., late Langworthy Professor of Physics in the Owens College, Victoria University, Manchester.

PRIMER OF PHYSICS. Illustrated. With Questions. 18mo. 1s.

LESSONS IN ELEMENTARY PHYSICS. Illustrated. Fcap. 8vo. 4s. 6d.

QUESTIONS. By Prof. T. H. CORE. Fcap. 8vo. 2s.

STEWART AND GEE.—LESSONS IN ELEMENTARY PRACTICAL PHYSICS. By BALFOUR STEWART, F.R.S., and W. W. HALDANE GEE, B.Sc. Cr. 8vo. Vol. I. GENERAL PHYSICAL PROCESSES. 6s. Vol. II. ELECTRICITY AND MAGNETISM. 7s. 6d. [Vol. III. OPTICS, HEAT, and SOUND. *In the Press.*

PRACTICAL PHYSICS FOR SCHOOLS AND THE JUNIOR STUDENTS OF COLLEGES. Gl. 8vo. Vol. I. ELECTRICITY AND MAGNETISM. 2s. 6d. [Vol. II. OPTICS, HEAT, AND SOUND. *In the Press.*

STOKES.—ON LIGHT. Burnett Lectures, delivered in Aberdeen in 1883-4-5. By Sir G. G. STOKES, F.R.S., Lucasian Professor of Mathematics in the University of Cambridge. First Course: ON THE NATURE OF LIGHT. Second Course: ON LIGHT AS A MEANS OF INVESTIGATION. Third Course: ON THE BENEFICIAL EFFECTS OF LIGHT. Cr. 8vo. 7s. 6d.

⁎ The 2d and 3d Courses may be had separately. Cr. 8vo. 2s. 6d. each.

STONE.—AN ELEMENTARY TREATISE ON SOUND. By W. H. STONE. Illustrated. Fcp. 8vo. 3s. 6d.

TAIT.—HEAT. By P. G. TAIT, Professor of Natural Philosophy in the University of Edinburgh. Cr. 8vo. 6s.

TAYLOR.—SOUND AND MUSIC. An Elementary Treatise on the Physical Constitution of Musical Sounds and Harmony, including the Chief Acoustical Discoveries of Professor Helmholtz. By SEDLEY TAYLOR, M.A. Illustrated. 2d Ed. Ex. Cr. 8vo. 8s. 6d.

ASTRONOMY

THOMPSON. — ELEMENTARY LESSONS IN ELECTRICITY AND MAGNETISM. By SILVANUS P. THOMPSON, Principal and Professor of Physics in the Technical College, Finsbury. Illustrated. New Ed., revised. Fcap. 8vo. 4s. 6d.

THOMSON.—Works by J. J. THOMSON, Professor of Experimental Physics in the University of Cambridge.
A TREATISE ON THE MOTION OF VORTEX RINGS. Adams Prize Essay, 1882. 8vo. 6s.
APPLICATIONS OF DYNAMICS TO PHYSICS AND CHEMISTRY. Cr. 8vo. 7s. 6d.

THOMSON.—Works by Sir W. THOMSON, F.R.S., Professor of Natural Philosophy in the University of Glasgow.
ELECTROSTATICS AND MAGNETISM, REPRINTS OF PAPERS ON. 2d Ed. 8vo. 18s.
POPULAR LECTURES AND ADDRESSES. 3 Vols. Illustrated. Cr. 8vo. Vol. I. CONSTITUTION OF MATTER. 6s.

TODHUNTER.—Works by ISAAC TODHUNTER, F.R.S.
NATURAL PHILOSOPHY FOR BEGINNERS. Part I. The properties of Solid and Fluid Bodies. 18mo. 3s. 6d. Part II. Sound, Light, and Heat. 18mo. 3s. 6d.
AN ELEMENTARY TREATISE ON LAPLACE'S, LAME'S, AND BESSEL'S FUNCTIONS. Crown 8vo. 10s. 6d.
A HISTORY OF THE MATHEMATICAL THEORIES OF ATTRACTION, AND THE FIGURE OF THE EARTH, from the time of Newton to that of Laplace. 2 vols. 8vo. 24s.

TURNER.—A COLLECTION OF EXAMPLES ON HEAT AND ELECTRICITY. By H. H. TURNER, Fellow of Trinity College, Cambridge. Cr. 8vo. 2s. 6d.

WRIGHT.—LIGHT: A Course of Experimental Optics, chiefly with the Lantern. By LEWIS WRIGHT. Illustrated. Cr. 8vo. 7s. 6d.

ASTRONOMY.

AIRY.—Works by Sir G. B. AIRY, K.C.B., formerly Astronomer-Royal.
POPULAR ASTRONOMY. 18mo. 4s. 6d.
GRAVITATION: an Elementary Explanation of the Principal Perturbations in the Solar System. 2d Ed. Cr. 8vo. 7s. 6d.

CHEYNE.—AN ELEMENTARY TREATISE ON THE PLANETARY THEORY. By C. H. H CHEYNE. With Problems. 3d Ed. Edited by Rev. A. FREEMAN, M.A., F.R.A.S. Cr. 8vo. 7s. 6d.

FORBES.—TRANSIT OF VENUS. By G. FORBES, Professor of Natural Philosophy in the Andersonian University, Glasgow. Illustrated. Cr. 8vo. 3s. 6d.

GODFRAY.—Works by HUGH GODFRAY, M.A., Mathematical Lecturer at Pembroke College, Cambridge.
A TREATISE ON ASTRONOMY. 4th Ed. 8vo. 12s. 6d.
AN ELEMENTARY TREATISE ON THE LUNAR THEORY, with a brief Sketch of the Problem up to the time of Newton. 2d Ed., revised. Cr. 8vo. 5s. 6d.

LOCKYER.—Works by J. NORMAN LOCKYER, F.R.S.
PRIMER OF ASTRONOMY. Illustrated. 18mo. 1s.
ELEMENTARY LESSONS IN ASTRONOMY.—With Spectra of the Sun, Stars, and Nebulæ, and numerous Illustrations. 36th Thousand. Revised throughout. Fcap. 8vo. 5s. 6d.
QUESTIONS ON LOCKYER'S ELEMENTARY LESSONS IN ASTRONOMY. By J. FORBES ROBERTSON. 18mo. 1s. 6d.
THE CHEMISTRY OF THE SUN. Illustrated. 8vo. 14s.
THE METEORIC HYPOTHESIS. Illustrated. 8vo. [In the Press.
THE EVOLUTION OF THE HEAVENS AND THE EARTH. Cr. 8vo. Illustrated. [In the Press.

NEWCOMB.—POPULAR ASTRONOMY. By S. NEWCOMB, LL.D., Professor U.S. Naval Observatory. Illustrated. 2d Ed., revised. 8vo. 18s.

HISTORICAL.

BALL.—A SHORT ACCOUNT OF THE HISTORY OF MATHEMATICS. By W. W. R. BALL. Cr. 8vo. 10s. 6d.

TODHUNTER.—Works by ISAAC TODHUNTER, F.R.S.
A HISTORY OF THE MATHEMATICAL THEORY OF PROBABILITY from the time of Pascal to that of Laplace. 8vo. 18s.
A HISTORY OF THE MATHEMATICAL THEORIES OF ATTRACTION, AND THE FIGURE OF THE EARTH, from the time of Newton to that of Laplace. 2 vols. 8vo. 24s.

NATURAL SCIENCES.

Chemistry; Physical Geography, Geology, and Mineralogy; Biology; Medicine.

(FOR MECHANICS, PHYSICS, AND ASTRONOMY, see *MATHEMATICS.*)

CHEMISTRY.

ARMSTRONG.—A MANUAL OF INORGANIC CHEMISTRY. By HENRY ARMSTRONG, F.R.S., Professor of Chemistry in the City and Guilds of London Technical Institute. Cr. 8vo. [*In preparation.*

COHEN.—THE OWENS COLLEGE COURSE OF PRACTICAL ORGANIC CHEMISTRY. By JULIUS B. COHEN, Ph.D., Assistant Lecturer on Chemistry in the Owens College, Manchester. With a Preface by Sir HENRY ROSCOE, F.R.S., and C. SCHORLEMMER, F.R.S. Fcap. 8vo. 2s. 6d.

COOKE.—ELEMENTS OF CHEMICAL PHYSICS. By JOSIAH P. COOKE, Jun., Erving Professor of Chemistry and Mineralogy in Harvard University. 4th Ed. 8vo. 21s.

FLEISCHER.—A SYSTEM OF VOLUMETRIC ANALYSIS. By EMIL FLEISCHER. Translated, with Notes and Additions, by M. M. P. MUIR, F.R.S.E. Illustrated. Cr. 8vo. 7s. 6d.

FRANKLAND.—A HANDBOOK OF AGRICULTURAL CHEMICAL ANALYSIS. By P. F. FRANKLAND, F.R.S., Professor of Chemistry in University College, Dundee. Cr. 8vo. 7s. 6d.

HARTLEY.—A COURSE OF QUANTITATIVE ANALYSIS FOR STUDENTS. By W. NOEL HARTLEY, F.R.S., Professor of Chemistry and of Applied Chemistry, Science and Art Department, Royal College of Science, Dublin. Gl. 8vo. 5s.

HIORNS.—PRACTICAL METALLURGY AND ASSAYING. A Text-book for the use of Teachers, Students, and Assayers. By ARTHUR H. HIORNS, Principal of the School of Metallurgy, Birmingham and Midland Institute. Illustrated. Gl. 8vo. 6s.
A TEXT-BOOK OF ELEMENTARY METALLURGY FOR THE USE OF STUDENTS. To which is added an Appendix of Examination Questions, embracing the whole of the Questions set in the three stages of the subject by the Science and Art Department for the past twenty years. By the Same. Gl. 8vo. 4s.
IRON AND STEEL MANUFACTURE. A Text-Book for Beginners. By the Same. Illustrated. Gl. 8vo. 3s. 6d.
MIXED METALS AND METALLIC ALLOYS. By the Same. [*In the Press.*

JONES.—THE OWENS COLLEGE JUNIOR COURSE OF PRACTICAL CHEMISTRY. By FRANCIS JONES, F.R.S.E., Chemical Master at the Grammar School, Manchester. With Preface by Sir HENRY ROSCOE, F.R.S. Illustrated. Fcp. 8vo. 2s. 6d.

CHEMISTRY

QUESTIONS ON CHEMISTRY. A Series of Problems and Exercises in Inorganic and Organic Chemistry. By the Same. Fcap. 8vo. 3s.

LANDAUER.—BLOWPIPE ANALYSIS. By J. LANDAUER. Authorised English Edition by J. TAYLOR and W. E. KAY, of Owens College, Manchester.
[*New Edition in Preparation.*]

LOCKYER.—THE CHEMISTRY OF THE SUN. By J. NORMAN LOCKYER, F.R.S. Illustrated. 8vo. 14s.

LUPTON.—CHEMICAL ARITHMETIC. With 1200 Problems. By S. LUPTON, M.A. 2d Ed., revised and abridged. Fcap. 8vo. 4s. 6d.

MELDOLA.—THE CHEMISTRY OF PHOTOGRAPHY. By RAPHAEL MELDOLA, F.R.S., Professor of Chemistry in the Technical College, Finsbury. Cr. 8vo. 6s.

MEYER. HISTORY OF CHEMISTRY. By ERNST VON MEYER. Translated by GEORGE MCGOWAN, Ph.D. 8vo. [*In the Press.*]

MIXTER.—AN ELEMENTARY TEXT-BOOK OF CHEMISTRY. By WILLIAM G. MIXTER, Professor of Chemistry in the Sheffield Scientific School of Yale College. 2d and revised Ed. Cr. 8vo. 7s. 6d.

MUIR.—PRACTICAL CHEMISTRY FOR MEDICAL STUDENTS. Specially arranged for the first M.B. Course. By M. M. P. MUIR, F.R.S.E., Fellow and Prælector in Chemistry at Gonville and Caius College, Cambridge. Fcap. 8vo. 1s. 6d.

MUIR AND WILSON.—THE ELEMENTS OF THERMAL CHEMISTRY. By M. M. P. MUIR, F.R.S.E.; assisted by D. M. WILSON. 8vo. 12s. 6d.

OSTWALD.—TEXT-BOOK OF GENERAL CHEMISTRY. By Prof. OSTWALD. Translated by JAMES WALKER. 8vo. [*In the Press.*]

RAMSAY.—EXPERIMENTAL PROOFS OF CHEMICAL THEORY FOR BEGINNERS. By WILLIAM RAMSAY, F.R.S., Professor of Chemistry in University College, London. Pott 8vo. 2s. 6d.

REMSEN.—Works by IRA REMSEN, Professor of Chemistry in the Johns Hopkins University, U.S.A.
COMPOUNDS OF CARBON: or, Organic Chemistry, an Introduction to the Study of. Cr. 8vo. 6s. 6d.
AN INTRODUCTION TO THE STUDY OF CHEMISTRY (INORGANIC CHEMISTRY). Cr. 8vo. 6s. 6d.
THE ELEMENTS OF CHEMISTRY. A Text Book for Beginners. Fcap. 8vo. 2s. 6d.
A TEXT-BOOK OF INORGANIC CHEMISTRY. 8vo. 16s.

ROSCOE.—Works by Sir HENRY E. ROSCOE, F.R.S., formerly Professor of Chemistry in the Owens College, Victoria University, Manchester.
PRIMER OF CHEMISTRY. Illustrated. With Questions. 18mo. 1s.
LESSONS IN ELEMENTARY CHEMISTRY, INORGANIC AND ORGANIC. With Illustrations and Chromolitho of the Solar Spectrum, and of the Alkalies and Alkaline Earths. Fcap. 8vo. 4s. 6d.

ROSCOE AND SCHORLEMMER.—INORGANIC AND ORGANIC CHEMISTRY. A Complete Treatise on Inorganic and Organic Chemistry. By Sir HENRY E. ROSCOE, F.R.S., and Prof. C. SCHORLEMMER, F.R.S. Illustrated. 8vo.
Vols. I. and II. INORGANIC CHEMISTRY. Vol. I.—The Non-Metallic Elements. 2d Ed. 21s. Vol. II. Part I.—Metals. 18s. Part II.—Metals. 18s.
Vol. III.—ORGANIC CHEMISTRY. THE CHEMISTRY OF THE HYDROCARBONS and their Derivatives. Five Parts. Parts I., II., and IV. 21s. Parts III. and V. 18s. each.

ROSCOE AND SCHUSTER.—SPECTRUM ANALYSIS. Lectures delivered in 1868. By Sir HENRY ROSCOE, F.R.S. 4th Ed., revised and considerably enlarged by the Author and by A. SCHUSTER, F.R.S., Ph.D., Professor of Applied Mathematics in the Owens College, Victoria University. With Appendices, Illustrations, and Plates. 8vo. 21s.

THORPE.—A SERIES OF CHEMICAL PROBLEMS, prepared with Special Reference to Sir HENRY Roscoe's Lessons in Elementary Chemistry, by T. E. THORPE, F.R.S., Professor of Chemistry in the Normal School of Science, South Kensington, adapted for the Preparation of Students for the Government, Science, and Society of Arts Examinations. With a Preface by Sir H. E. ROSCOE, F.R.S. New Ed., with Key. 18mo. 2s.

THORPE AND RÜCKER.—A TREATISE ON CHEMICAL PHYSICS. By Prof. T. E. THORPE, F.R.S., and Prof. A. W. RÜCKER, F.R.S. Illustrated. 8vo.
[*In preparation.*
WRIGHT.—METALS AND THEIR CHIEF INDUSTRIAL APPLICATIONS. By C. ALDER WRIGHT, Lecturer on Chemistry in St. Mary's Hospital School. Ex. fcap. 8vo. 3s. 6d.

PHYSICAL GEOGRAPHY, GEOLOGY, AND MINERALOGY.

BLANFORD.—THE RUDIMENTS OF PHYSICAL GEOGRAPHY FOR THE USE OF INDIAN SCHOOLS; with a Glossary of Technical Terms employed. By H. F. BLANFORD, F.G.S. Illustrated. Cr. 8vo. 2s. 6d.
FERREL.—A POPULAR TREATISE ON THE WINDS. Comprising the General Motions of the Atmosphere, Monsoons, Cyclones, Tornadoes, Waterspouts, Hailstorms, &c. By WILLIAM FERREL, M.A., Member of the American National Academy of Sciences. 8vo. 18s.
FISHER.—PHYSICS OF THE EARTH'S CRUST. By the Rev. OSMOND FISHER, M.A., F.G.S., Hon. Fellow of King's College, London. 2d Ed., altered and enlarged. 8vo. 12s.
GEIKIE.—Works by ARCHIBALD GEIKIE, LL.D., F.R.S., Director-General of the Geological Survey of Great Britain and Ireland.
PRIMER OF PHYSICAL GEOGRAPHY. Illustrated. With Questions. 18mo. 1s.
ELEMENTARY LESSONS IN PHYSICAL GEOGRAPHY. Illustrated. Fcap. 8vo. 4s. 6d. QUESTIONS ON THE SAME. 1s. 6d.
PRIMER OF GEOLOGY. Illustrated. 18mo. 1s.
CLASS BOOK OF GEOLOGY. Illustrated. New and Cheaper Edition.
TEXT-BOOK OF GEOLOGY. Illustrated. 2d Ed., 7th Thousand, revised and enlarged. 8vo. 28s.
OUTLINES OF FIELD GEOLOGY. Illustrated. Ex. fcap. 8vo. 3s. 6d.
THE SCENERY AND GEOLOGY OF SCOTLAND, VIEWED IN CONNEXION WITH ITS PHYSICAL GEOLOGY. Illustrated. Cr. 8vo. 12s. 6d.
HUXLEY.—PHYSIOGRAPHY. An Introduction to the Study of Nature. By T. H. HUXLEY, F.R.S. Illustrated. New and Cheaper Edition. Cr. 8vo. 6s.
LOCKYER.—OUTLINES OF PHYSIOGRAPHY—THE MOVEMENTS OF THE EARTH. By J. NORMAN LOCKYER, F.R.S., Examiner in Physiography for the Science and Art Department. Illustrated. Cr. 8vo. Sewed, 1s. 6d.
PHILLIPS.—A TREATISE ON ORE DEPOSITS. By J. ARTHUR PHILLIPS, F.R.S. Illustrated. 8vo. 25s.
ROSENBUSCH AND IDDINGS.—MICROSCOPICAL PHYSIOGRAPHY OF THE ROCK-MAKING MINERALS: AN AID TO THE MICROSCOPICAL STUDY OF ROCKS. By H. ROSENBUSCH. Translated and Abridged by J. P. IDDINGS. Illustrated. 8vo. 24s.

BIOLOGY.

ALLEN.—ON THE COLOURS OF FLOWERS, as Illustrated in the British Flora. By GRANT ALLEN. Illustrated. Cr. 8vo. 3s. 6d.
BALFOUR.—A TREATISE ON COMPARATIVE EMBRYOLOGY. By F. M. BALFOUR, F.R.S., Fellow and Lecturer of Trinity College, Cambridge. Illustrated. 2d Ed., reprinted without alteration from the 1st Ed. 2 vols. 8vo. Vol. I. 18s. Vol. II. 21s.
BALFOUR AND WARD.—A GENERAL TEXT-BOOK OF BOTANY. By ISAAC BAYLEY BALFOUR, F.R.S., Professor of Botany in the University of Edinburgh, and H. MARSHALL WARD, F.R.S., Professor of Botany in the Royal Indian Engineering College, Cooper's Hill. 8vo. [*In preparation.*
BETTANY.—FIRST LESSONS IN PRACTICAL BOTANY. By G. T. BETTANY. 18mo. 1s.

BIOLOGY 35

BOWER.—A COURSE OF PRACTICAL INSTRUCTION IN BOTANY. By F. O. BOWER, D.Sc., Regius Professor of Botany in the University of Glasgow. Cr. 8vo. 10s. 6d.

CHURCH AND SCOTT.—MANUAL OF VEGETABLE PHYSIOLOGY. By Professor A. H. CHURCH, and D. H. SCOTT, D.Sc., Lecturer in the Normal School of Science. Illustrated. Cr. 8vo. [*In preparation.*

COPE.—THE ORIGIN OF THE FITTEST. Essays on Evolution. By E. D. COPE, M.A., Ph.D. 8vo. 12s. 6d.

COUES.—FIELD ORNITHOLOGY AND GENERAL ORNITHOLOGY. By ELLIOTT COUES, M.A. Illustrated. 8vo. [*In the Press.*

DARWIN.—MEMORIAL NOTICES OF CHARLES DARWIN, F.R.S., &c. By T. H. HUXLEY, F.R.S., G. J. ROMANES, F.R.S., ARCHIBALD GEIKIE, F.R.S., and W. T. THISELTON DYER, F.R.S. Reprinted from *Nature*. With a Portrait. Cr. 8vo. 2s. 6d.

EIMER.—ORGANIC EVOLUTION AS THE RESULT OF THE INHERITANCE OF ACQUIRED CHARACTERS ACCORDING TO THE LAWS OF ORGANIC GROWTH. By Dr. G. H. THEODOR EIMER. Translated by J. T. CUNNINGHAM, F.R.S.E., late Fellow of University College, Oxford. 8vo. 12s. 6d.

FEARNLEY.—A MANUAL OF ELEMENTARY PRACTICAL HISTOLOGY. By WILLIAM FEARNLEY. Illustrated. Cr. 8vo. 7s. 6d.

FLOWER AND GADOW.—AN INTRODUCTION TO THE OSTEOLOGY OF THE MAMMALIA. By W. H. FLOWER, F.R.S., Director of the Natural History Departments of the British Museum. Illustrated. 3d Ed. Revised with the assistance of HANS GADOW, Ph.D., Lecturer on the Advanced Morphology of Vertebrates in the University of Cambridge. Cr. 8vo. 10s. 6d.

FOSTER.—Works by MICHAEL FOSTER, M.D., Professor of Physiology in the University of Cambridge.

PRIMER OF PHYSIOLOGY. Illustrated. 18mo. 1s.

A TEXT-BOOK OF PHYSIOLOGY. Illustrated. 5th Ed., largely revised. In Three Parts. 8vo. Part I., comprising Book I. Blood—The Tissues of Movement, The Vascular Mechanism. 10s. 6d. Part II., comprising Book II. The Tissues of Chemical Action, with their Respective Mechanisms—Nutrition. 10s. 6d. [Part III. *In the Press.*

FOSTER AND BALFOUR.—THE ELEMENTS OF EMBRYOLOGY. By Prof. MICHAEL FOSTER, M.D., and the late F. M. BALFOUR, F.R.S., Professor of Animal Morphology in the University of Cambridge. 2d Ed., revised. Edited by A. SEDGWICK, M.A., Fellow and Assistant Lecturer of Trinity College, Cambridge, and W. HEAPE, M.A., late Demonstrator in the Morphological Laboratory of the University of Cambridge. Illustrated. Cr. 8vo. 10s. 6d.

FOSTER AND LANGLEY.—A COURSE OF ELEMENTARY PRACTICAL PHYSIOLOGY AND HISTOLOGY. By Prof. MICHAEL FOSTER, M.D., and J. N. LANGLEY, F.R.S., Fellow of Trinity College, Cambridge. 6th Ed. Cr. 8vo. 7s. 6d.

GAMGEE.—A TEXT-BOOK OF THE PHYSIOLOGICAL CHEMISTRY OF THE ANIMAL BODY. Including an Account of the Chemical Changes occurring in Disease. By A. GAMGEE, M.D., F.R.S. Illustrated. 8vo. Vol. I. 18s.

GOODALE.—PHYSIOLOGICAL BOTANY. I. Outlines of the Histology of Phænogamous Plants. II. Vegetable Physiology. By GEORGE LINCOLN GOODALE, M.A., M.D., Professor of Botany in Harvard University. 8vo. 10s. 6d.

GRAY.—STRUCTURAL BOTANY, OR ORGANOGRAPHY ON THE BASIS OF MORPHOLOGY. To which are added the Principles of Taxonomy and Phytography, and a Glossary of Botanical Terms. By Prof. ASA GRAY, LL.D. 8vo. 10s. 6d.

THE SCIENTIFIC PAPERS OF ASA GRAY. Selected by C. SPRAGUE SARGENT. 2 vols. Vol. I. Reviews of Works on Botany and Related Subjects, 1834-1887. Vol. II. Essays, Biographical Sketches, 1841-1886. 8vo. 21s.

HAMILTON.—A SYSTEMATIC AND PRACTICAL TEXT-BOOK OF PATHOLOGY. By D. J. HAMILTON, F.R.S.E., Professor of Pathological Anatomy in the University of Aberdeen. Illustrated. 8vo. Vol. I. 25s.

NATURAL SCIENCES

HOOKER.—Works by Sir JOSEPH HOOKER, F.R.S., &c.
PRIMER OF BOTANY. Illustrated. 18mo. 1s.
THE STUDENT'S FLORA OF THE BRITISH ISLANDS. 3d Ed., revised. Gl. 8vo. 10s. 6d.

HOWES.—AN ATLAS OF PRACTICAL ELEMENTARY BIOLOGY. By G. B. HOWES, Assistant Professor of Zoology, Normal School of Science and Royal School of Mines. With a Preface by Prof. T. H. HUXLEY, F.R.S. 4to. 14s.

HUXLEY.—Works by Prof. T. H. HUXLEY, F.R.S.
INTRODUCTORY PRIMER OF SCIENCE. 18mo. 1s.
LESSONS IN ELEMENTARY PHYSIOLOGY. Illustrated. Fcap. 8vo. 4s. 6d.
QUESTIONS ON HUXLEY'S PHYSIOLOGY. By T. ALCOCK, M.D. 18mo. 1s. 6d.

HUXLEY AND MARTIN.—A COURSE OF PRACTICAL INSTRUCTION IN ELEMENTARY BIOLOGY. By Prof. T. H. HUXLEY, F.R.S., assisted by H. N. MARTIN, F.R.S., Professor of Biology in the Johns Hopkins University, U.S.A. New Ed., revised and extended by G. B. HOWES and D. H. SCOTT, Ph.D., Assistant Professors, Normal School of Science and Royal School of Mines. With a Preface by T. H. HUXLEY, F.R.S. Cr. 8vo. 10s. 6d.

KLEIN.—Works by E. KLEIN, F.R.S., Lecturer on General Anatomy and Physiology in the Medical School of St. Bartholomew's Hospital, Professor of Bacteriology at the College of State Medicine, London.
MICRO-ORGANISMS AND DISEASE. An Introduction into the Study of Specific Micro-Organisms. Illustrated. 3d Ed., revised. Cr. 8vo. 6s.
THE BACTERIA IN ASIATIC CHOLERA. Cr. 8vo. 5s.

LANG.—TEXT-BOOK OF COMPARATIVE ANATOMY. By Dr. ARNOLD LANG, Professor of Zoology in the University of Zurich, Translated by H. M. BERNARD, M.A., and M. BERNARD. 2 vols. 8vo. [In the Press.

LANKESTER.—Works by E. RAY LANKESTER, F.R.S., Professor of Zoology in University College, London.
A TEXT-BOOK OF ZOOLOGY. 8vo. [In preparation.
DEGENERATION: A CHAPTER IN DARWINISM. Illustrated. Cr. 8vo. 2s. 6d.
THE ADVANCEMENT OF SCIENCE. Occasional Essays and Addresses. 8vo. 10s. 6d.

LUBBOCK.—Works by the Right Hon. Sir JOHN LUBBOCK, F.R.S., D.C.L.
THE ORIGIN AND METAMORPHOSES OF INSECTS. Illustrated. Cr. 8vo. 3s. 6d.
ON BRITISH WILD FLOWERS CONSIDERED IN RELATION TO INSECTS. Illustrated. Cr. 8vo. 4s. 6d.
FLOWERS, FRUITS, AND LEAVES. Illustrated. 2d Ed. Cr. 8vo. 4s. 6d.
SCIENTIFIC LECTURES. 2d Ed. 8vo. 8s. 6d.
FIFTY YEARS OF SCIENCE. Being the Address delivered at York to the British Association, August 1881. 5th Ed. Cr. 8vo. 2s. 6d.

MARTIN AND MOALE.—ON THE DISSECTION OF VERTEBRATE ANIMALS. By Prof. H. N. MARTIN and W. A. MOALE. Cr. 8vo. [In preparation.

MIVART.—LESSONS IN ELEMENTARY ANATOMY. By ST. GEORGE MIVART, F.R.S., Lecturer on Comparative Anatomy at St. Mary's Hospital. Illustrated. Fcap. 8vo. 6s. 6d.

MULLER.—THE FERTILISATION OF FLOWERS. By HERMANN MÜLLER. Translated and Edited by D'ARCY W. THOMPSON, B.A., Professor of Biology in University College, Dundee. With a Preface by C. DARWIN, F.R.S. Illustrated. 8vo. 21s.

OLIVER.—Works by DANIEL OLIVER, F.R.S., late Professor of Botany in University College, London.
LESSONS IN ELEMENTARY BOTANY. Illustrated. Fcap. 8vo. 4s. 6d.
FIRST BOOK OF INDIAN BOTANY. Illustrated. Ex. fcap. 8vo. 6s. 6d.

PARKER.—Works by T. JEFFREY PARKER, F.R.S., Professor of Biology in the University of Otago, New Zealand

MEDICINE

A COURSE OF INSTRUCTION IN ZOOTOMY (VERTEBRATA). Illustrated. Cr. 8vo. 8s. 6d.
LESSONS IN ELEMENTARY BIOLOGY. Illustrated. Cr. 8vo. [*In the Press.*
PARKER AND BETTANY.—THE MORPHOLOGY OF THE SKULL. By Prof. W. K. PARKER, F.R.S., and G. T. BETTANY. Illustrated. Cr. 8vo. 10s. 6d.
ROMANES.—THE SCIENTIFIC EVIDENCES OF ORGANIC EVOLUTION. By GEORGE J. ROMANES, F.R.S., Zoological Secretary of the Linnean Society. Cr. 8vo. 2s. 6d.
SEDGWICK.—A SUPPLEMENT TO F. M. BALFOUR'S TREATISE ON EMBRYOLOGY. By ADAM SEDGWICK, F.R.S., Fellow and Lecturer of Trinity College, Cambridge. Illustrated. 8vo. [*In preparation.*
SHUFELDT.—THE MYOLOGY OF THE RAVEN (*Corvus corax Sinuatus*). A Guide to the Study of the Muscular System in Birds. By R. W. SHUFELDT. Illustrated. 8vo. [*In the Press.*
SMITH.—DISEASES OF FIELD AND GARDEN CROPS, CHIEFLY SUCH AS ARE CAUSED BY FUNGI. By W. G. SMITH, F.L.S. Illustrated. Fcap. 8vo. 4s. 6d.
STEWART AND CORRY.—A FLORA OF THE NORTH-EAST OF IRELAND. Including the Phanerogamia, the Cryptogamia Vascularis, and the Muscineæ. By S. A. STEWART, Curator of the Collections in the Belfast Museum, and the late T. H. CORRY, M.A., Lecturer on Botany in the University Medical and Science Schools, Cambridge. Cr. 8vo. 5s. 6d.
WALLACE.—DARWINISM: An Exposition of the Theory of Natural Selection, with some of its Applications. By ALFRED RUSSEL WALLACE, LL.D., F.R.S. 3d Ed. Cr. 8vo. 9s.
WARD.—TIMBER AND SOME OF ITS DISEASES. By H. MARSHALL WARD, F.R.S., Professor of Botany in the Royal Indian Engineering College, Cooper's Hill. Illustrated. Cr. 8vo. 6s.
WIEDERSHEIM.—ELEMENTS OF THE COMPARATIVE ANATOMY OF VERTEBRATES. By Prof. R. WIEDERSHEIM. Adapted by W. NEWTON PARKER, Professor of Biology in the University College of South Wales and Monmouthshire. With Additions. Illustrated. 8vo. 12s. 6d.

MEDICINE.

BLYTH.—A MANUAL OF PUBLIC HEALTH. By A. WYNTER BLYTH, M.R.C.S. 8vo. [*In the Press.*
BRUNTON.—Works by T. LAUDER BRUNTON, M.D., F.R.S., Examiner in Materia Medica in the University of London, in the Victoria University, and in the Royal College of Physicians, London.
A TEXT-BOOK OF PHARMACOLOGY, THERAPEUTICS, AND MATERIA MEDICA. Adapted to the United States Pharmacopœia by F. H. WILLIAMS, M.D., Boston, Mass. 3d Ed. Adapted to the New British Pharmacopœia, 1885. 8vo. 21s.
TABLES OF MATERIA MEDICA: A Companion to the Materia Medica Museum. Illustrated. Cheaper Issue. 8vo. 5s.
ON THE CONNECTION BETWEEN CHEMICAL CONSTITUTION AND PHYSIOLOGICAL ACTION, BEING AN INTRODUCTION TO MODERN THERAPEUTICS. Croonian Lectures. 8vo. [*In the Press.*
GRIFFITHS.—LESSONS ON PRESCRIPTIONS AND THE ART OF PRESCRIBING. By W. HANDSEL GRIFFITHS. Adapted to the Pharmacopœia, 1885. 18mo. 3s. 6d.
HAMILTON.—A TEXT-BOOK OF PATHOLOGY, SYSTEMATIC AND PRACTICAL. By D. J. HAMILTON, F.R.S.E., Professor of Pathological Anatomy, University of Aberdeen. Illustrated. Vol. I. 8vo. 25s.
KLEIN.—Works by E. KLEIN, F.R.S., Lecturer on General Anatomy and Physiology in the Medical School of St. Bartholomew's Hospital, London.
MICRO-ORGANISMS AND DISEASE. An Introduction into the Study of Specific Micro-Organisms. Illustrated. 3d Ed., revised. Cr. 8vo. 6s.
THE BACTERIA IN ASIATIC CHOLERA. Cr. 8vo. 5s.

D

WHITE.—A TEXT-BOOK OF GENERAL THERAPEUTICS. By W. HALE
WHITE, M.D., Senior Assistant Physician to and Lecturer in Materia Medica at
Guy's Hospital. Illustrated. Cr. 8vo. 8s. 6d.
ZIEGLER—MACALISTER.—TEXT-BOOK OF PATHOLOGICAL ANATOMY
AND PATHOGENESIS. By Prof. E. ZIEGLER. Translated and Edited by
DONALD MACALISTER, M.A., M.D., Fellow and Medical Lecturer of St. John's
College, Cambridge. Illustrated. 8vo.
Part I.—GENERAL PATHOLOGICAL ANATOMY. 2d Ed. 12s. 6d.
Part II.—SPECIAL PATHOLOGICAL ANATOMY. Sections I.-VIII. 2d Ed.
12s. 6d. Sections IX.-XII. 12s. 6d.

HUMAN SCIENCES.

Mental and Moral Philosophy; Political Economy; Law and Politics;
Anthropology; Education.

MENTAL AND MORAL PHILOSOPHY.

BOOLE.—THE MATHEMATICAL ANALYSIS OF LOGIC. Being an Essay
towards a Calculus of Deductive Reasoning. By GEORGE BOOLE. 8vo. 5s.
CALDERWOOD.—HANDBOOK OF MORAL PHILOSOPHY. By Rev. HENRY
CALDERWOOD, LL.D., Professor of Moral Philosophy in the University of
Edinburgh. 14th Ed., largely rewritten. Cr. 8vo. 6s.
CLIFFORD.—SEEING AND THINKING. By the late Prof. W. K. CLIFFORD,
F.R.S. With Diagrams. Cr. 8vo. 8s. 6d.
JARDINE.—THE ELEMENTS OF THE PSYCHOLOGY OF COGNITION. By
Rev. ROBERT JARDINE, D.Sc. 3d Ed., revised. Cr. 8vo. 6s. 6d.
JEVONS.—Works by W. STANLEY JEVONS, F.R.S.
PRIMER OF LOGIC. 18mo. 1s.
ELEMENTARY LESSONS IN LOGIC; Deductive and Inductive, with Copious
Questions and Examples, and a Vocabulary of Logical Terms. Fcap. 8vo. 3s. 6d.
THE PRINCIPLES OF SCIENCE. A Treatise on Logic and Scientific Method.
New and revised Ed. Cr. 8vo. 12s. 6d.
STUDIES IN DEDUCTIVE LOGIC. 2d Ed. Cr. 8vo. 6s.
PURE LOGIC: AND OTHER MINOR WORKS. Edited by R. ADAMSON,
M.A., LL.D., Professor of Logic at Owens College, Manchester, and HARRIET
A. JEVONS. With a Preface by Prof. ADAMSON. 8vo. 10s. 6d.
KANT—MAX MULLER.—CRITIQUE OF PURE REASON. By IMMANUEL KANT.
2 vols. 8vo. 16s. each. Vol. I. HISTORICAL INTRODUCTION, by LUD-
WIG NOIRÉ; Vol. II. CRITIQUE OF PURE REASON, translated by F. MAX
MÜLLER.
KANT—MAHAFFY AND BERNARD.—KANT'S CRITICAL PHILOSOPHY FOR
ENGLISH READERS. By J. P. MAHAFFY, D.D., Professor of Ancient History
in the University of Dublin, and JOHN H. BERNARD, B.D., Fellow of Trinity
College, Dublin. A new and complete Edition in 2 vols. Cr. 8vo.
Vol. I. THE KRITIK OF PURE REASON EXPLAINED AND DEFENDED. 7s. 6d.
Vol. II. THE PROLEGOMENA. Translated with Notes and Appendices. 6s.
KEYNES.—FORMAL LOGIC, Studies and Exercises in. Including a Generalisation
of Logical Processes in their application to Complex Inferences. By JOHN
NEVILLE KEYNES, M.A. 2d Ed., revised and enlarged. Cr. 8vo. 10s. 6d.
McCOSH.—Works by JAMES McCOSH, D.D., President of Princeton College.
PSYCHOLOGY. Cr. 8vo.
I. THE COGNITIVE POWERS. 6s. 6d.
II. THE MOTIVE POWERS. 6s. 6d.
FIRST AND FUNDAMENTAL TRUTHS: being a Treatise on Metaphysics.
Ex. cr. 8vo. 9s.

POLITICAL ECONOMY 39

MAURICE.—MORAL AND METAPHYSICAL PHILOSOPHY. By F. D. MAURICE, M.A., late Professor of Moral Philosophy in the University of Cambridge. Vol. I.—Ancient Philosophy and the First to the Thirteenth Centuries. Vol. II.—Fourteenth Century and the French Revolution, with a glimpse into the Nineteenth Century. 4th Ed. 2 vols. 8vo. 16s.

RAY.—A TEXT-BOOK OF DEDUCTIVE LOGIC FOR THE USE OF STUDENTS. By P. K. RAY, D.Sc., Professor of Logic and Philosophy, Presidency College, Calcutta. 4th Ed. Globe 8vo. 4s. 6d.

SIDGWICK.—Works by HENRY SIDGWICK, LL.D. D.C.L., Knightbridge Professor of Moral Philosophy in the University of Cambridge.
THE METHODS OF ETHICS. 3d Ed. 8vo. 14s. A Supplement to the 2d Ed., containing all the important Additions and Alterations in the 3d Ed. 8vo. 6s.
OUTLINES OF THE HISTORY OF ETHICS, for English Readers. 2d Ed., revised. Cr. 8vo. 3s. 6d.

VENN.—Works by JOHN VENN, F.R.S., Examiner in Moral Philosophy in the University of London.
THE LOGIC OF CHANCE. An Essay on the Foundations and Province of the Theory of Probability, with special Reference to its Logical Bearings and its Application to Moral and Social Science. 3d Ed., rewritten and greatly enlarged. Cr. 8vo. 10s. 6d
SYMBOLIC LOGIC. Cr. 8vo. 10s. 6d.
THE PRINCIPLES OF EMPIRICAL OR INDUCTIVE LOGIC. 8vo. 18s.

POLITICAL ECONOMY.

BOHM-BAWERK.—CAPITAL AND INTEREST. Translated by WILLIAM SMART, M.A. 8vo. 14s.

CAIRNES.—THE CHARACTER AND LOGICAL METHOD OF POLITICAL ECONOMY. By J. E. CAIRNES. Cr. 8vo. 6s.
SOME LEADING PRINCIPLES OF POLITICAL ECONOMY NEWLY EXPOUNDED. By the Same. 8vo. 14s.

COSSA.—GUIDE TO THE STUDY OF POLITICAL ECONOMY. By Dr. L. COSSA. Translated. With a Preface by W. S. JEVONS, F.R.S. Cr. 8vo. 4s. 6d.

FAWCETT.—POLITICAL ECONOMY FOR BEGINNERS, WITH QUESTIONS. By Mrs. HENRY FAWCETT. 7th Ed. 18mo. 2s. 6d.
TALES IN POLITICAL ECONOMY. By the Same. Cr. 8vo. 3s.

FAWCETT.—A MANUAL OF POLITICAL ECONOMY. By Right. Hon. HENRY FAWCETT, F.R.S. 7th Ed., revised. With a Chapter on "State Socialism and the Nationalisation of the Land," and an Index. Cr. 8vo. 12s. 6d.
AN EXPLANATORY DIGEST of the above. By C. A. WATERS, B.A. Cr. 8vo. 2s. 6d.

GUNTON.—WEALTH AND PROGRESS: A Critical Examination of the Wages Question and its Economic Relation to Social Reform. By GEORGE GUNTON. Cr. 8vo. 6s.

HOWELL.—THE CONFLICTS OF CAPITAL AND LABOUR. Historically and Economically considered, being a History and Review of the Trade Unions of Great Britain, showing their origin, Progress, Constitution, and Objects, in their varied Political, Social, Economical, and Industrial Aspects. By GEORGE HOWELL, M.P. 2d Ed. revised. Cr. 8vo. 6s.

JEVONS.— Works by W. STANLEY JEVONS, F.R.S.
PRIMER OF POLITICAL ECONOMY. 18mo. 1s.
THE THEORY OF POLITICAL ECONOMY. 3d Ed., revised. 8vo. 10s. 6d.

KEYNES.—THE SCOPE AND METHOD OF POLITICAL ECONOMY. By J. N. KEYNES, M.A. [In preparation.

MARSHALL.—THE ECONOMICS OF INDUSTRY. By A. MARSHALL, M.A., Professor of Political Economy in the University of Cambridge, and MARY P. MARSHALL. Ex. fcap. 8vo. 2s. 6d.

MARSHALL.—THE PRINCIPLES OF ECONOMICS. By ALFRED MARSHALL, M.A. 2 vols. 8vo. [Vol. I. Shortly.

PALGRAVE.—A DICTIONARY OF POLITICAL ECONOMY. By various Writers. Edited by R. H. INGLIS PALGRAVE. [*In the Press.*
SIDGWICK.—THE PRINCIPLES OF POLITICAL ECONOMY. By HENRY SIDGWICK, LL.D., D.C.L., Knightbridge Professor of Moral Philosophy in the University of Cambridge. 2d Ed., revised. 8vo. 16s.
WALKER.—Works by FRANCIS A. WALKER, M.A.
  FIRST LESSONS IN POLITICAL ECONOMY. Cr. 8vo. 5s.
  A BRIEF TEXT-BOOK OF POLITICAL ECONOMY. Cr. 8vo. 6s. 6d.
  POLITICAL ECONOMY. 2d Ed., revised and enlarged. 8vo. 12s. 6d.
  THE WAGES QUESTION. 8vo. 14s.
WICKSTEED.—ALPHABET OF ECONOMIC SCIENCE. By PHILIP H. WICKSTEED, M.A. Part I. Elements of the Theory of Value or Worth. Gl. 8vo. 2s. 6d.

LAW AND POLITICS.

ADAMS AND CUNNINGHAM.—THE SWISS CONFEDERATION. By Sir F. O. ADAMS and C. CUNNINGHAM. 8vo. 14s.
ANGLO-SAXON LAW, ESSAYS ON.—Contents: Anglo-Saxon Law Courts, Land and Family Law, and Legal Procedure. 8vo. 18s
BALL.—THE STUDENT'S GUIDE TO THE BAR. By WALTER W. R. BALL, M.A., Fellow and Assistant Tutor of Trinity College, Cambridge. 4th Ed., revised. Cr. 8vo. 2s. 6d.
BIGELOW.—HISTORY OF PROCEDURE IN ENGLAND FROM THE NORMAN CONQUEST. The Norman Period, 1066-1204. By MELVILLE M. BIGELOW, Ph.D., Harvard University. 8vo. 16s.
BRYCE.—THE AMERICAN COMMONWEALTH. By JAMES BRYCE, M.P., D.C.L., Regius Professor of Civil Law in the University of Oxford. Two Volumes. Ex. cr. 8vo. 25s. Part I. The National Government. Part II. The State Governments. Part III. The Party System. Part IV. Public Opinion. Part V. Illustrations and Reflections. Part VI. Social Institutions.
BUCKLAND.—OUR NATIONAL INSTITUTIONS. A Short Sketch for Schools. By ANNA BUCKLAND. With Glossary. 18mo. 1s.
DICEY.—INTRODUCTION TO THE STUDY OF THE LAW OF THE CONSTITUTION. By A. V. DICEY, B.C.L., Vinerian Professor of English Law in the University of Oxford. 3d Ed. 8vo. 12s. 6d.
DILKE.—PROBLEMS OF GREATER BRITAIN. By the Right Hon. Sir CHARLES WENTWORTH DILKE. With Maps. 2 vols. 8vo. 36s.
DONISTHORPE.—INDIVIDUALISM: A System of Politics. By WORDSWORTH DONISTHORPE. 8vo. 14s.
ENGLISH CITIZEN, THE.—A Series of Short Books on his Rights and Responsibilities. Edited by HENRY CRAIK, LL.D. Cr. 8vo. 3s. 6d. each.
  CENTRAL GOVERNMENT. By H. D. TRAILL, D.C.L.
  THE ELECTORATE AND THE LEGISLATURE. By SPENCER WALPOLE.
  THE POOR LAW. By Rev. T. W. FOWLE, M.A.
  THE NATIONAL BUDGET; THE NATIONAL DEBT; TAXES AND RATES. By A. J. WILSON.
  THE STATE IN RELATION TO LABOUR. By W. STANLEY JEVONS, LL.D.
  THE STATE AND THE CHURCH. By the Hon. ARTHUR ELLIOT, M.P.
  FOREIGN RELATIONS. By SPENCER WALPOLE.
  THE STATE IN ITS RELATION TO TRADE. By Sir T. H. FARRER, Bart.
  LOCAL GOVERNMENT. By M. D. CHALMERS, M.A.
  THE STATE IN ITS RELATION TO EDUCATION. By HENRY CRAIK, LL.D.
  THE LAND LAWS. By Sir F. POLLOCK, Bart., Professor of Jurisprudence in the University of Oxford.
  COLONIES AND DEPENDENCIES. Part I. INDIA. By J. S. COTTON, M.A. II. THE COLONIES. By E. J. PAYNE, M.A.
  JUSTICE AND POLICE. By F. W. MAITLAND.
  THE PUNISHMENT AND PREVENTION OF CRIME. By Colonel Sir EDMUND DU CANE, K.C.B., Chairman of Comissioners of Prisons.

HOLMES.—THE COMMON LAW. By O. W. HOLMES Jun. Demy 8vo. 12s.

MAITLAND.—PLEAS OF THE CROWN FOR THE COUNTY OF GLOUCESTER BEFORE THE ABBOT OF READING AND HIS FELLOW JUSTICES ITINERANT, IN THE FIFTH YEAR OF THE REIGN OF KING HENRY THE THIRD, AND THE YEAR OF GRACE 1221. By F. W. MAITLAND. 8vo. 7s. 6d.

PATERSON.—Works by JAMES PATERSON, Barrister-at-Law.
COMMENTARIES ON THE LIBERTY OF THE SUBJECT, AND THE LAWS OF ENGLAND RELATING TO THE SECURITY OF THE PERSON. Cheaper Issue. Two Vols. Cr. 8vo. 21s.
THE LIBERTY OF THE PRESS, SPEECH, AND PUBLIC WORSHIP. Being Commentaries on the Liberty of the Subject and the Laws of England. Cr. 8vo. 12s.

PHILLIMORE.—PRIVATE LAW AMONG THE ROMANS. From the Pandects. By J. G. PHILLIMORE, Q.C. 8vo. 16s.

POLLOCK.—ESSAYS IN JURISPRUDENCE AND ETHICS. By Sir FREDERICK POLLOCK, Bart., Corpus Christi Professor of Jurisprudence in the University of Oxford. 8vo. 10s. 6d.
INTRODUCTION TO THE HISTORY OF THE SCIENCE OF POLITICS. By the same. Cr. 8vo. 2s. 6d.

RICHEY.—THE IRISH LAND LAWS. By ALEXANDER G. RICHEY, Q.C., Deputy Regius Professor of Feudal English Law in the University of Dublin. Cr. 8vo. 3s. 6d.

SIDGWICK.—THE ELEMENTS OF POLITICS. By HENRY SIDGWICK, LL.D. 8vo. [In the Press.

STEPHEN.—Works by Sir J. FITZJAMES STEPHEN, Q.C., K.C.S.I., a Judge of the High Court of Justice, Queen's Bench Division.
A DIGEST OF THE LAW OF EVIDENCE. 5th Ed., revised and enlarged. Cr. 8vo. 6s.
A DIGEST OF THE CRIMINAL LAW: CRIMES AND PUNISHMENTS. 4th Ed., revised. 8vo. 16s.
A DIGEST OF THE LAW OF CRIMINAL PROCEDURE IN INDICTABLE OFFENCES. By Sir J. F. STEPHEN, K.C.S.I., and H. STEPHEN, LL.M., of the Inner Temple, Barrister-at-Law. 8vo. 12s. 6d.
A HISTORY OF THE CRIMINAL LAW OF ENGLAND. Three Vols. 8vo. 48s.
GENERAL VIEW OF THE CRIMINAL LAW OF ENGLAND. 2d Ed. 8vo. 14s. The first edition of this work was published in 1863. The new edition is substantially a new work, intended as a text-book on the Criminal Law for University and other Students, adapted to the present day.

ANTHROPOLOGY.

FLOWER.—FASHION IN DEFORMITY, as Illustrated in the Customs of Barbarous and Civilised Races. By Prof. FLOWER, F.R.S. Illustrated. Cr. 8vo. 2s. 6d.

FRAZER.—THE GOLDEN BOUGH. A Study in Comparative Religion. By J. G. FRAZER, M.A., Fellow of Trinity College, Cambridge. 2 vols. 8vo. 28s.

M'LENNAN.—THE PATRIARCHAL THEORY. Based on the papers of the late JOHN F. M'LENNAN. Edited by DONALD M'LENNAN, M.A., Barrister-at-Law. 8vo. 14s.
STUDIES IN ANCIENT HISTORY. Comprising a Reprint of "Primitive Marriage." An inquiry into the origin of the form of capture in Marriage Ceremonies. 8vo. 16s.

TYLOR.—ANTHROPOLOGY. An Introduction to the Study of Man and Civilisation. By E. B. TYLOR, F.R.S. Illustrated. Cr. 8vo. 7s. 6d.

EDUCATION.

ARNOLD.—REPORTS ON ELEMENTARY SCHOOLS. 1852-1882. By MATTHEW ARNOLD, D.C.L. Edited by the Right Hon. Sir FRANCIS SANDFORD, K.C.B. Cheaper Issue. Cr. 8vo. 3s. 6d.

BALL.—THE STUDENT'S GUIDE TO THE BAR. By WALTER W. R. BALL, M.A., Fellow and Assistant Tutor of Trinity College, Cambridge. 4th Ed., revised. Cr. 8vo. 2s. 6d.
BLAKISTON.—THE TEACHER. Hints on School Management. A handbook for Managers, Teachers' Assistants, and Pupil Teachers. By J. R. BLAKISTON. Cr. 8vo. 2s. 6d. (Recommended by the London, Birmingham, and Leicester School Boards.)
CALDERWOOD.—ON TEACHING. By Prof. HENRY CALDERWOOD. New Ed. Ex. fcap. 8vo. 2s. 6d.
FITCH.—NOTES ON AMERICAN SCHOOLS AND TRAINING COLLEGES. Reprinted from the Report of the English Education Department for 1888-89, with permission of the Controller of H.M.'s Stationery Office. By J. G. FITCH, M.A. Gl. 8vo. 2s. 6d.
GEIKIE.—THE TEACHING OF GEOGRAPHY. A Practical Handbook for the use of Teachers. By ARCHIBALD GEIKIE, F.R.S., Director-General of the Geological Survey of the United Kingdom. Cr. 8vo. 2s.
GLADSTONE.—OBJECT TEACHING.—A Lecture delivered at the Pupil-Teacher Centre, William Street Board School, Hammersmith. By J. H. GLADSTONE, F.R.S. With an Appendix. Cr. 8vo. 3d.
SPELLING REFORM FROM A NATIONAL POINT OF VIEW. By the same. Cr. 8vo. 1s. 6d.
HERTEL.—OVERPRESSURE IN HIGH SCHOOLS IN DENMARK. By Dr. HERTEL. Translated by C. G. SÖRENSEN. With Introduction by Sir J. CRICHTON-BROWNE, F.R.S. Cr. 8vo. 3s. 6d.

TECHNICAL KNOWLEDGE.

(SEE ALSO MECHANICS, LAW, AND MEDICINE.)

Civil and Mechanical Engineering; Military and Naval Science; Agriculture; Domestic Economy; Book-Keeping.

CIVIL AND MECHANICAL ENGINEERING.

ALEXANDER AND THOMSON.—ELEMENTARY APPLIED MECHANICS. By T. ALEXANDER, Professor of Civil Engineering, Trinity College, Dublin, and A. W. THOMSON, Lecturer in Engineering at the Technical College, Glasgow. Part II. TRANSVERSE STRESS. Cr. 8vo. 10s. 6d.
CHALMERS.—GRAPHICAL DETERMINATION OF FORCES IN ENGINEERING STRUCTURES. By J. B. CHALMERS, C.E. Illustrated. 8vo. 24s.
COTTERILL.—APPLIED MECHANICS: an Elementary General Introduction to the Theory of Structures and Machines. By J. H. COTTERILL, F.R.S., Professor of Applied Mechanics in the Royal Naval College, Greenwich. 2d Ed. 8vo. 18s.
COTTERILL AND SLADE.—ELEMENTARY MANUAL OF APPLIED MECHANICS. By Prof. J. H. COTTERILL and J. H. SLADE. Cr. 8vo. [In the Press.
KENNEDY.—THE MECHANICS OF MACHINERY. By A. B. W. KENNEDY, F.R.S. Illustrated. Cr. 8vo. 12s. 6d.
REULEAUX.—THE KINEMATICS OF MACHINERY. Outlines of a Theory of Machines. By Prof. F. REULEAUX. Translated and Edited by Prof. A. B. W. KENNEDY, F.R.S. Illustrated. 8vo. 21s.
WHITHAM.—STEAM-ENGINE DESIGN. For the Use of Mechanical Engineers, Students, and Draughtsmen. By J. M. WHITHAM, Professor of Engineering, Arkansas Industrial University. Illustrated. 8vo. 25s.
YOUNG.—SIMPLE PRACTICAL METHODS OF CALCULATING STRAINS ON GIRDERS, ARCHES, AND TRUSSES. With a Supplementary Essay on Economy in Suspension Bridges. By E. W. YOUNG, C.E. With Diagrams. 8vo. 7s. 6d.

AGRICULTURE—DOMESTIC ECONOMY 43

MILITARY AND NAVAL SCIENCE.

AITKEN.—THE GROWTH OF THE RECRUIT AND YOUNG SOLDIER. With a view to the selection of "Growing Lads" for the Army, and a Regulated System of Training for Recruits. By Sir W. AITKEN, F.R.S., Professor of Pathology in the Army Medical School. Cr. 8vo. 8s. 6d.

ARMY PRELIMINARY EXAMINATION, 1882-1889, Specimens of Papers set at the. With Answers to the Mathematical Questions. Subjects: Arithmetic, Algebra, Euclid, Geometrical Drawing, Geography, French, English Dictation. Cr. 8vo. 3s. 6d.

MERCUR.—ELEMENTS OF THE ART OF WAR. Prepared for the use of Cadets of the United States Military Academy. By JAMES MERCUR, Professor of Civil Engineering at the United States Academy, West Point, New York. 2d Ed., revised and corrected. 8vo. 17s.

PALMER.—TEXT BOOK OF PRACTICAL LOGARITHMS AND TRIGONOMETRY.—By J. H. PALMER, Head Schoolmaster, R.N., H.M.S. *Cambridge*, Devonport. Gl. 8vo. 4s. 6d.

ROBINSON.—TREATISE ON MARINE SURVEYING. Prepared for the use of younger Naval Officers. With Questions for Examinations and Exercises principally from the Papers of the Royal Naval College. With the results. By Rev. JOHN L. ROBINSON, Chaplain and Instructor in the Royal Naval College, Greenwich. Illustrated. Cr. 8vo. 7s. 6d.

SANDHURST MATHEMATICAL PAPERS, for Admission into the Royal Military College, 1881-1889. Edited by E. J. BROOKSMITH, B.A., Instructor in Mathematics at the Royal Military Academy, Woolwich. Cr. 8vo. [*Immediately.*

SHORTLAND.—NAUTICAL SURVEYING. By the late Vice-Admiral SHORTLAND, LL.D. 8vo. 21s.

WILKINSON.—THE BRAIN OF AN ARMY. A Popular Account of the German General Staff. By SPENSER WILKINSON. Cr. 8vo. 2s. 6d.

WOLSELEY.—Works by General Viscount WOLSELEY, G.C.M.G.
THE SOLDIER'S POCKET-BOOK FOR FIELD SERVICE. 5th Ed., revised and enlarged. 16mo. Roan. 5s.
FIELD POCKET-BOOK FOR THE AUXILIARY FORCES. 16mo. 1s. 6d.

WOOLWICH MATHEMATICAL PAPERS, for Admission into the Royal Military Academy, Woolwich, 1880-1888 inclusive. Edited by E. J. BROOKSMITH, B.A., Instructor in Mathematics at the Royal Military Academy, Woolwich. Cr. 8vo. 6s.

AGRICULTURE.

FRANKLAND.—AGRICULTURAL CHEMICAL ANALYSIS, A Handbook of. By PERCY F. FRANKLAND, F.R.S., Professor of Chemistry, University College, Dundee. Founded upon *Leitfaden für die Agriculture Chemiche Analyse*, von Dr. F. KROCKER. Cr. 8vo. 7s. 6d.

SMITH.—DISEASES OF FIELD AND GARDEN CROPS, CHIEFLY SUCH AS ARE CAUSED BY FUNGI. By WORTHINGTON G. SMITH, F.L.S., Illustrated. Fcap. 8vo. 4s. 6d.

TANNER.—ELEMENTARY LESSONS IN THE SCIENCE OF AGRICULTURAL PRACTICE. By HENRY TANNER, F.C.S., M.R.A.C., Examiner in the Principles of Agriculture under the Government Department of Science. Fcap. 8vo. 3s. 6d.
FIRST PRINCIPLES OF AGRICULTURE. By the same. 18mo. 1s.
THE PRINCIPLES OF AGRICULTURE. By the same. A Series of Reading Books for use in Elementary Schools. Ex. fcap. 8vo.
  I. The Alphabet of the Principles of Agriculture. 6d.
  II. Further Steps in the Principles of Agriculture. 1s.
  III. Elementary School Readings on the Principles of Agriculture for the third stage. 1s.

WARD.—TIMBER AND SOME OF ITS DISEASES. By H. MARSHALL WARD, M.A., F.L.S., F.R.S., Fellow of Christ's College, Cambridge, Professor of Botany at the Royal Indian Engineering College, Cooper's Hill. With Illustrations. Cr. 8vo. 6s.

DOMESTIC ECONOMY.

BARKER.—FIRST LESSONS IN THE PRINCIPLES OF COOKING. By LADY BARKER. 18mo. 1s.

BERNERS.—FIRST LESSONS ON HEALTH. By J. BERNERS. 18mo. 1s.

BLYTH.—A MANUAL OF PUBLIC HEALTH. By A. WYNTER BLYTH, M.R.C.S. 8vo. [*In the Press.*

COOKERY BOOK.—THE MIDDLE CLASS COOKERY BOOK. Edited by the Manchester School of Domestic Cookery. Fcap. 8vo. 1s. 6d.

CRAVEN.—A GUIDE TO DISTRICT NURSES. By Mrs. DACRE CRAVEN (*née* FLORENCE SARAH LEES), Hon. Associate of the Order of St. John of Jerusalem, &c. Cr 8vo. 2s. 6d.

FREDERICK.—HINTS TO HOUSEWIVES ON SEVERAL POINTS, PARTICULARLY ON THE PREPARATION OF ECONOMICAL AND TASTEFUL DISHES. By Mrs. FREDERICK. Cr. 8vo. 1s.

GRAND'HOMME.—CUTTING-OUT AND DRESSMAKING. From the French of Mdlle. E. GRAND'HOMME. With Diagrams. 18mo. 1s.

JEX-BLAKE.—THE CARE OF INFANTS. A Manual for Mothers and Nurses. By SOPHIA JEX-BLAKE, M.D., Lecturer on Hygiene at the London School of Medicine for Women. 18mo. 1s.

RATHBONE.—THE HISTORY AND PROGRESS OF DISTRICT NURSING FROM ITS COMMENCEMENT IN THE YEAR 1859 TO THE PRESENT DATE, including the foundation by the Queen of the Queen Victoria Jubilee Institute for Nursing the Poor in their own Homes. By WILLIAM RATHBONE, M.P. Cr. 8vo. 2s. 6d.

TEGETMEIER.—HOUSEHOLD MANAGEMENT AND COOKERY. With an Appendix of Recipes used by the Teachers of the National School of Cookery. By W. B. TEGETMEIER. Compiled at the request of the School Board for London. 18mo. 1s.

WRIGHT.—THE SCHOOL COOKERY-BOOK. Compiled and Edited by C. E. GUTHRIE WRIGHT, Hon. Sec. to the Edinburgh School of Cookery. 18mo. 1s.

BOOK-KEEPING.

THORNTON.—FIRST LESSONS IN BOOK-KEEPING. By J. THORNTON. Cr. 8vo. 2s. 6d. KEY. Oblong 4to. 10s. 6d.

PRIMER OF BOOK-KEEPING. By the Same. 18mo. 1s. [*Key Immediately*

GEOGRAPHY.

(SEE ALSO PHYSICAL GEOGRAPHY.)

BARTHOLOMEW.—THE ELEMENTARY SCHOOL ATLAS. By JOHN BARTHOLOMEW, F.R.G.S. 4to. 1s.

This Elementary Atlas is designed to illustrate the principal text-books on Elementary Geography.

PHYSICAL AND POLITICAL SCHOOL ATLAS, Consisting of 80 Maps and complete Index. By the Same. Prepared for the use of Senior Pupils. Royal 4to. [*In the Press.*

THE LIBRARY REFERENCE ATLAS OF THE WORLD. By the Same. A Complete Series of 84 Modern Maps. With Geographical Index to 100,000 places. Half-morocco. Gilt edges. Folio. £2:12:6 net.

* This work has been designed with the object of supplying the public with a thoroughly complete and accurate atlas of Modern Geography, in a convenient reference form, and at a moderate price.

CLARKE.—CLASS-BOOK OF GEOGRAPHY. By C. B. CLARKE, F.R.S. New Ed., revised 1889, with 18 Maps. Fcap. 8vo. Paper covers, 3s. Cloth, 3s. 6d.

GEIKIE.—Works by ARCHIBALD GEIKIE, F.R.S., Director-General of the Geological Survey of the United Kingdom.

THE TEACHING OF GEOGRAPHY. A Practical Handbook for the use of Teachers. Cr. 8vo. 2s.
GEOGRAPHY OF THE BRITISH ISLES. 18mo. 1s.
GREEN.—A SHORT GEOGRAPHY OF THE BRITISH ISLANDS. By JOHN RICHARD GREEN and A. S. GREEN. With Maps. Fcap. 8vo. 3s. 6d.
GROVE.—A PRIMER OF GEOGRAPHY. By Sir GEORGE GROVE, D.C.L. Illustrated. 18mo. 1s
KIEPERT.—A MANUAL OF ANCIENT GEOGRAPHY. By Dr. H. KIEPERT. Cr. 8vo. 5s.
MACMILLAN'S GEOGRAPHICAL SERIES.—Edited by ARCHIBALD GEIKIE, F.R.S., Director-General of the Geological Survey of the United Kingdom.
  THE TEACHING OF GEOGRAPHY. A Practical Handbook for the Use of Teachers. By ARCHIBALD GEIKIE, F.R.S. Cr. 8vo. 2s.
  MAPS AND MAP-MAKING. By W. A. ELDERTON. [*In the Press.*
  GEOGRAPHY OF THE BRITISH ISLES. By A. GEIKIE, F.R.S. 18mo. 1s.
  AN ELEMENTARY CLASS-BOOK OF GENERAL GEOGRAPHY. By H. R. MILL, D.Sc, Lecturer on Physiography and on Commercial Geography in the Heriot-Watt College, Edinburgh. Illustrated. Cr. 8vo. 3s. 6d.
  GEOGRAPHY OF THE BRITISH COLONIES. By G. M. DAWSON and A. SUTHERLAND. [*In preparation.*
  GEOGRAPHY OF EUROPE. By J. SIME, M.A. Illustrated. Gl. 8vo. [*In the Press.*
  GEOGRAPHY OF INDIA. By H. F. BLANFORD, F.G.S. [*In the Press.*
  GEOGRAPHY OF NORTH AMERICA. By Prof. N. S. SHALER. [*In preparation.*
  ADVANCED CLASS-BOOK OF THE GEOGRAPHY OF BRITAIN.
  ** Other volumes will be announced in due course.
STRACHEY.—LECTURES ON GEOGRAPHY. By General RICHARD STRACHEY, R.E. Cr. 8vo. 4s. 6d.

HISTORY.

ARNOLD.—THE SECOND PUNIC WAR. Being Chapters from THE HISTORY OF ROME, by the late THOMAS ARNOLD, D.D., Headmaster of Rugby. Edited, with Notes, by W. T. ARNOLD, M.A. With 8 Maps. Cr. 8vo. 5s. 6d.
ARNOLD.—THE ROMAN SYSTEM OF PROVINCIAL ADMINISTRATION TO THE ACCESSION OF CONSTANTINE THE GREAT. By W. T. ARNOLD, M.A. Cr. 8vo. 6s.
BEESLY.—STORIES FROM THE HISTORY OF ROME. By Mrs. BEESLY. Fcap. 8vo. 2s. 6d.
BRYCE.—Works by JAMES BRYCE, M.P., D.C.L., Regius Professor of Civil Law in the University of Oxford.
  THE HOLY ROMAN EMPIRE. 9th Ed. Cr. 8vo. 7s. 6d.
    ** Also a *Library Edition.* Demy 8vo. 14s.
  THE AMERICAN COMMONWEALTH. 2 vols. Ex. cr. 8vo. 25s. Part I. The National Government. Part II. The State Governments. Part III. The Party System. Part IV. Public Opinion. Part V. Illustrations and Reflections. Part VI. Social Institutions.
BUCKLEY.—A HISTORY OF ENGLAND FOR BEGINNERS. By ARABELLA B. BUCKLEY. With Maps and Tables. Gl. 8vo. 3s.
BURY.—A HISTORY OF THE LATER ROMAN EMPIRE FROM ARCADIUS TO IRENE, A.D. 395-800. By JOHN B. BURY, M.A., Fellow of Trinity College, Dublin. 2 vols. 8vo. 32s.
ENGLISH STATESMEN, TWELVE. Cr. 8vo. 2s. 6d. each.
  WILLIAM THE CONQUEROR. By EDWARD A. FREEMAN, D.C.L., LL.D.
  HENRY II. By Mrs. J. R. GREEN.

HISTORY

EDWARD I. By F. YORK POWELL. [*In preparation.*
HENRY VII. By JAMES GAIRDNER.
CARDINAL WOLSEY. By Professor M. CREIGHTON.
ELIZABETH. By E. S. BEESLY. [*In preparation.*
OLIVER CROMWELL. By FREDERIC HARRISON.
WILLIAM III. By H. D. TRAILL.
WALPOLE. By JOHN MORLEY.
CHATHAM. By JOHN MORLEY. [*In preparation.*
PITT. By JOHN MORLEY. [*In preparation.*
PEEL. By J. R. THURSFIELD. [*In the Press.*

FISKE.—Works by JOHN FISKE, formerly Lecturer on Philosophy at Harvard University.
 THE CRITICAL PERIOD IN AMERICAN HISTORY, 1783-1789. Ex. cr. 8vo. 10s. 6d.
 THE BEGINNINGS OF NEW ENGLAND; or, The Puritan Theocracy in its Relations to Civil and Religious Liberty. Cr. 8vo. 7s. 6d.

FREEMAN.—Works by EDWARD A. FREEMAN, D.C.L., Regius Professor of Modern History in the University of Oxford, &c.
 OLD ENGLISH HISTORY. With Maps. Ex. fcap. 8vo. 6s.
 A SCHOOL HISTORY OF ROME. Cr. 8vo. [*In preparation.*
 METHODS OF HISTORICAL STUDY. 8vo. 10s. 6d.
 THE CHIEF PERIODS OF EUROPEAN HISTORY. Six Lectures. With an Essay on Greek Cities under Roman Rule. 8vo. 10s. 6d.
 HISTORICAL ESSAYS. First Series. 4th Ed. 8vo. 10s. 6d.
 HISTORICAL ESSAYS. Second Series. 3d Ed., with additional Essays. 8vo. 10s. 6d.
 HISTORICAL ESSAYS. Third Series. 8vo. 12s.
 THE GROWTH OF THE ENGLISH CONSTITUTION FROM THE EARLIEST TIMES. 4th Ed. Cr. 8vo. 5s.
 GENERAL SKETCH OF EUROPEAN HISTORY. Enlarged, with Maps, etc. 18mo. 3s. 6d.
 PRIMER OF EUROPEAN HISTORY. 18mo. 1s. (*History Primers.*)

FRIEDMANN.—ANNE BOLEYN. A Chapter of English History, 1527-1536. By PAUL FRIEDMANN. 2 vols. 8vo. 28s.

FYFFE.—A SCHOOL HISTORY OF GREECE. By C. A. FYFFE, M.A., late Fellow of University College, Oxford. Cr. 8vo. [*In preparation.*

GREEN.—Works by JOHN RICHARD GREEN, LL.D., late Honorary Fellow of Jesus College, Oxford.
 A SHORT HISTORY OF THE ENGLISH PEOPLE. New and Revised Ed. With Maps, Genealogical Tables, and Chronological Annals. Cr. 8vo. 8s. 6d. 150th Thousand.
 Also the same in Four Parts. With the corresponding portion of Mr. Tait's "Analysis." Crown 8vo. 3s. each. Part I. 607-1265. Part II. 1204-1553. Part III. 1540-1689. Part IV. 1660-1873.
 HISTORY OF THE ENGLISH PEOPLE. In four vols. 8vo. 16s. each.
  Vol. I.—Early England, 449-1071; Foreign Kings, 1071-1214; The Charter, 1214-1291; The Parliament, 1307-1461. With 8 Maps.
  Vol. II.—The Monarchy, 1461-1540; The Reformation, 1540-1603.
  Vol. III.—Puritan England, 1603-1660; The Revolution, 1660-1688. With four Maps.
  Vol. IV.—The Revolution, 1688-1760; Modern England, 1760-1815. With Maps and Index.
 THE MAKING OF ENGLAND. With Maps. 8vo. 16s.
 THE CONQUEST OF ENGLAND. With Maps and Portrait. 8vo. 18s.
 ANALYSIS OF ENGLISH HISTORY, based on Green's "Short History of the English People." By C. W. A. TAIT, M.A., Assistant Master at Clifton College. Crown 8vo. 3s. 6d.

HISTORY

READINGS FROM ENGLISH HISTORY. Selected and Edited by JOHN RICHARD GREEN. Three Parts. Gl. 8vo. 1s. 6d. each. I. Hengist to Cressy. II. Cressy to Cromwell. III. Cromwell to Balaklava.

GUEST.—LECTURES ON THE HISTORY OF ENGLAND. By M. J. GUEST. With Maps. Cr. 8vo. 6s.

HISTORICAL COURSE FOR SCHOOLS.—Edited by E. A. FREEMAN, D.C.L., Regius Professor of Modern History in the University of Oxford. 18mo.
GENERAL SKETCH OF EUROPEAN HISTORY. By E. A. FREEMAN, D.C.L. New Ed., revised and enlarged. With Chronological Table, Maps, and Index. 3s. 6d.
HISTORY OF ENGLAND. By EDITH THOMPSON. New Ed., revised and enlarged. With Coloured Maps. 2s. 6d.
HISTORY OF SCOTLAND. By MARGARET MACARTHUR. 2s.
HISTORY OF ITALY. By Rev. W. HUNT, M.A. New Ed. With Coloured Maps. 3s. 6d.
HISTORY OF GERMANY. By J. SIME, M.A. New Ed., revised. 3s.
HISTORY OF AMERICA. By JOHN A. DOYLE. With Maps. 4s. 6d.
HISTORY OF EUROPEAN COLONIES. By E. J. PAYNE, M.A. With Maps. 4s. 6d.
HISTORY OF FRANCE. By CHARLOTTE M. YONGE. With Maps. 3s. 6d.
HISTORY OF GREECE. By EDWARD A. FREEMAN, D.C.L. [*In preparation.*
HISTORY OF ROME. By EDWARD A. FREEMAN, D.C.L. [*In preparation.*

HISTORY PRIMERS.—Edited by JOHN RICHARD GREEN, LL.D. 18mo. 1s. each.
ROME. By Rev. M. CREIGHTON, M.A., Dixie Professor of Ecclesiastical History in the University of Cambridge. Maps.
GREECE. By C. A. FYFFE, M.A., late Fellow of University College, Oxford. Maps.
EUROPE. By E. A. FREEMAN, D.C.L. Maps.
FRANCE. By CHARLOTTE M. YONGE.
GREEK ANTIQUITIES. By Rev. J. P. MAHAFFY, D.D. Illustrated.
CLASSICAL GEOGRAPHY. By H. F. TOZER, M.A.
GEOGRAPHY. By Sir G. GROVE, D.C.L. Maps.
ROMAN ANTIQUITIES. By Prof. WILKINS, Litt.D. Illustrated.

HOLE.—A GENEALOGICAL STEMMA OF THE KINGS OF ENGLAND AND FRANCE. By Rev. C. HOLE. On Sheet. 1s.

JENNINGS.—CHRONOLOGICAL TABLES. A synchronistic arrangement of the events of Ancient History (with an Index). By Rev. ARTHUR C. JENNINGS. 8vo. 5s.

LABBERTON.—NEW HISTORICAL ATLAS AND GENERAL HISTORY. By R. H. LABBERTON. 4to. New Ed., revised and enlarged. 15s.

LETHBRIDGE.—A SHORT MANUAL OF THE HISTORY OF INDIA. With an Account of INDIA AS IT IS. The Soil, Climate, and Productions; the People, their Races, Religions, Public Works, and Industries; the Civil Services, and System of Administration. By Sir ROPER LETHBRIDGE, Fellow of the Calcutta University. With Maps. Cr. 8vo. 5s.

MAHAFFY.—GREEK LIFE AND THOUGHT FROM THE AGE OF ALEXANDER TO THE ROMAN CONQUEST. By Rev. J. P. MAHAFFY, D.D., Fellow of Trinity College, Dublin. Cr. 8vo. 12s. 6d.
THE GREEK WORLD UNDER ROMAN SWAY. From Plutarch to Polybius. By the same Author. Cr. 8vo. [*In the Press.*

MARRIOTT.—THE MAKERS OF MODERN ITALY: MAZZINI, CAVOUR, GARIBALDI. Three Lectures. By J. A. R. MARRIOTT, M.A., Lecturer in Modern History and Political Economy, Oxford. Cr. 8vo. 1s. 6d.

MICHELET.—A SUMMARY OF MODERN HISTORY. Translated by M. C. M. SIMPSON. Gl. 8vo. 4s. 6d.

NORGATE.—ENGLAND UNDER THE ANGEVIN KINGS. By KATE NORGATE. With Maps and Plans. 2 vols. 8vo. 32s.

OTTÉ.—SCANDINAVIAN HISTORY. By E. C. OTTÉ. With Maps. Gl. 8vo. 6s.
SEELEY.—Works by J. R. SEELEY, M.A., Regius Professor of Modern History in the University of Cambridge.
  THE EXPANSION OF ENGLAND. Crown 8vo. 4s. 6d.
  OUR COLONIAL EXPANSION. Extracts from the above. Cr. 8vo. Sewed. 1s.
TAIT.—ANALYSIS OF ENGLISH HISTORY, based on Green's "Short History of the English People." By C. W. A. TAIT, M.A., Assistant Master at Clifton. Cr. 8vo. 3s. 6d.
WHEELER.—Works by J. TALBOYS WHEELER.
  A PRIMER OF INDIAN HISTORY. Asiatic and European. 18mo. 1s.
  COLLEGE HISTORY OF INDIA, ASIATIC AND EUROPEAN. With Maps. Cr. 8vo. 3s. 6d.
  A SHORT HISTORY OF INDIA AND OF THE FRONTIER STATES OF AFGHANISTAN, NEPAUL, AND BURMA. With Maps. Cr. 8vo. 12s.
YONGE.—Works by CHARLOTTE M. YONGE.
  CAMEOS FROM ENGLISH HISTORY. Ex. fcap. 8vo. 5s. each. (1) FROM ROLLO TO EDWARD II. (2) THE WARS IN FRANCE. (3) THE WARS OF THE ROSES. (4) REFORMATION TIMES. (5) ENGLAND AND SPAIN. (6) FORTY YEARS OF STUART RULE (1603–1643). (7) REBELLION AND RESTORATION (1642–1678.)
  EUROPEAN HISTORY. Narrated in a Series of Historical Selections from the Best Authorities. Edited and arranged by E. M. SEWELL and C. M. YONGE. Cr. 8vo. First Series, 1003–1154. 6s. Second Series, 1088–1228. 6s.
  THE VICTORIAN HALF CENTURY—A JUBILEE BOOK. With a New Portrait of the Queen. Cr. 8vo., paper covers, 1s. Cloth, 1s. 6d.

ART.

ANDERSON.—LINEAR PERSPECTIVE AND MODEL DRAWING. A School and Art Class Manual, with Questions and Exercises for Examination, and Examples of Examination Papers. By LAURENCE ANDERSON. Illustrated. 8vo. 2s.
COLLIER.—A PRIMER OF ART. By the Hon. JOHN COLLIER. Illustrated. 18mo. 1s.
COOK.—THE NATIONAL GALLERY: A POPULAR HANDBOOK TO. By EDWARD T. COOK, with a preface by JOHN RUSKIN, LL.D., and Selections from his Writings. 3d Ed. Cr. 8vo. Half Morocco, 14s.
  ₊ Also an Edition on large paper, limited to 250 copies. 2 vols. 8vo.
DELAMOTTE.—A BEGINNER'S DRAWING BOOK. By P. H. DELAMOTTE, F.S.A. Progressively arranged. New Ed., improved. Cr. 8vo. 3s. 6d.
ELLIS.—SKETCHING FROM NATURE. A Handbook for Students and Amateurs. By TRISTRAM J. ELLIS. Illustrated by H. STACY MARKS, R.A., and the Author. New Ed., revised and enlarged. Cr. 8vo. 3s. 6d.
GROVE.—A DICTIONARY OF MUSIC AND MUSICIANS. A.D. 1450—1889. Edited by Sir GEORGE GROVE, D.C.L. In four vols. 8vo. Price 21s. each. Also in Parts.
  Parts I. to XIV., Parts XIX.—XXII., 3s. 6d. each. Parts XV., XVI., 7s. Parts XVII., XVIII., 7s. Parts XXIII.—XXV. (Appendix), 9s.
  A COMPLETE INDEX TO THE ABOVE. By MRS. E. WODEHOUSE. 8vo. 7s. 6d.
HUNT.—TALKS ABOUT ART. By WILLIAM HUNT. With a Letter from Sir J. E. MILLAIS, Bart., R.A. Cr. 8vo. 3s. 6d.
MELDOLA.—THE CHEMISTRY OF PHOTOGRAPHY. By RAPHAEL MELDOLA, F.R.S., Professor of Chemistry in the Technical College, Finsbury. Cr. 8vo. 6s.
TAYLOR.—A PRIMER OF PIANOFORTE PLAYING. By FRANKLIN TAYLOR. Edited by Sir GEORGE GROVE. 18mo. 1s.

TAYLOR.—A SYSTEM OF SIGHT-SINGING FROM THE ESTABLISHED MUSICAL NOTATION; based on the Principle of Tonic Relation, and Illustrated by Extracts from the Works of the Great Masters. By SEDLEY TAYLOR. 8vo. [*In the Press.*

TYRWHITT.—OUR SKETCHING CLUB. Letters and Studies on Landscape Art. By Rev. R. ST. JOHN TYRWHITT. With an authorised Reproduction of the Lessons and Woodcuts in Prof. Ruskin's "Elements of Drawing." 4th Ed. Cr. 8vo. 7s. 6d.

DIVINITY.

ABBOTT.—BIBLE LESSONS. By Rev. EDWIN A. ABBOTT, D.D. Cr. 8vo. 4s. 6d.

ABBOTT—RUSHBROOKE.—THE COMMON TRADITION OF THE SYNOPTIC GOSPELS, in the Text of the Revised Version. By Rev. EDWIN A. ABBOTT, D.D., and W. G. RUSHBROOKE, M.L. Cr. 8vo. 3s. 6d.

ARNOLD.—Works by MATTHEW ARNOLD.
  A BIBLE-READING FOR SCHOOLS,—THE GREAT PROPHECY OF ISRAEL'S RESTORATION (Isaiah, Chapters xl.-lxvi.) Arranged and Edited for Young Learners. 18mo. 1s.
  ISAIAH XL.—LXVI. With the Shorter Prophecies allied to it. Arranged and Edited, with Notes. Cr. 8vo. 5s.
  ISAIAH OF JERUSALEM, IN THE AUTHORISED ENGLISH VERSION. With Introduction, Corrections and Notes. Cr. 8vo. 4s. 6d.

BENHAM.—A COMPANION TO THE LECTIONARY. Being a Commentary on the Proper Lessons for Sundays and Holy Days. By Rev. W. BENHAM, B.D. Cr. 8vo. 4s. 6d.

CASSEL.—MANUAL OF JEWISH HISTORY AND LITERATURE; preceded by a BRIEF SUMMARY OF BIBLE HISTORY. By Dr. D. CASSEL. Translated by Mrs. H. LUCAS. Fcap. 8vo. 2s. 6d.

CROSS.—BIBLE READINGS SELECTED FROM THE PENTATEUCH AND THE BOOK OF JOSHUA. By Rev. JOHN A. CROSS. 2d Ed., enlarged, with Notes. Gl. 8vo. 2s. 6d.

DRUMMOND.—THE STUDY OF THEOLOGY, INTRODUCTION TO. By JAMES DRUMMOND, LL.D., Professor of Theology in Manchester New College, London. Cr. 8vo. 5s.

FARRAR.—Works by the Venerable Archdeacon F. W. FARRAR, D.D., F.R.S., Archdeacon and Canon of Westminster.
  THE HISTORY OF INTERPRETATION. Being the Bampton Lectures, 1885. 8vo. 16s.
  THE MESSAGES OF THE BOOKS. Being Discourses and Notes on the Books of the New Testament. 8vo. 14s.

GASKOIN.—THE CHILDREN'S TREASURY OF BIBLE STORIES. By Mrs. HERMAN GASKOIN. Edited with Preface by Rev. G. F. MACLEAR, D.D. 18mo. 1s. each. Part I.—OLD TESTAMENT HISTORY. Part II.—NEW TESTAMENT. Part III.—THE APOSTLES: ST. JAMES THE GREAT, ST. PAUL, AND ST. JOHN THE DIVINE.

GOLDEN TREASURY PSALTER.—Students' Edition. Being an Edition of "The Psalms Chronologically arranged, by Four Friends," with briefer Notes. 18mo. 3s. 6d.

GREEK TESTAMENT.—Edited, with Introduction and Appendices, by Bishop WESTCOTT and Dr. F. J. A. HORT. Two Vols. Cr. 8vo. 10s. 6d. each. Vol. I. The Text. Vol. II. Introduction and Appendix.
  SCHOOL EDITION OF TEXT. 12mo, cloth. 4s. 6d. 18mo, morocco, gilt edges. 6s. 6d.
  GREEK TESTAMENT, SCHOOL READINGS IN THE. Being the outline of the life of our Lord, as given by St. Mark, with additions from the Text of the other Evangelists. Arranged and Edited, with Notes and Vocabulary, by Rev. A. CALVERT, M.A. Fcap. 8vo. 4s. 6d.

DIVINITY

THE GOSPEL ACCORDING TO ST. MATTHEW. Being the Greek Text as revised by Bishop WESTCOTT and Dr. HORT. With Introduction and Notes by Rev. A. SLOMAN, M.A., Headmaster of Birkenhead School. Fcap. 8vo. 2s. 6d.

THE GOSPEL ACCORDING TO ST. MARK. Being the Greek Text as revised by Bishop WESTCOTT and Dr. HORT. With Introduction and Notes by Rev. J. O. F. MURRAY, M.A., Lecturer at Emmanuel College, Cambridge. Fcap. 8vo. [*In preparation.*

THE GOSPEL ACCORDING TO ST. LUKE. Being the Greek Text as revised by Bishop WESTCOTT and Dr. HORT. With Introduction and Notes by Rev. JOHN BOND, M.A. [*In preparation.*

THE ACTS OF THE APOSTLES. Being the Greek Text as revised by Bishop WESTCOTT and Dr. HORT. With Explanatory Notes by T. E. PAGE, M.A., Assistant Master at the Charterhouse. Fcap. 8vo. 4s. 6d.

GWATKIN.—CHURCH HISTORY TO THE BEGINNING OF THE MIDDLE AGES. By H. M. GWATKIN, M.A. 8vo. [*In preparation.*

HARDWICK.—Works by Archdeacon HARDWICK.

A HISTORY OF THE CHRISTIAN CHURCH. Middle Age. From Gregory the Great to the Excommunication of Luther. Edited by W. STUBBS, D.D., Bishop of Oxford. With 4 Maps. Cr. 8vo. 10s. 6d.

A HISTORY OF THE CHRISTIAN CHURCH DURING THE REFORMATION. 9th. Ed. Edited by Bishop STUBBS. Cr. 8vo. 10s. 6d.

HOOLE.—THE CLASSICAL ELEMENT IN THE NEW TESTAMENT. Considered as a proof of its Genuineness, with an Appendix on the Oldest Authorities used in the Formation of the Canon. By CHARLES H. HOOLE, M.A., Student of Christ Church, Oxford. 8vo. 10s. 6d.

JENNINGS AND LOWE.—THE PSALMS, WITH INTRODUCTIONS AND CRITICAL NOTES. By A. C. JENNINGS, M.A.; assisted in parts by W. H. LOWE, M.A. In 2 vols. 2d Ed., revised. Cr. 8vo. 10s. 6d. each.

KIRKPATRICK.—THE MINOR PROPHETS. Warburtonian Lectures. By Rev. Prof. KIRKPATRICK. [*In preparation.*

KUENEN.—PENTATEUCH AND BOOK OF JOSHUA: an Historico-Critical Inquiry into the Origin and Composition of the Hexateuch. By A. KUENEN. Translated by P. H. WICKSTEED, M.A. 8vo. 14s.

LIGHTFOOT.—Works by the Right Rev. J. B. LIGHTFOOT, D.D., late Bishop of Durham.

ST. PAUL'S EPISTLE TO THE GALATIANS. A Revised Text, with Introduction, Notes, and Dissertations. 9th Ed., revised. 8vo. 12s.

ST. PAUL'S EPISTLE TO THE PHILIPPIANS. A Revised Text, with Introduction, Notes, and Dissertations. 9th. Ed., revised. 8vo. 12s.

ST. CLEMENT OF ROME—THE TWO EPISTLES TO THE CORINTHIANS. A Revised Text, with Introduction and Notes. 2 Vols. 8vo. [*In the Press.*

ST. PAUL'S EPISTLES TO THE COLOSSIANS AND TO PHILEMON. A Revised Text, with Introductions, Notes, and Dissertations. 8th Ed., revised. 8vo. 12s.

THE APOSTOLIC FATHERS. Part II. ST. IGNATIUS—ST. POLYCARP. Revised Texts. With Introductions, Notes, Dissertations, and Translations. 2d Ed. 3 vols. 8vo. 48s.

THE APOSTOLIC FATHERS. Abridged Edition. With short Introductions, Greek Text, and English Translation. 8vo. [*In the Press.*

ESSAYS ON THE WORK ENTITLED "SUPERNATURAL RELIGION." (Reprinted from the *Contemporary Review*). 8vo. 10s. 6d.

MACLEAR.—Works by the Rev. G. F. MACLEAR, D.D., Warden of St. Augustine's College, Canterbury.

ELEMENTARY THEOLOGICAL CLASS-BOOKS.

A SHILLING BOOK OF OLD TESTAMENT HISTORY. With Map. 18mo.

A SHILLING BOOK OF NEW TESTAMENT HISTORY. With Map. 18mo. These works have been carefully abridged from the Author's large manuals.

A CLASS-BOOK OF OLD TESTAMENT HISTORY. Maps. 18mo. 4s. 6d.

A CLASS BOOK OF NEW TESTAMENT HISTORY, including the Connection of the Old and New Testaments. With maps. 18mo. 5s. 6d.

DIVINITY 51

AN INTRODUCTION TO THE THIRTY-NINE ARTICLES. 18mo.
AN INTRODUCTION TO THE CREEDS. 18mo. 2s. 6d. [*In the Press.*
A CLASS-BOOK OF THE CATECHISM OF THE CHURCH OF ENGLAND. 18mo. 1s. 6d.
A FIRST CLASS-BOOK OF THE CATECHISM OF THE CHURCH OF ENGLAND. With Scripture Proofs. 18mo. 6d.
A MANUAL OF INSTRUCTION FOR CONFIRMATION AND FIRST COMMUNION. WITH PRAYERS AND DEVOTIONS. 32mo. 2s.
MAURICE.—THE LORD'S PRAYER, THE CREED, AND THE COMMANDMENTS. To which is added the Order of the Scriptures. By Rev. F. D. MAURICE, M.A. 18mo. 1s.
THE PENTATEUCH AND BOOK OF JOSHUA: an Historico-Critical Inquiry into the Origin and Composition of the Hexateuch. By A. KUENEN, Professor of Theology at Leiden. Translated by P. H. WICKSTEED, M.A. 8vo. 14s.
PROCTER.—A HISTORY OF THE BOOK OF COMMON PRAYER, with a Rationale of its Offices. By Rev. F. PROCTER. 18th Ed., revised and enlarged. Cr. 8vo. 10s. 6d.
PROCTER AND MACLEAR.—AN ELEMENTARY INTRODUCTION TO THE BOOK OF COMMON PRAYER. Re-arranged and supplemented by an Explanation of the Morning and Evening Prayer and the Litany. By Rev. F. PROCTER and Rev. Dr. MACLEAR. New and enlarged Edition, containing the Communion Service and the Confirmation and Baptismal Offices. 18mo. 2s. 6d.
THE PSALMS, WITH INTRODUCTIONS AND CRITICAL NOTES. By A. C. JENNINGS, M.A., Jesus College, Cambridge; assisted in parts by W. H. LOWE. M.A., Hebrew Lecturer at Christ's College, Cambridge. In 2 vols. 2d Ed., revised. Cr. 8vo. 10s. 6d. each.
RAMSAY.—THE CATECHISER'S MANUAL; or, the Church Catechism Illustrated and Explained. By Rev. ARTHUR RAMSAY. 18mo. 1s. 6d.
RYLE.—AN INTRODUCTION TO THE CANON OF THE OLD TESTAMENT. By Rev. H. E. RYLE, Hulsean Professor of Divinity in the University of Cambridge. Cr. 8vo. [*In preparation.*
SIMPSON.—AN EPITOME OF THE HISTORY OF THE CHRISTIAN CHURCH DURING THE FIRST THREE CENTURIES, AND OF THE REFORMATION IN ENGLAND. By Rev. WILLIAM SIMPSON. 7th Ed. Fcap. 8vo. 3s. 6d.
ST. JAMES' EPISTLE.—The Greek Text with Introduction and Notes. By Rev. JOSEPH MAYOR, M.A., Professor of Moral Philosophy in King's College, London. 8vo. [*In the Press.*
ST. JOHN'S EPISTLES.—The Greek Text, with Notes and Essays. By Right Rev. B. F. WESTCOTT, D.D., Bishop of Durham. 2d Ed., revised. 8vo. 12s. 6d.
ST. PAUL'S EPISTLES.—THE EPISTLE TO THE ROMANS. Edited by the Very Rev. C. J. VAUGHAN, D.D., Dean of Llandaff. 5th Ed. Cr. 8vo. 7s. 6d.
THE TWO EPISTLES TO THE CORINTHIANS, A COMMENTARY ON. By the late Rev. W. KAY, D.D., Rector of Great Leghs, Essex. 8vo. 9s.
THE EPISTLE TO THE GALATIANS. Edited by the Right Rev. J. B. LIGHTFOOT, D.D. 9th Ed. 8vo. 12s.
THE EPISTLES TO THE EPHESIANS, THE COLOSSIANS, AND PHILEMON; with Introductions and Notes, and an Essay on the Traces of Foreign Elements in the Theology of these Epistles. By Rev. J. LLEWELYN DAVIES, M.A. 8vo. 7s. 6d.
THE EPISTLE TO THE PHILIPPIANS. By the Right Rev. J. B. LIGHTFOOT, D.D. 9th Ed. 8vo. 12s.
THE EPISTLE TO THE PHILIPPIANS, with Translation, Paraphrase, and Notes for English Readers. By the Very Rev. C. J. VAUGHAN, D.D. Cr. 8vo. 5s.
THE EPISTLE TO THE COLOSSIANS AND TO PHILEMON. By the Right Rev. J. B. LIGHTFOOT, D.D. 8th Ed. 8vo. 12s.
THE EPISTLE TO THE THESSALONIANS, COMMENTARY ON THE GREEK TEXT. By JOHN EADIE, D.D. Edited by Rev. W. YOUNG, M.A., with Preface by Prof. CAIRNS. 8vo. 12s.

DIVINITY

THE EPISTLE TO THE HEBREWS.—In Greek and English. With Critical and Explanatory Notes. Edited by Rev. F. RENDALL, M.A. Cr. 8vo. 6s.
  THE ENGLISH TEXT, WITH COMMENTARY. By the same Editor. Cr. 8vo. 7s. 6d.
  THE GREEK TEXT. With Notes by C. J. VAUGHAN, D.D., Dean of Llandaff. Cr. 8vo. 7s. 6d.
  THE GREEK TEXT. With Notes and Essays by Bishop WESTCOTT, D.D. 8vo. 14s.

WESTCOTT.—Works by the Right Rev. BROOKE FOSS WESTCOTT, D.D., Bishop of Durham.
  A GENERAL SURVEY OF THE HISTORY OF THE CANON OF THE NEW TESTAMENT DURING THE FIRST FOUR CENTURIES. 6th Ed. With Preface on "Supernatural Religion." Cr. 8vo. 10s. 6d.
  INTRODUCTION TO THE STUDY OF THE FOUR GOSPELS. 7th Ed. Cr. 8vo. 10s. 6d.
  THE BIBLE IN THE CHURCH. A Popular Account of the Collection and Reception of the Holy Scriptures in the Christian Churches. 18mo. 4s. 6d.
  THE EPISTLES OF ST. JOHN. The Greek Text, with Notes and Essays. 2d Ed., revised. 8vo. 12s. 6d.
  THE EPISTLE TO THE HEBREWS. The Greek Text, with Notes and Essays. 8vo. 14s.
  SOME THOUGHTS FROM THE ORDINAL. Cr. 8vo. 1s. 6d.

WESTCOTT AND HORT.—THE NEW TESTAMENT IN THE ORIGINAL GREEK. The Text, revised by the Right Rev. Bishop WESTCOTT and Dr. F. J. A. HORT. 2 vols. Cr. 8vo. 10s. 6d. each. Vol. I. Text. Vol. II. Introduction and Appendix.
  SCHOOL EDITION OF TEXT. 12mo. 4s. 6d. 18mo. Morocco, gilt edges. 6s. 6d.

WILSON.—THE BIBLE STUDENT'S GUIDE to the more Correct Understanding of the English Translation of the Old Testament, by reference to the original Hebrew. By WILLIAM WILSON, D.D., Canon of Winchester. 2d Ed., carefully revised. 4to. 25s.

WRIGHT.—THE COMPOSITION OF THE FOUR GOSPELS. A Critical Enquiry. By Rev. ARTHUR WRIGHT., M.A., Fellow and Tutor of Queen's College, Cambridge. Cr. 8vo. 5s.

WRIGHT.—THE BIBLE WORD-BOOK: A Glossary of Archaic Words and Phrases in the Authorised Version of the Bible and the Book of Common Prayer. By W. ALDIS WRIGHT, M.A., Vice-Master of Trinity College, Cambridge. 2d Ed., revised and enlarged. Cr. 8vo. 7s. 6d.

YONGE.—SCRIPTURE READINGS FOR SCHOOLS AND FAMILIES. By CHARLOTTE M. YONGE. In Five Vols. Ex. fcp. 8vo. 1s. 6d. each. With Comments. 3s. 6d. each.
  FIRST SERIES.—GENESIS TO DEUTERONOMY. SECOND SERIES.—From JOSHUA to SOLOMON. THIRD SERIES.—The KINGS and the PROPHETS. FOURTH SERIES.—The GOSPEL TIMES. FIFTH SERIES.—APOSTOLIC TIMES.

ZECHARIAH—THE HEBREW STUDENT'S COMMENTARY ON ZECHARIAH, HEBREW AND LXX. With Excursus on Syllable-dividing, Metheg, Initial Dagesh, and Siman Rapheh. By W. H. LOWE, M.A., Hebrew Lecturer at Christ's College, Cambridge. 8vo. 10s. 6d.

Printed by R. & R. CLARK, *Edinburgh.*

www.ingramcontent.com/pod-product-compliance
Lightning Source LLC
Chambersburg PA
CBHW032138230426
43672CB00011B/2376